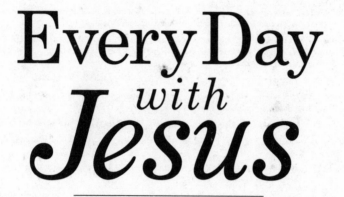

Every Day with Jesus

DAILY JOY *for the* JOURNEY

365 Devotions to Draw You Closer to Him

Guideposts
Guideposts.org

Published by Guideposts Books & Inspirational Media
39 Old Ridgebury Road, Suite 27
Danbury, CT 06810
Guideposts.org

Acknowledgments

Every attempt has been made to credit the sources of copyrighted material used in this book. If any such acknowledgment has been inadvertently omitted or miscredited, receipt of such information would be appreciated.

Scripture quotations marked (AMP) are taken from *The Amplified Bible* and *The Amplified Bible, Classic Edition*. Copyright © 2015 by The Lockman Foundation, La Habra, CA 90631. All rights reserved. Copyright © 1954, 1958, 1962, 1964, 1965, 1987 by The Lockman Foundation. Used by permission. www.Lockman.org

Scripture quotations marked (ERV) are taken from *Easy-to-Read Version Bible*. Copyright © 2006 by Bible League International.

Scripture quotations marked (ESV) are taken from the *Holy Bible, English Standard Version*. Copyright © 2001 by Crossway Bibles, a division of Good News Publishers. Used by permission. All rights reserved.

Scripture quotations marked (GNT) are taken from *Good News Translation*. Copyright © 1992 by American Bible Society.

Scripture quotations marked (GW) are taken from *God's Word Translation*. Copyright © 1995 by God's Word to the Nations. Used by permission of Baker Publishing Group.

Scripture quotations marked (HCSB) are taken from the *Holman Christian Standard Bible*. Copyright © 1999, 2000, 2002, 2003 by Holman Bible Publishers, Nashville, Tennessee. All rights reserved.

Scripture quotations marked (ICB) are taken from *The Holy Bible, International Children's Bible*. Copyright © 1986, 1988, 1999, 2015 by Tommy Nelson, a division of Thomas Nelson. Used by permission.

Scripture quotations marked (ISV) are taken from the *International Standard Version of the Bible*. Copyright © 1995–2014 by ISV Foundation. All rights reserved internationally. Used by permission of Davidson Press, Inc.

Scripture quotations marked (KJV) are taken from *The King James Version of the Bible*.

Scripture quotations marked (MSG) are taken from *The Message*. Copyright © 1993, 1994, 1995, 1996, 2000, 2001, 2002 by Eugene H. Peterson.

Scripture quotations marked (NASB) are taken from the *New American Standard Bible*. Copyright © 1960, 1962, 1963, 1968, 1971, 1972, 1973, 1975, 1977, 1995 by The Lockman Foundation. Used by permission. www.Lockman.org

Scripture quotations marked (NCV) are taken from the *New Century Version*. Copyright © 2005 by Thomas Nelson, Inc. Used by permission. All rights reserved.

Scripture quotations marked (NIV) are taken from two editions: *The Holy Bible, New International Version, NIV.* Copyright © 1973, 1978, 1984, 2011 by Biblica. All rights reserved worldwide. *The Holy Bible, New International Version.* Copyright © 1973, 1978, 1984 by International Bible Society. Used by permission of Zondervan Bible Publishers.

Scripture quotations marked (NKJV) are taken from *The Holy Bible, New King James Version*. Copyright © 1983, 1985, 1990, 1997 by Thomas Nelson, Inc.

Scripture quotations marked (NLT) are taken from *The Holy Bible, New Living Translation*. Copyright © 1996. Used by permission of Tyndale House Publishers, Inc., Wheaton, Illinois 60189. All rights reserved.

Scripture quotations marked (NRSV) are taken from the *New Revised Standard Version Bible*. Copyright © 1989 by the Division of Christian Education of the National Council of the Churches of Christ in the U.S.A. Used by permission. All rights reserved.

Scripture quotations marked (RSV) are taken from the *Revised Standard Version of the Bible*. Copyright © 1946, 1952, 1971 by the Division of Christian Education of the National Council of the Churches of Christ in the U.S.A. Used by permission. All rights reserved.

Scripture quotations marked (TLB) are taken from *The Living Bible*. Copyright © 1971 by Tyndale House Foundation. Used by permission of Tyndale House Publishers, Inc., Carol Stream, Illinois 60188. All rights reserved.

Cover and interior design by Müllerhaus
Indexed by Maria A. Sullivan
Typeset by Aptara

ISBN: 978-1-948649-00-1
ISBN: 978-0-8249-0964-2 (ePub)
ISBN: 978-0-8249-0965-9 (ePDF)

Printed and bound in the United States of America
10 9 8 7 6 5 4 3 2 1

Introduction

Growing up in my family, the teachings of Jesus were the foundation of our faith walk. The stories in the Bible taught me about His love and compassion for all people. It doesn't matter what gender, race, or social class a person is; Jesus loves everyone. This unconditional love is what drew me to Him. In my early teens, I decided to follow Jesus and live by His teachings. I learned early on that without Jesus's grace, it would be impossible to live for Him. Forty plus years later, I still continue to deepen my relationship with Jesus and experience the power of His love. And what better way to do so than to spend a few minutes each and every day with Him.

Every Day with Jesus consists of 365 devotionals, one for each day of the year, which will draw you closer to Jesus and deepen your faith. Through heartfelt stories of hope and grace, the writers share their personal walk with Jesus. In reading these devotionals, you will be encouraged by the Bible verses that affirm His love and presence in your life. Each prayer will give you the strength to live out your faith with boldness, humility, and the courage needed in times of doubt. Be renewed by Jesus's life changing words; discover what it means to be Jesus's disciple and learn how to shine His light, especially for those in despair and darkness.

Making Jesus our first priority in life takes discipline and a daily commitment. *Every Day with Jesus* will deepen your passion for Him; there is a word of wisdom for you within every devotional. When your faith is tested, doubts overrun your thoughts, and fear overwhelms you, Jesus is with you. As Jesus said, "In this world you will have trouble. But take heart! I have overcome the world" (John 16:33). Jesus's daily presence reminds us that in following Him, we will find peace and an abundant life in return.

Faithfully Yours,

Rev. Dr. Pablo R. Diaz

My Precious One,

As the new year begins, I want to invite you into a new and better life with Me. I am your Messiah—the One Who came to save you from the old life and deliver you into the new. Because you belong to Me, you are a new creation. You became new the moment you accepted Me into your life, and in Me you are also becoming new every day. It's a process, being conformed to My image. Be patient in hope and be kind to yourself as you grow and change. Like the snow that falls, flake by flake, I make all things beautiful in My time. When you feel discouraged just remember: My mercies are new for you every morning; every moment is a fresh start.

No matter what, you will never hear Me say that you are out of chances. There's no conclusion to my compassion, no limit to My love for you. With Me you can always begin again.

I see you, where you are at this very moment. I know the unique challenges you are facing this year, the old things you want to leave behind. Nothing is hidden from Me. I understand your smallest concerns and the deepest desires of your heart. I have come to you to help you. I will meet you where you are. You don't have to wait until things are different before you accept my invitation. Take My hand. Trust in Me with all of your heart, and let Me lead you. I will make your path straight. Let's walk together through this year in newness of life.

I love you forever.

Anyone united with the Messiah gets a fresh start, is created new. The old life is gone. —2 Corinthians 5:17 (MSG)

> I know your deeds. See, I have placed before you an open door that no one can shut. I know that you have little strength, yet you have kept my word and have not denied my name. —Revelation 3:8 (NIV)

On New Year's Day, we celebrate with family and dear friends over a good-luck meal that consists of savory pork and black-eyed peas, a dish I cook every year. Knowing who is coming, I prepare the meal with a little extra TLC. I anticipate that first knock on the front door. It always makes my heart leap with joy. After all, these are the most special people in my life coming to dinner. It makes me grateful for this time to start fresh, begin anew, and welcome in a new year with the people dearest to me.

As each loved one arrives, we exchange hugs and smiles. Delightful aromas of what I've prepared waft through the air. The anticipation of a good meal mingles with love and happiness as we all join hands and pray, "Lord, make us thankful for these and all our many blessings," followed by, "God is great! God is good!"

Our gathering is a simple reminder that Jesus's front door is always open. Through Him are new possibilities and new prospects for the year to come. It fills me with such joyful anticipation. I welcome and embrace it. And I expect to walk through the new year upholding His glorious name. What a great way to start the new year!

—*Mary E. Williams*

"Cheers to a new year and another chance for us to get it right."
—*Oprah Winfrey*

 JESUS, please be my strength and guide my every step through this new year. Amen.

> Jesus answered, "Can you make the friends of the bridegroom fast while he is with them? But the time will come when the bridegroom will be taken from them; in those days they will fast." —Luke 5:34-35 (NIV)

Can you imagine going to a wedding where the bride and groom say, "Sorry, no food or drink—and don't even think about a moist slice of vanilla-cream wedding cake!"? That's a gathering I'd rather not attend. Weddings are supposed to be parties full of life, plates of good food, and laughter—not restrictive fasts. Here's the rub: Life has rhythms of both fasting and feasting. Christmas holidays, Thanksgiving dinners, summers at the lake on Fourth of July—these are not times to fast. The events and food are part of the celebration. I can actually smell the months of November and December—cheddar-cheese biscuits, sticky pecan pie, and homemade syrup spilling over thick slices of my Skier's French Toast on Christmas morning. I don't want to spend those months eating lettuce!

But come January it's time to hunker down. I focus and fast so I can take care of this body that I love. When Jesus walked the earth, it wasn't time to fast. His years on earth were to be enjoyed with bread, wine, figs, and honey. The time for fasting would come. The cross made sure of that. When we adapt to the rhythms of feasting and fasting, intentionality sets in and we know we're living as He intended.

—*Gari Meacham*

"There has to be a way to live with health and maturity and intention
while still honoring the part of me that loves to eat, that sees food
as a way to nurture and nourish both my body and my spirit."
—*Shauna Niequist*

JESUS, I need to live in a healthy balance of fasting and feasting. Please show me how. Amen.

> **No one can serve two masters. Either you will hate the one and love the other, or you will be devoted to the one and despise the other. You cannot serve both God and money. —Matthew 6:24 (NIV)**

As a twentysomething, I became part of a team that formed a small corporation. Our shared goal was to build a successful business and reap a huge profit. The business plan was solid, but it demanded every bit of my time and money to get it off the ground.

The first eight months were the hardest, but the allure of success kept me going. I devoted sixteen-hour workdays without earning any income, often giving up weekends and personal time to achieve my dream. Finally, my sacrifices began to pay off.

Within two years, I was flush with the thrill of driving a sporty new car, living in a new home in the suburbs, and taking luxury vacations. But it didn't take long before lunch dates at trendy restaurants lost their allure and relationships with my business partners began to crumble. We were all groveling at the altar of money.

During that same time, I met a family that lived on a very modest income but had more joy and more faith in God than anyone I knew. I wanted that for myself. Their influence led me to put my faith in Christ. I decided to sell my share of the business and focus on Him. I soon discovered that following Jesus is the richest way to live.

—*Barb Howe*

"A life is either all spiritual or not spiritual at all. No man can serve two masters. Your life is shaped by the end you live for. You are made in the image of what you desire."
—*Thomas Merton*

 JESUS, may I never forget that Your loving presence in my life is a far greater prize than any of the things money can buy. Amen.

> Then Jesus told him, "Because you have seen me, you have believed; blessed are those who have not seen and yet have believed." —John 20:29 (NIV)

I have the mind of a skeptic, and I sometimes doubt both the truth of the Scriptures and that still, small voice that would have me obey God. I ask myself, *On what then do I place my trust? My own reason? My limited experiences? The press? Scientists?*

It's a question of trust of the unseen. I say that because I do trust that my car's brakes will work when I need them to, and I have faith that a chair will hold my weight. I exercise faith in doing all the mundane things involved with living my daily life. Why, then, is God's Word the object of my skepticism? Yes, the Bible is filled with miracles, and yes, it claims to be the foundation of life itself, so it should be held to a high standard—and it is! Generations of scholars, translators, and archaeologists have meticulously worked to bring me the eyewitness accounts of Jesus, as all these men and women were carried along by the same Spirit that had the power to raise Jesus from the dead.

I recognize that my faith isn't in the scholars, archaeologists, translators, publishers or printers. My faith is in Jesus. Doubt and skepticism remain issues I must overcome, as they are often reserved for what the Word of God says about me and my faith more than about the truth of Who He is or what He's done. But acknowledging that truth is a step toward righteousness, which ultimately brings me closer to Him.

—*Michael Berrier*

"A little faith will bring your soul to heaven,
but a lot of faith will bring heaven to your soul."
—*Dwight L. Moody*

I BELIEVE in You, Lord Jesus, though I have not yet seen the scars on Your body. And I believe that in the end I will see You face to face, because You have told me so. Amen.

> Then Jesus declared, "I am the bread of life. Whoever comes to me will never go hungry, and whoever believes in me will never be thirsty."
> —John 6:35 (NIV)

When I was a child, my mom made cheese toast when I didn't feel well or simply needed a snack. It wasn't fancy. She took a piece of bread, topped it with cheddar cheese, and warmed it in the oven—the basic ingredients of bread and cheese melted into something delightful. I make it in my own kitchen now, but it never tastes as good as my mother's version.

I still equate cheese toast with comfort and home. To me, it represents more than food. Cheese toast means someone is taking care of me. It reminds me of being loved by my mother.

When Jesus says, "I am the Bread of Life," He means more than a physical loaf of bread. We require physical food to survive, but Jesus is essential for our spiritual survival. By providing the bread analogy, Jesus used a term we easily understand. Our bodies need food and water, but our souls hunger and thirst for Jesus. Only He can provide the type of bread and water that will satisfy our spirits.

We were created to be in a relationship with Jesus. Just as we need to eat food each day to keep our bodies healthy and strong, we need to spend time with Jesus every day to receive spiritual nourishment.

—*Allison K. Flexer*

"When you eat, I want you to think of God, of the holiness of hands that feed us, of the provision we are given every time we eat."
—*Shauna Niequist*

 JESUS, just like bread, you are essential to our lives. Nourish us with Your eternal bread and water. Amen.

I have come as a light to shine in this dark world, so that all who put their trust in me will no longer remain in the dark. —John 12:46 (NLT)

There's something absolutely breathtaking about a full moon. Its soft glow shines through the night sky. Moonlight is used in ballads, romance novels, and even romantic movies. It's appealing. It's easy to look upon and yet gives enough light to see in the darkest of night. It can guide you if you're lost and help you find your way home. It's truly a beauty to be marveled at.

When I think about Jesus being the Light to shine in the dark, I don't see the bright sun—though He's brilliant like the sun—because the sun can be scorching, blinding, and harsh. But the moon reflects the sun's light, absorbing its harshness, and draws people in. And with all the smaller stars surrounding it, it's a painting waiting to be captured.

At night, when I sit on my dock over the pond, I like to imagine all of Jesus's followers as stars and Jesus, like the moon, as the brightest light—the most radiant—front and center. Sitting there, gazing up at all that wonder, is a perfect reminder to me that we can draw more people to a soft light that shines beautifully than we can with harsh light that burns and withers. People need kindness that leads to repentance—not sharp words of condemnation. How I shine matters.

—*Jessica R. Patch*

"There are two kinds of light—the glow that illuminates, and the glare that obscures."
—*James Thurber*

 JESUS, let my light be a thing of beauty that attracts and points people in darkness straight to You. Amen.

> I pray they will be one, Father, just as you are in me and I am in you. I pray that they also will be in us, so that the world will believe that you sent me.
> —John 17:21 (CEB)

It was part of a conversation I had decades ago—just a few words, but they ended up changing my life. I'd gone to a minister for some spiritual advice. I told him how I'd grown up in a good church, had gone to Sunday school, and read lots of spiritual books, but something was missing. That's when he asked me a question: "Do you know God?"

I hesitated. "I don't know," I said. It occurred to me that I knew God the way I knew my best friends' parents. They might ask me to call them by their first names, and I would say, "Sure, Mr. and Mrs. Johns." These were formal relationships, nothing personal.

"How do you get to know God?" I asked.

"You spend time with God every day," this good man said. "That means sitting quietly in prayer. It might be only for five minutes, but it's five minutes dedicated to listening to Jesus and learning Who Jesus is to you. You should do it every day."

So I began a spiritual practice that hasn't stopped since. Sometimes it's on a subway train, sometimes on the sofa, and sometimes in a busy office. To know someone you must spend time with them, listening, learning, and loving.

—*Rick Hamlin*

"The irony is that while God doesn't need us but still wants us,
we desperately need God but don't really want Him most of the time."
—*Francis Chan*

 JESUS, every day is another day to get to know You, and knowing You is knowing the Father. Amen.

For all those who exalt themselves will be humbled, and those who humble themselves will be exalted. —Luke 14:11 (NIV)

Early on in my relationship with my husband, my father-in-law impressed me as a man who appreciated knowledge and sharing truth. That's why the path he chose in seeking fulfillment surprised me.

He followed in his father's footsteps, choosing to pledge his heart to a fraternity in which he clung to secrets, and pursued significance and recognition through man-made degrees. As his father had done before him, he reached the highest honors.

My father-in-law resented his youngest son's choice to break the generational tradition and give his heart to Jesus and follow His ways instead. The tension lay just below the surface of their relationship decade after decade, until cancer ravaged my father-in-law's body.

In the end he lay on his sickbed, abandoned by those he knew in the fellowship. It was then he saw that my husband and I, followers of Jesus—not his secret-society buddies—stood by him and cared for him. We had the answers he desperately sought in his last days on earth. When my father-in-law finally humbled himself and expressed his need for Jesus, we had the privilege of helping him find his faith before he was ushered into heaven and into the arms of his Savior.

—*Mona Hodgson*

*"I have been driven many times upon my knees by the overwhelming
conviction that I had nowhere else to go."*
—*Abraham Lincoln*

JESUS, You alone are worthy of praise. I need you. I exalt You, Lord. Be high and lifted up in my life. Amen.

> Even the Spirit of truth, whom the world cannot receive, because it neither sees him nor knows him. You know him, for he dwells with you and will be in you. —John 14:17 (ESV)

I have often asked myself, *Why me?* Why did I recognize and accept Jesus, when it seems like so many in this world can neither see Him nor accept Him?

God sent an odd assortment of Christian characters—unlikely neighbors, colleagues, and friends—into my story at a time when I was longing for meaning. Despite my intellectual bent and worldly ways, I couldn't help but be persuaded that Jesus was indeed Who He claimed to be. And I couldn't help but surrender to Him, despite the odds.

Jesus tells us here that our path to Him is supernatural. It is the Holy Spirit living alongside and inside of us Who enables us to see and accept Jesus, from the point of salvation and thereafter. And it's only by opening my heart to Christ that the Spirit of truth takes up residence.

There was really nothing in me before, apart from a life that wasn't working for me, that would cause me to be open-minded enough to accept Christ and receive the Holy Spirit.

The Bible uses many other terms to describe the Holy Spirit and His work, including "Encourager," "Helper," "Counselor," and "Advocate." I count on the Holy Spirit living in me to reveal truth, inform my thoughts and actions, and shine brightly enough to help others recognize and accept Jesus for Who He is.

—Isabella Yosuico

"I desire each of my followers to be a Light-bearer. The Holy Spirit who lives in you can shine from your face, making me visible to people around you."
—*Sarah Young*

 LORD JESUS, help me more deeply sense and reflect Your Spirit within me, so that I might reveal You to an unseeing world. Amen.

I am the good shepherd; I know my sheep and my sheep know me. My sheep listen to my voice; I know them, and they follow me. —John 10:14, 27 (NIV)

After delivering an item to my children's school, I heard a voice as I walked out the front entrance.

"Mom!"

Students crowded the hallway, but one voice caused my heart to jump and made me pause.

I turned to see my son walking toward me. Because I know him and have listened to his voice since the day he was born, his call rose above the crowd.

Jesus describes Himself as our Shepherd, the One Who takes care of us and knows us. He doesn't just casually know us, but He has an intimate knowledge of us. And the more time we spend with Jesus, the better we know Him and recognize His voice.

I've learned over the years to listen for Jesus's voice, the still small sound that comes through clearly in solitude and the loving Scripture verses intended to offer guidance for me every day. The more I train myself to listen, the more recognizable He becomes and I can follow Him better.

—*Amelia Rhodes*

"The heart and soul of the Christian life is learning to hear God's voice and then developing the courage to do what he asks us to do."
—*Bill Hybels*

JESUS, I desire to hear Your voice throughout the day. Please grant me courage to do what You say. Amen.

> Whoever acknowledges me before others, I will also acknowledge before my Father in heaven. But whoever disowns me before others, I will disown before my Father in heaven. —Matthew 10:32-33 (NIV)

A close friend of mine had a morning ritual she performed before sending her children off to school. The ritual consisted of a series of visual checks to ensure they were ready to leave the house. Hair brushed: check. Teeth brushed: check. Clothes match: check. There were probably a few more "checks" I am forgetting, but I remember that the final item was the most important. She would say something like, "Remember, you are a [last name]. Everything you say and do today reflects not just on you but also on our family."

Unsurprisingly, her children grew up to become admirable adults. To this day they bring honor to the family name. I truly want to do the same for my family name—and for the name of Jesus, Who connected His reputation to mine when He took me in many years ago and made me a part of His family of faith.

Everywhere I go, I face a choice of acknowledging or disowning Jesus by my words and actions. In everything I do, I want to remember that I am His and that all I do reflects not just on me but also on Him. I want nothing less than to disown Him by my actions. I want nothing more than to acknowledge Jesus and His love, grace, mercy, and beauty in everything I say and do every day.

—*Bob Hostetler*

"The greatest single cause of atheism in the world today is Christians who acknowledge Jesus with their lips and walk out the door and deny Him by their lifestyle. That is what an unbelieving world simply finds unbelievable."
—*Brennan Manning*

 LORD JESUS, let my every word and deed today acknowledge You and bring honor to Your Name. Amen.

I have given them your word and the world has hated them, for they are not of the world any more than I am of the world. —John 17:14 (NIV)

Accepting the job had been a terrible mistake. I didn't fit in. Part of the "problem" was my faith. Few of the other workers practiced any religion at all, and those who did worshipped a god by a different name.

The larger source of their discomfort was my perspective. Seeing my life through the hope and peace Jesus provided left my colleagues suspicious. Soon I sensed a chill whenever entering a room in my workplace. Though I'd often heard of people suffering from persecution, the sting of rejection, when aimed at me personally, hurt. With care, I walked a thin line.

The longer I stayed, the more stress filled my world. I prayed to the Lord for delivery, and I waited. Months, then years passed.

My relationship with my colleagues remained the same—strained but livable. Then a change occurred in my heart as something new came alive and grew day by day. I became stronger, more focused on Christ's perfect will for me, until there was no longer any doubt. One morning, following prayer, I took the final leap of faith and submitted my resignation.

Starting over as an inspirational writer challenges me. But there is no reward greater than knowing I'm exactly where Jesus wants me to be. That's quite the promotion!

—*Heidi Gaul*

"May God in His mercy lead us through these times;
but above all, may He lead us to Himself."
—*Dietrich Bonhoeffer*

 LORD JESUS, continue walking me through the tough times and leading me toward the joy found in Your will. Amen.

> **Stop judging by mere appearances, but instead judge correctly.**
> **—John 7:24 (NIV)**

I stood in Maria's kitchen, trying to mask my frustration. One of the other women was putting down moms like me, who worked outside the home, labeling our choice as "unbiblical." I swallowed my fear of confrontation and told her about my husband's frequent medical bills and reductions in hours that made it impossible for us to live on one income. I shared the wonderful things God did because I had to work, like opening doors for me to write. I loved my work! I waited for her to soften. She didn't, so I decided against telling her that I survived on one income now because my husband had left.

Lord, what else should I say?

Nothing. I stopped trying to defend myself and accepted the moment as a lesson in what can happen when we make snap judgments.

"Stop judging by mere appearances." Jesus's words remind me that He also encountered harsh judgment—even in the process of healing—from those who cared only about society's rules. Recalling the conversation in Maria's kitchen, I felt challenged to be mindful of my own tendency to point fingers based on assumptions. How many times have I let my interpretation of what's "right" be so important that I failed to see Jesus at work in someone's life?

As we go out into a world filled with people who may or may not live according to our standards, I hope we follow the example of Jesus, Who possessed the grace to see beyond mere appearances.

—Jeanette Hanscome

"It is the property of fools, to be always judging." —*Thomas Fuller*

 LORD, forgive me for judging by appearances. I don't want to be like the Pharisees; I want to be like You. Amen.

You pore over the Scriptures because you think you have eternal life in them, yet they testify about Me. —John 5:39 (HCSB)

As an art and history teacher for many years, one of the easiest things for my students to learn was ROYGBIV, the acronym that stands for the sequence of colors in the rainbow. However, I knew not to assume that just because they could recite the colors and mix them together they could instantly paint a masterpiece.

But it seemed that every year I had a few students who were convinced they could create a great painting just because they'd mastered the ins and outs of color mixing. Wrong. They were soon humbled and had to admit there was way more to learn in order to become a true artist.

Jesus acknowledged that the teachers and scribes were diligently searching Scripture, but they were doing it not to glorify God but rather to draw praise and honor to themselves. They could recite the letter of the law but had a vague understanding of the Spirit behind it.

Dietrich Bonhoeffer, a German pastor known for resisting Hitler, knew that people, even those who claim to follow the Bible, are likely to latch onto their own ideas about life and God. He wrote about it extensively to his brother, and I can't help but agree.

Pride can get the best of us. Whether we're attempting to master a new skill or, more importantly, trying to deepen our walk with Jesus, we must first remember the foundation—those basic truths on which we must build, learn, and grow.

—*Angie Spady*

"One cannot simply read the Bible, like other books. One must be prepared really to enquire of it. Only then will it reveal itself. Only if we expect from it the ultimate answer, shall we receive it." —Dietrich Bonhoeffer

JESUS, thank You for Your Word and for reminding me that I cannot just memorize it. Help me to tuck it deeply into my heart and get to know You personally. Amen.

> **For whoever wants to save their life will lose it, but whoever loses their life for me will find it. —Matthew 16:25 (NIV)**

I have a serious sweet tooth. Jokingly, I've been known to refer to it more as an entire mouth of sweet teeth. Whether this just comes naturally or is a product of growing up eating dessert after dinner every night, the result is the same. I crave something sweet after pretty much every meal…and for snacking…and just whenever the mood strikes me. Knowing this, it's not surprising that self-denial isn't something I'm particularly good at by nature.

"It's Hard to Be a Christian" was the title of a sermon by Dr. Martin Luther King Jr., in which he talks candidly about self-denial. Dr. King was talking about much more than my junk-food habits. He was talking about pride and ego. His words made me self-reflect. I asked myself, *Do I call the shots in my life or have I willingly surrendered to the "pressing concerns of God's kingdom?" And what do those concerns have to do with me?* What is abundantly clear is that putting Jesus first and myself second isn't necessarily easy. It takes discipline. The good news—the gospel message—is that the result of submitting our lives to Christ, which seems like giving it all up, is actually to receive true life!

—*Wayne Adams*

"Jesus never left men with such illusions. He made it crystal clear that His gospel was difficult. It demands that we subordinate our clamoring egos to the pressing concerns of God's kingdom. This is the meaning of self-denial."
—*Martin Luther King Jr.*

 DEAR JESUS, please give us the strength to put You first in our lives. Thank You that when we deny ourselves and submit to You, we find true love and life in return. Amen.

For my Father's will is that everyone who looks to the Son and believes in him shall have eternal life, and I will raise them up at the last day.
—John 6:40 (NIV)

The doctor must have been mistaken. A diagnosis such as this happened to other people, not to my family. A hemorrhaging tumor in my husband's brain wasn't part of the plan. At least, it hadn't been part of our plan.

Even before the shock had time to dissipate, the surgery was scheduled and I notified loved ones. With all the preparations made, we waited. Time stretched before us, the empty days dragging.

Life, the way I'd lived it before, had ended. Every minute spent with my husband became precious, as I wondered how many more moments God would grant him. We didn't talk about it, but I suspected that, like me, he also was fighting a private battle against an unseen but powerful enemy: terror. Would he survive? Would we need a miracle?

Through it all, Jesus walked with us. We sensed His presence and prayed constantly, welcoming His responses. When we flipped open the Bible, He spoke to us with words of quiet reassurance. On days when doubts overran our thoughts and our faith flagged, He held us close.

On the morning of the surgery, we were ready. Each day, we'd grown in our relationship with Christ, learning to trust Him as the Great Physician. There was no room for fear.

The operation was successful, and my husband is fine. And our faith? Stronger than ever before.

—*Heidi Gaul*

"Faith sees the invisible, believes the unbelievable, and receives the impossible."
—*Corrie ten Boom*

JESUS, Your magnificent love heals the sick, just as Your sacrifice overcame death. I praise Your holy name. Amen.

> Truly I tell you, if anyone says to this mountain, "Go, throw yourself into the sea," and does not doubt in their heart but believes that what they say will happen, it will be done for them. Therefore I tell you, whatever you ask for in prayer, believe that you have received it, and it will be yours. —Mark 11:23–24 (NIV)

I gazed out my kitchen window at a majestic range of mountains called the Collegiate Peaks. They were intimidating, imposing, and immovable.

So was the mountain in my living room.

It was a mountain of worry with icy peaks of fear. On this particular morning, I had anxiety about a troubled relationship. Words had left bruises only grace would heal, and years of history and hurts had resurfaced as fresh scars.

The mountains in my mind seemed as impassable and impossible as the mountains outside my window—yet Jesus promises we can stand at the base of our insurmountable obstacles and call to Him for help.

I began to pray, not knowing how or when this relationship would untangle, and Jesus brought to my mind other mountains we had conquered together. Sometimes He had lifted me over their peaks, and other times He had detoured me around them. Sometimes He simply whisks a mountain away and sweeps up the debris!

My faith strengthened, I put on the only mountain-climbing gear we ever need: bold, confident, expectant prayer.

—*Amy Lively*

"When I turned my focus around, I realized that God is alive beyond mountains and oceans of my fear if I can but turn around right where I am each time the mountains or oceans threaten to overwhelm me." —Keith Miller

 JESUS, there's a mountain in front of me today. I don't know how You will remove it, but I trust You to do exactly what I need, when I need it, in a way that I might not expect. Amen.

Jesus touched their eyes and said, "Because of your faith, you will be healed." —Matthew 9:29 (CEV)

There's a reason for the old saying "Seeing is believing."

By the time we're adults, most of us have become a little jaded because we know we can't trust everything we're told.

"Next time it'll be different."

"If you elect me, I'll lower your taxes."

"The check is in the mail."

Even Thomas the disciple, who knew Jesus so well and had witnessed so many of His miracles, refused to believe that Jesus had risen after the crucifixion. He told Jesus he'd believe it when he saw the nail marks in the palms of His hands.

Jesus performed a miracle for people who didn't have Thomas's firsthand experience. The two blind men Jesus healed had only heard of His power, but still they made it their business to find Him. They called out, "Son of David, have pity on us." Jesus asked if they believed He could make them see. When they said, "Yes, Lord," He healed them.

These men had not seen Jesus's miracles with their own eyes. They hadn't seen anything for years. And Jesus told them that they would be healed because of their faith—not because of their determination to get to Jesus, not because He felt sorry for them, but because they believed without seeing.

—*Michelle Rapkin*

"Any concern too small to be turned into a prayer is too small to be made into a burden." —Corrie ten Boom

JESUS, thank You for Your love and Your care for me. Please give me faith like the blind men whom You healed. Help me to be confident in Your love and Your care. Amen.

THE TRUTH WILL SET YOU FREE

> So Jesus said to the Jews who had believed him, "If you abide in my word, you are truly my disciples, and you will know the truth, and the truth will set you free." —John 8:31-32 (ESV)

I want to be set free. I want freedom from jealousy and anger and strife. I want freedom from the fear of failing as a mother and from the frustration of unproductive days. I want freedom from my vices—wasting time with technology and chasing rabbit trails in my mind.

I want freedom, and it feels like I am wired to strive for it—to work and sweat and become "better" at developing a holiness in my spirit.

Jesus tells us the way to freedom comes from knowing truth, and the only way to know truth is by abiding in the Word. That's good news, because the Word is a welcome place for distracted wanderers like me to abide.

The hard work of abiding is not about my strength or endurance or willpower to change my wandering heart (thank goodness). The hard work of abiding is about trusting that Jesus opens the door to a home with everything we need for life.

This is the truth that sets me free. I do not have to chase freedom from failure and frustration and vice. When I abide in the Word, I actively believe that Jesus is my safe shelter, my steadfast provider, and my certain rest. He worked and sweated so that I can find my freedom in Him.

—*Caroline Kolts*

"In sharing our weaknesses [Jesus] gives us strength and imparts through his companionship a life that has the quality of eternity." —*Dallas Willard*

 JESUS, give me patience to abide in Your presence so I can know truth and experience freedom. Amen.

> One night the Lord spoke to Paul in a vision: "Do not be afraid; keep on speaking, do not be silent. For I am with you, and no one is going to attack and harm you, because I have many people in this city." —Acts 18:9-10 (NIV)

When I was young, I became lost in a tidal swamp deep in the heart of old Florida. Well after dark, I found a woodsy road and began to follow it. The night was cold and inky black. Only a sandy strip of road stretched ahead, disappearing into darkness. No stars shone through the thick tree canopy, where limbs draped with mossy fingers undulated and whispered. Creatures rustled in the underbrush, their movements furtive and quick. I shivered, quickening my steps, and a chill crept up my neck as I imagined panthers, bears, and other creatures padding softly behind me or watching, licking long fangs and waiting for the right moment to strike. I walked faster and faster, gulping air in choppy breaths, my fears overwhelming me.

It was then that I began to sing. My voice, at first cracked and weak, grew bolder and stronger as the melodies pushed against the darkness around me. I sang songs from my childhood, hymns from church, and solos I'd heard my father sing. I sang the Lord's Prayer, hanging on every word, singing as if I were standing in a church by a blushing bride and her husband-to-be. If anyone had heard me, they would have thought a lunatic walked the road that night. But the songs comforted me and chased away fear. And I knew I was not alone.

—*J. Mason Williams*

"Now, God be praised, that to believing souls gives
light in darkness, comfort in despair."
—*William Shakespeare*

 LORD, give me the strength to know You are always there. Yours is the face I seek. Amen.

> **Then Jesus said to them, "The Son of Man is Lord of the Sabbath."**
> **—Luke 6:5 (NIV)**

I love Sunday afternoon naps. Everyone in my family does. It's not at all unusual for all of us to sleep for an hour or two after lunch, before we head back to church.

Our culture doesn't make room for naps. In a world where busyness and achievement are gods, there is no space for intentional rest. Jesus offered a different perspective about Sabbath.

When David and his men were hungry, they ate the bread set aside for worship. This act wasn't rooted in disregard for the God's holiness but in their belief of His provision.

We might not haggle over consecrated bread, but we are often constrained by a narrow view of Sabbath, of rest and worship. While our schedules are dictated by to-do lists, Jesus offers a reminder that He is Lord of all.

Understanding rest as an opportunity to trust the Lord's provision is challenging. Some view intentional rest as laziness. Jesus points to a greater truth: our salvation is tied to our relationship with Him.

Naps, like the bread, aren't holy of themselves. But learning to trust in the Lord's provision for us is a vital part of our worship and growth as believers.

—*Teri Lynne Underwood*

"Rest is a matter of wisdom, not law."
—*Woodrow Kroll*

 JESUS, help me trust Your provision. Teach me the value of rest in a world that values busyness. Amen.

> Jesus did not let him, but said, "Go home to your own people and tell them how much the Lord has done for you, and how he has had mercy on you."
> —Mark 5:19 (NIV)

I met Victor at church. He was a man on fire for Jesus. Joy radiated in his eyes and smile, and I asked him what had brought him to faith.

Victor had been a part of the crime world when he was a teen ager. He spent five years in prison for his cartel involvement. When he was released, he vowed to stay clean. But the lure of money challenged Victor to return to his old ways. His choices made him a wanted man once again, and he escaped to Mexico, where he lived as a fugitive for five more years. There, he searched for meaning and purpose in his life. A young woman introduced him to Jesus by telling him the story of Paul's conversion. That introduction led him to Jesus, and he never let Him go.

Victor married the young woman and returned to the States. Depression hit him hard while he was adapting to his new life. But his Christian employer became his mentor. When my friend Victor chose to seek out a Christian lawyer to help him face the crimes he'd committed, he turned to his mentor for guidance. Together they met with the lawyer, who helped facilitate a miracle. Victor learned his slate had been wiped clean—just as Jesus had done for him eternally. He enrolled in college and graduated with skills to help others not only succeed but also find Jesus.

After he finished his story, I was weeping.

Victor continues to inspire my life, and we remain close friends. Because of his testimony, I'm encouraged to reach out to those the world believes are in need. As Victor has proven, hope rises when we give our lives to Jesus Christ.

—DiAnn Mills

"The best and most beautiful things in the world cannot be seen or even touched— they must be felt with the heart." —Helen Keller

DEAR JESUS, help me to reveal Your love to my family and friends by my thoughts, words, and actions. You are the joy of a believer's life. Amen.

> **Just as the living Father sent me and I live because of the Father, so the one who feeds on me will live because of me. —John 6:57 (NIV)**

My quiet time alone with God in the morning had gotten boring, monotonous, and stuffy. I tried a different devotional book, but I still felt unmoved. Then a friend asked me how I was doing. I admitted that my time with God wasn't as meaningful as it had been. I realized, after that admission, the problem was with me—not God. God is never boring!

"Are you spending time with Jesus, or with your devotional book?" Her question made me stop and think. Was it possible that I was just going through the motions, reading the Word of God but not connecting with the Author?

Jesus wanted me to sit and concentrate on Him, not so much on my journal, books, or prayer notebook. Feeling fulfilled didn't come from those things; it came from the Reason behind it all: Jesus. As I mindfully acknowledged Jesus's presence with me, He brought to my mind verses—His words—that comforted, encouraged, and directed me in the next steps of my journey.

Refreshed and excited, I began a new journey, each day spending time with the living God.

—*Nancy Sebastian Kuch*

"The power of effective habits is not in the seclusion, or the silence, or the journal, but in whom you find in the habit…if you find more of God, you have found resources far beyond yourself to address your deepest, most desperate needs."
—*Marshall Segal*

 JESUS, thank You for being willing—and desiring—to meet with me each day. You make my time each morning come alive as You feed me. Amen.

> I am in them and You are in Me. May they be made completely one, so the world may know You have sent Me and have loved them as You have loved Me. —John 17:23 (HCSB)

Change is hard. Regardless of our age, being taken out of our comfort zone is something we rarely choose on our own. But when my husband and I became empty nesters, we made the decision that he should accept a job offer in the Southwest, an area we'd only visited a few times and primarily read about in travel brochures. Although we were filled with the anticipation of a rousing new adventure, we were also filled with apprehension. What if we couldn't find a church where our souls could thrive and be in unity with others? The fear of achieving this number-one priority led to weeks of soul-searching and intense prayer.

In John 17:23, Jesus's prayer is that those in a covenant with God must desire unity with Him as God's Son. By reading God's Word, doing His will, and exercising faith, we can prepare to live in the same way He does and for all eternity.

Just a few weeks after moving to New Mexico, we found a wonderful church filled with believers who sing His praises to the rooftop. They welcomed us with open arms, and in unity we love spreading the good news of Jesus throughout our town. A reason to rejoice, for sure!

—*Angie Spady*

"Jesus welcomes all who come to Him. . . He's the door; He's the way. He loves you and will receive you if you will come to Him sincerely." —James MacDonald

JESUS, thank You for guiding my steps each day and for providing me with so many opportunities to be in sweet union with You. Oh, how I love You! Amen.

LOSING OUR WAY

Blessed is he who does not take offense at me. —Matthew 11:6 (NASB)

Growing up in the foothills of Colorado, most weekends you could find me skiing with my friends down snow-packed mountains. Back then I was a bit of a rebel, and I often led the pack off the trail into dense forests covered with low-hanging branches that darkened the light of the sun. At first the freedom of rebellion was thrilling. But soon the thrill of traveling an unpredictable path confused my friends and me, and we got so deep in the powdered snow that the real path, although nearby, seemed a million miles away. We couldn't see it because of the low branches, and the sights and sounds of the ski slope were replaced with the unsure footing of a doubtful path.

Sometimes it feels like we've lost our way, even though the way is near to us. That happened to the followers of John the Baptist. Jesus told them to go back to John, who was in prison, and tell him that He was the Truth they shouldn't stumble over. In their fear and confusion over John's imprisonment, it seemed they'd lost their way and fell into doubt. In times of trouble or disappointment, the true path of Jesus is closer than we think. We've simply lost our bearings and must keep from stumbling away from the truth.

—*Gari Meacham*

"Peace has never been about a place. It has always been about a person."
—*Jennifer Dukes Lee*

 JESUS, I've lost my way and can't see the real path. Bring me back to You and keep me from doubting Your truth and direction. Amen.

> **Righteous Father, the world does not know you, but I know you; and these know that you have sent me. I made your name known to them, and I will make it known, so that the love with which you have loved me may be in them, and I in them. —John 17: 25-26 (NRSV)**

When I first became Christian, it was the gospel of John that caught my attention. And I fell in love with chapter 17: a whole chapter in which Jesus just pours His heart out! When I first read it, I felt like I was caught up in a web of love that Jesus spins around Himself, His Heavenly Father, and His friends. Today's two verses are the end of that soliloquy. My heart beats stronger when I read them, as I imagine Jesus's voice quavering while He prays in the presence of His friends.

I hear heartache in Jesus's voice here, and I also hear in His prayer an acknowledgment of three crucial aspects of Christianity: the power of witness, the authenticity of connection, and the nature of love.

How bittersweet it must have been to say, "The world does not know you, God, but I know you." His mission wasn't to conquer the world in the name of God. His mission was to share God's love with whomever was there to receive it. A precious few people recognized Jesus's real and intimate connection with God. Jesus simply loved them, and He knew that through that love each of those precious few could experience God's presence inside their very souls. This is how real Christianity spreads: when we love one an other with the same love through which God loves us.

—*Lizzie Berne DeGear*

"Love takes off the masks that we fear we cannot live
without and know we cannot live within."
—James Baldwin

JESUS, I bear witness to Your connection to God, and I vow to let You open up my soul, letting the love I feel there be part of the continuing story. Amen.

SPIRIT WELLNESS

> When Jesus saw him lying there and learned that he had been in this condition for a long time, he asked him, "Do you want to get well?"
> —John 5:6 (NIV)

My life is halfway over, I figured. *Why not spend the second half of it healthy—and why not do it before my big, almost-surprise fortieth birthday party?* I invested in a weight-loss and wellness program a friend of mine raved about. I did pretty well the first couple of weeks, rigorously taking the right packets at the right time, drinking my water, and eating the recommended snacks and meals.

It was boring, tedious, and difficult, requiring a lot of planning and preparation. But I had the birthday party dangling like a carrot in front of me, so I plugged on. When it became apparent I wasn't going to experience a miraculous loss of four pant sizes by Saturday, I let up a little. Then a lot. Then completely.

Getting well is hard work.

When Jesus encountered a man who had been unwell for a long time, the question Jesus asked seems obvious: "Do you want to get well?" Who wouldn't want to get well after thirty-eight years of suffering? But as I so often do, the man in the story responded with excuses and complaints about why wellness was impossible and unlikely for him. Jesus ordered him, "Stand up, pick up your mat, and walk!"

Perhaps Jesus recognizes the significant difference between being well and getting well.

Being well is easy, but getting well is an everyday exercise in trust, obedience, and faithfulness.

—*Amy Lively*

"There is an expression among even the most advanced runners that getting your shoes on is the hardest part of any workout." —Kathrine Switzer

 JESUS, I do want to be well, physically, spiritually, emotionally, and relationally. Please help me take the first difficult steps with You. Amen.

See that you don't tell this to anyone. But go, show yourself to the priest and offer the sacrifices that Moses commanded for your cleansing, as a testimony to them. —Mark 1:44 (NIV)

"Mom" flashed on the caller ID. I dreaded another tension-filled conversation.

"I've had a wake-up call from God." Her tone was reflective and somber. "I want to change."

A racing heart had landed my otherwise healthy mother in the hospital. Old wounds and issues had plagued our relationship. Her desire to change was welcome.

Shortly after her release, she suffered a major stroke and was rushed to the ER again, this time with only a slim chance of survival.

Three days later, in the hospital, my mom held a brand-new grandson. My brother's son was born during my mom's amazing recovery.

"Miracle" became the buzzword in family conversations.

On her first Sunday home, my mom drove, which was against doctor's orders.

"I had to go to church and thank Jesus," she explained. Her voice sounded different, peaceful. "Something has changed in my heart…in ways I can't explain. All of this was meant to happen. Jesus gave me a full physical, mental, and spiritual healing."

The Lord used my mother's heart issue to spur a desire to change and blessed her with miracles that became testimonies. She became a new creation in Christ.

Now our relationship is restored, and others in our family are leaning toward the voice of their Creator.

—Holly Michael

"Those blessings are sweetest that are won with prayer and worn with thanks."
—Thomas Goodwin

JESUS, thank You for Your many miracles, big and small. We pray that our lives become testimonies of Your great love. Amen.

Blessed are those who mourn, for they will be comforted.
—Matthew 5:4 (NIV)

At the retreat center, where I spoke that day, Sarah sat on the chair in front of me, head in hands, not meeting my gaze.

Two friends flanked her, gently encouraging her to share her story with me. I was a stranger to her, but one who already understood her story.

Through agonizing whispers, she told us about the abuse she'd suffered as a child. It was the kind of story that makes you weep, and wish you could shake the responsible adults into repentance.

"You can be set free," I told her. "It won't happen overnight, or even a hundred overnights, but I believe Jesus will bring you comfort—even after so much pain."

She looked up, her hair obscuring her face. "You really believe that?"

I nodded, and then we prayed together. I poured out my own anguish over her story.

Two years later, Sarah sat across from me at a Tex-Mex restaurant in my town, her eyes reflecting newfound joy. She recounted her journey from the time we prayed together up to that moment—an extraordinary journey of healing. Jesus truly did comfort her. Sarah now wanted to boldly encourage others and help bring comfort to those burdened by their own painful stories.

From mourning to comfort, from imprisonment to freedom, Sarah experienced Jesus's radical intervention, and now she longs for others also to experience it.

—*Mary DeMuth*

"God's strength makes us strong; His comfort comforts us. With Him we no longer run; we rest." —Dillon Burroughs

 JESUS, I really need Your comfort. I trust You'll transform me and help me become a comforter for others. Amen.

Now this is eternal life: that they know you, the only true God, and Jesus Christ, whom you have sent. —John 17:3 (NIV)

The first time the concept of eternal life had real meaning for me was the day my eleven-year-old son went to heaven. Killed in a freak bus accident, he was here one minute, gone the next. Brokenhearted, my life changed forever.

Shortly after, I was considering all I held dear: family, friends, hearth, and home. Still I longed to step into the hereafter and hug my boy again. The desire was so strong, I felt like I was outside of my body, watching someone who looked like me survive.

Though yearning for the rapture or anything powerful enough to send me heavenward, I focused on Jesus—the One Who gave His life, so eternity was possible for my child and for me. This was my hope in the midst of my deepest grief. He comforted and kept me, holding me close like a most beloved daughter.

Then a day came when I knew it was time to live in this world again. Driving home from work, I thought about buying new mini blinds. Mini blinds! Why was I thinking about something so mundane and worldly, after all that had happened in the past year? But I somehow knew He was gently encouraging me to embrace my everyday life once again. With deep knowledge of His matchless grace, His loving care, and His presence with me always, I could take some steps on my own.

Jesus walks beside me still, ever the bridge to my son, reminding me of His promise of eternal life.

—*Cathy Elliott*

"Jesus has given me eternal life in Him. Let them take my life here, but God holds me in the palm of His hand and no one can take Him from me." —Francine Rivers

LORD, may we know the one true God and accept the promise of eternal life through Jesus Christ. Amen.

> **Whoever believes in him is not condemned, but whoever does not believe stands condemned already because they have not believed in the name of God's one and only Son. —John 3:18 (NIV)**

The feeling of guilt is sometimes I find hard to escape. I feel guilty for not being a better father. *Do I spend enough time with my kids? Am I fully present when with them?* Could I be a better husband? *Did I do those things my wife asked me to?* Am I a good person in general? *Do I care for my neighbor? The planet?* If I'm being honest, it sometimes seems as if the Bible was actually the source of my guilt. I mean, if we stand "condemned already" before we even believe in Jesus Christ, doesn't that mean we're starting from a guilty perspective?

Thankfully, my more rational self is reminded, probably with some divine clarification, that this isn't really what's happening and is not how I should be reacting to this passage. Although, as John Calvin appropriately reminds us, we begin life separated from God by sin. Jesus Christ frees us from condemnation as we come to faith in Him. So, whereas I should still work to be a better father (put down my phone!), husband (listen more!), and human (care for God's creation!), I don't need to constantly feel guilty or under a state of judgment. Jesus Christ sets us free to live in joy and love, as we work together to build His kingdom.

—*Wayne Adams*

"I have said that all parts of the soul were possessed by sin after
Adam deserted the fountain of righteousness." —John Calvin

DEAR JESUS, thank You for freeing us from the guilt of condemnation. Please help me to live in the light of Your love and grace. Amen.

Love Letter from Jesus
LOVE

My Beautiful One,

You are loved. You are honored. I have called you by name. You are valued and worthy and prized. Hear My words, and keep them in your heart forever, because they are truth—the truth that sets you free. It doesn't matter what anyone else says or thinks, because I am God. I created you. And here is what I say: there is no flaw in you.

You are so precious to Me, so important, that I laid down my life so I could be with you forever. No love is greater than My love for you. I am yours, and you are Mine. Nothing can ever come between us. Whatever you go through—great joy or difficulty, deep water or fire—you are never alone. I am with you always.

When you see beauty in the world, think of Me—in the uniqueness of each snowflake that falls, in the eyes of a child, in all the colors of the sunset and in the sounds of music. All of these things belong to Me, and I freely give them for you to enjoy.

Also, though, when you encounter fear, hate, or pain, turn your thoughts to Me. Fix your eyes on Me. Remember that even though these things are real and part of the world, I have overcome the world. You can find strength, peace, and hope in Me. My grace is enough for you. Through Me you can overcome. The darkness seems powerful sometimes, but I am the Light of the World. My love is stronger—always stronger—and it casts out fear. Love always wins.

I love you forever.

"As the Father has loved me, so have I loved you. Now remain in my love." John 15:9 (NIV)

> Jesus replied, "You are in error because you do not know the Scriptures or the power of God. At the resurrection people will neither marry nor be given in marriage; they will be like the angels in heaven." —Matthew 22:29–30 (NIV)

"Look how young they are," I whispered, smiling at the adoring look my young niece gave her husband-to-be as they recited their wedding vows. My wife of thirty-five years eyed me quizzically. "We were ten years younger when we got married," she observed.

So young, I thought. We knew nothing of life and the trials it would bring, or how life and time would shape our future selves. In fact, though we thought we knew each other, we only really began to know each other after we joined as one.

But we were committed to each other. We fiercely loved each other and were willing to support each other in all things. We were eager and excited to take on the world, focused on each other and ready to live, love, and laugh together…and, yes, to cry as well.

Jesus is likewise committed to us. We come to Him like blushing brides and uncertain husbands, desperately young in our faith, but committed, focused, and willing to grow closer to Him. Not perfect. Not unblemished. But willing to join with Him in this life and be with Him in the next.

In return, He loves us fiercely, laughing and crying with us as an ever-present soul mate.

That is an "I do" to believe in.

—*J. Mason Williams*

"A good marriage isn't something you find; it's something you make."
—*Gary L. Thomas*

 JESUS, thank You for Your love. You know I am not perfect, yet You love me with a steadfast love that will never fail. For that, I am forever grateful. Amen.

> Jesus answered them, "It is not the healthy who need a doctor, but the sick. I have not come to call the righteous, but sinners to repentance."
> —Luke 5:31–32 (NIV)

Every day, I take my dog to a nearby park, where she chases squirrels. Over time, I've become acquainted with three people who don't seem to have a home. They're in the park 365 days a year, no matter what the weather. I don't know much about them, but I do know that they have kind hearts and hard lives. Occasionally it has occurred to me that I should invite them to church. But I'm not sure they'd fit in.

Recently, one of them, Terri, invited me to *her* church. She had been recently baptized and was very happy about her newfound fellowship. That Sunday I went to a small community-center room rented by a Christian ministry that serves those who are especially vulnerable. I walked in and immediately knew that everyone was welcome there. I slowly realized something else: I was actually the one in need of help, as my hesitation to invite them to my church made me more like a Pharisee, who needs to repent, than like Jesus, Who loves us all the same.

Since then, I've gone back there to worship service several times. Each time, I've felt Jesus there with us.

—*Michelle Rapkin*

"He measures our lives by how we love." —Francis Chan

DEAR JESUS, please forgive me for my pharisaical tendencies. Please help me to remember that You have a soft spot for those who recognize they need help and healing. Amen.

> Beware of practicing your piety before others in order to be seen by them; for then you have no reward from your Father in heaven. So whenever you give alms, do not sound a trumpet before you, as the hypocrites do in the synagogues and in the streets, so that they may be praised by others. Truly I tell you, they have received their reward. —Matthew 6:1-2 (NRSV)

It was so tempting. The boy in my second-grade class, the one who never wore a coat in the winter, had just sat down next to me on the school bus. If he was wearing the same short-sleeve shirt he usually did, it was now hidden under a new wool jacket. When his older sister walked past me to take a seat, I noticed her normally bare legs were now covered in warm stockings. I stole a shy sideways glance at him; then I thought about the promise I had made to my parents.

A week before, when they had asked me why I was crying, I told them about the brother and sister who were always shivering when they got on the bus. My parents listened with concern—then they asked me what Jesus would do. "Help," I said. They made me promise never to tell anyone before doing so, explaining that it was important not to embarrass the family. I nodded and vowed to keep the secret. Shoes and clothing began arriving at our house, along with canned goods and supplies. Items were carefully packaged; then they disappeared. I knew where Billy got his coat, but I wasn't telling. Instead, I held this secret close to my heart—and, in a sense, I held him, too, in Jesus's name.

—*Andrea Raynor*

"It is one of those beautiful compensations of this life that no one can sincerely try to help another without helping himself."
—*Ralph Waldo Emerson*

 DEAR JESUS, help me give as You have called us to give and to live as You have called us to live. My secret treasure is safe with You. Amen.

> The third time [Jesus] said to him, "Simon son of John, do you love me?" Peter was hurt because Jesus asked him the third time, "Do you love me?" He said, "Lord, you know all things; you know that I love you." Jesus said, "Feed my sheep." —John 21:17 (NIV)

I'd done it again. I'd had every opportunity to tell my neighbor about Christ's love, yet I remained silent. That afternoon, I felt deep despair. *How could I have done that?* I berated myself. *Why didn't I speak up?*

After Peter denied knowing Jesus, three times on the night of Christ's arrest (see John 18:15-18, 25-27), he must have carried that same sense of shame. He must have remembered that Jesus had pronounced Peter the rock on which Jesus would build His church (see Matthew 16:18). I wonder if that knowledge increased Peter's anguish. I wonder if he thought, as I often do, *How can Jesus forgive me? How can He use me when I can't even stand up for Him?*

Yet after His resurrection, Jesus asked Peter three times, "Do you love Me?" When Peter responded yes, Jesus told him, "Feed My sheep." Why three times? Because in giving Peter a chance to say, "I love You," for every time he'd said, "I don't know Him," Jesus was showing that God's grace is greater than our disgrace. And for every "Feed My sheep," Jesus was saying, "You still have a purpose."

Jesus offers us immeasurable grace to cover our faults and the reassurance that our purpose is still intact, no matter how many times we mess up. Hallelujah!

—*Ginger Kolbaba*

> *"God specializes in giving people a fresh start."*
> —*Rick Warren*

JESUS, You don't leave me in my despair. Thank You that You offer grace and purpose that cover my failings. Amen.

> "A farmer went out to sow his seed. As he was scattering the seed, some fell along the path, and the birds came and ate it up. Some fell on rocky places, where it did not have much soil. It sprang up quickly, because the soil was shallow. But when the sun came up, the plants were scorched, and they withered because they had no root. Other seed fell among thorns, which grew up and choked the plants. Still other seed fell on good soil, where it produced a crop…" —Matthew 13:3–8 (NIV)

As someone who likes organization and order, I noticed something interesting about the above parable. The farmer didn't plant the seed in nice, organized rows. He scattered it across a wide area and in many types of soil.

Personally, I would have chosen a more orderly approach to avoid negative outcomes. I'm an accountant, and my husband is an engineer. We both like to manage projects, keep things in order, and minimize risk. It wouldn't have occurred to me to scatter the seeds randomly, but I've never been much of a gardener—or a risk-taker.

The farmer sowed widely and had varied results. Regardless of the outcome, he didn't discriminate in the places he sowed.

This principle can apply to sharing the love of Jesus with others. We can sow widely and share the love of Jesus with everyone, not just people we think will receive it well and not only in places where we feel comfortable. Sharing our faith can mean taking a risk.

When we share Jesus with others, we can't know what type of soil the seed will land upon. Jesus calls us to be the sowers, but only He can change hearts. The seeds we plant may be the beginning of Jesus's work in someone's life.

—*Allison K. Flexer*

"Most people need love and acceptance a lot more than they need advice."
—*Bob Goff*

 JESUS, teach us to love others and reflect You in our words and actions. Let the soil of our hearts be rich so our faith can grow. Amen.

> He told them, "This is what is written: The Messiah will suffer and rise from the dead on the third day, and repentance for the forgiveness of sins will be preached in his name to all nations, beginning at Jerusalem." —Luke 24:46–47 (NIV)

A woman selling makeup door to door brought me to Jesus. Between lipstick samples and bubble baths, she'd drop a Scripture here or a parable there. At first her enthusiasm struck me as odd, and I was embarrassed for her.

Twentysomething and confident, I considered religion a crutch for the weak. The idea of a God loving me enough to die for my sins seemed overwhelming, even a bit scary. But every two weeks she returned, and I'd invite her in. After a while, I stopped thinking of how impossible the whole salvation story sounded and started believing. Months later, I began attending a local Bible study with her. I used to say that, thanks to her, I was not only prettier on the outside but on the inside, too.

Like a young girl in love, the more I knew of Him, the more I wanted to know—and the more I needed to share Him with others. Telling others about Jesus wasn't easy, especially in my circle of friends. Some of them laughed at my zeal, while others became angry with me and ended our relationship. But not all. A few, as my cosmetics supplier and I were, were forever changed when we met Jesus.

Many years have passed, but I'm still that girl. He's still my Savior, the greatest hero of all. And He always will be.

—*Heidi Gaul*

"There are two ways of spreading light; to be the candle or the mirror that reflects it."
—*Edith Wharton*

 JESUS, give me boldness in my faith. Help me spread Your light to those in darkness. Amen.

> Jesus reached for a little child, placed him among the Twelve, and embraced him. Then he said, "Whoever welcomes one of these children in my name welcomes me; and whoever welcomes me isn't actually welcoming me but rather the one who sent me." —Mark 9:36–37 (CEB)

My younger son, Timothy, was in fifth grade, and I was taking him to school. Soon he would be making this trip on his own. He wouldn't need my guidance. But the time spent together was sweet while it lasted. We practiced state capitals on the subway. "North Dakota?" I asked. "Bismarck," he said. "What about Nebraska?" "Lincoln," he said. "How 'bout multiplication? Eight times nine?" "Seventy-two," he said. What did he need me for?

We got off the subway and walked, Tim looking to see if any of his friends were around with backpacks slung over shoulders. A child gets to a stage where his or her peers matter more than any parent. We stopped at the busy intersection and waited. Then the light changed, and we stepped off the curb. He reached up and held my hand. Still reaching up and trusting.

There's a lot about a childlike spirit to embrace—innocence, imagination, and creativity. But when Jesus welcomed that child, I wonder if He was reminding the disciples that childlike trust is crucial by grabbing hold of our Father's outstretched hand.

—*Rick Hamlin*

"It is a great consolation for me to remember that the Lord, to whom I had drawn near in humble and childlike faith, has suffered and died for me, and that He will look on me in love and compassion." —Wolfgang Amadeus Mozart

DAY AFTER DAY in life's journey, Christ Jesus, I step out in faith, looking both directions, taking a deep breath, and then grabbing hold of your hand.

> The King will reply, "Truly I tell you, whatever you did for one of the least of these brothers and sisters of mine, you did for me." —Matthew 25:40 (NIV)

Some birthdays are more memorable than others. Sixteen birthdays ago, on April 2, was one of those celebrations for me.

My husband's eyes twinkled mischievously as he handed me a big box. Inside was a stuffed dog. "Is this supposed to be the puppy I wanted?" I pouted. Then I opened the card. *"I'm waiting for you,"* it read, right above a picture of a Jack Russell puppy. I was so surprised that I cried.

We named her YoYo because, boy, could she jump! Up and down she hopped at the door or at the base of a palm tree where a squirrel had climbed, outside our Florida home. She stopped only to eat, lick my face, or snuggle beside me on the couch. She rarely left my side—except to chase squirrels! But YoYo is old now. I have to clean up her accidents and remind her to eat. She can barely see and sleeps most of the day in her favorite spot, which is anywhere near me. I am thankful Jesus gave me such a loving companion. She has given me all the love she has to give, and she now needs me to give her all the help I can to make her last days comfortable.

My birthday gift has come full circle. It is such a blessing to care for my sweet little puppy in her last days with me.

—*Mary E. Williams*

"If there are no dogs in heaven, then when I die I want to go where they went."
—*Will Rogers*

THANK YOU, Jesus, for bringing such love into my life! When YoYo's time comes, please wrap her in Your arms and pet her for me.

> **A second is equally important: "Love your neighbor as yourself."**
> **—Matthew 22:39** (NLT)

I don't love everything about myself. There are some features I would change. Smaller nose. Thinner thighs. Straighter hair. But to be honest, most of the time, I am consumed by an inflated sense of self-interest and self-preservation—despite my flaws. In short, I love myself.

Popular wisdom might paraphrase Jesus's words as such: "Love God with all your heart and then love yourself, because you can't succeed unless you love yourself." But Jesus said the greatest commandment was first to love God and then to love the people next door and at my job—as much as I love myself.

I must admit, some people are not easy for me to love. The angry person who spouts off. The negative person, who says the idea will fail. The know-it-all. The liar, who habitually says something is bigger or better than it is. Does Jesus mean for me to love these people? Yes. Love them in spite of their flawed characters.

When I love Jesus, the overflow falls on others. This kind of love requires me to love them without expecting anything in return for my love. Not *"I'll show love to her, and she will invite me to the next event."* Instead, *I love her as I love myself. Unconditionally. Completely.*

—Karen Porter

"Don't wait for other people to be loving, giving, compassionate, grateful, forgiving, generous, or friendly…lead the way!" —Steve Maraboli

DEAR JESUS, give me love for my neighbors, coworkers, family, and friends. Remind me to love them as You do. Amen.

But he said, "I must proclaim the good news of the kingdom of God to the other towns also, because that is why I was sent." —Luke 4:43 (NIV)

I met Myo at the Thailand-Myanmar border. To me, the man personified Apostle Paul, a nomad on a mission. His skin the color of acorns, Myo was small in physical stature with dark hair and eyes. He wore a T-shirt, an ankle-length cylinder of fabric called a *longyi* tied at his waist, and flip-flops. Myo sported a smile that made me feel welcome and appreciated. He invited the mission team I'd tagged along with to join him on his rounds through three villages that day. So began my first venture into Burma.

In his own village, Myo led my sister and me up into a small home covered by a thatched roof. We sat on a mat and prayed with a young mother and her newborn. Then my nephew and I walked with Myo to the market in town to find formula for the baby and nutritional biscuits for the mama. Purposefulness and faithfulness to his calling marked Myo's countenance and movements. In the leper and brick-making villages, Myo consistently served those in need. He proclaimed the unfailing love of Christ and was at His service doing good works, which was a way of worshipping the Savior Who has redeemed us.

Jesus's example shows me that my mission is essentially the same: to proclaim the good news of His kingdom wherever I am and by any means I have.

—*Mona Hodgson*

"I do not pray for success; I ask for faithfulness." —*Mother Teresa*

LORD JESUS, help me be faithful to proclaim You when and where You lead me. Amen.

> Then he turned toward the woman and said to Simon, "Do you see this woman? I came into your house. You did not give me any water for my feet, but she wet my feet with her tears and wiped them with her hair." —Luke 7:44 (NIV)

The older woman with shoulder-length, bleached blond hair and a big smile stepped into the center aisle of our church and swayed to the beat of the worship band. She raised her hands, and her long peasant skirt billowed around her. Then she beckoned others to join her. People smiled. Some even waved. One brave soul of an older man joined her, rocking back and forth with her. While I was bouncing a bit to the beat, something inside of me wanted to step into a discomfort zone with her. I just couldn't. *Just a bit too much*, I thought.

Or was it?

Jesus loves extravagant worship. The woman in the story in Luke gave everything she had to Jesus—her tears, her expensive perfume, her messed-up hair, and her reputation. While Simon did not provide even a minimal gesture of hospitality—water for Jesus to wash his feet—the woman ministered to Jesus in an extravagant way. She stooped down so Jesus would be honored.

Over-the-top worship demonstrates our love for Jesus, our gratitude for His life and sacrifice, and our recognition of His lordship. His life-giving example inspires us to give of ourselves as we worship, as we work, and as we serve others.

—*Janet Holm McHenry*

"Jesus paid it all,
All to Him I owe;
Sin had left a crimson stain,
He washed it white as snow."
—*Elvina M. Hall*

 JESUS, You are worthy of my extravagant worship. I love You, adore You, and give You my most-high praise. Amen.

> Do not judge others, and you will not be judged. For you will be treated as you treat others. The standard you use in judging is the standard by which you will be judged. —Matthew 7:1-2 (NLT)

My daughter came into my room with her cell phone and showed me a photo a girl had posted on social media. The photo was of my daughter, with slanderous words about her appearance underneath her picture.

Immediately, my blood pressure rose. I thought of a million things I wanted to say or do to that girl, none of them godly. I might have even mentioned a few to my daughter.

Calmly, she put the phone down. "I'm not going to do anything but be kind and treat her with respect," my daughter said. "Her home life is so bad. She can't help but act out like this. She doesn't know Jesus." At first I was shocked, then utterly convicted. I've always taught my children to treat others as they'd want to be treated, but I guess I hadn't learned the lesson for myself.

My daughter knows many students who aren't believers. They come from all sorts of backgrounds and lifestyles, and yet they respect her and her faith. When they're struggling or have questions, it's her they seek out. They know they'll receive zero judgment. Jesus never judged. He said He didn't come to do that but to save the lost through unconditional love.

When I find myself in a situation in which I might be prone to judge, I remember my daughter's words and this truth: Jesus loves. And I am to follow Christ and model His behavior.

—*Jessica R. Patch*

"If you judge people, you have no time to love them."
—*Mother Teresa*

 JESUS, help me refrain from judging others and see people as You see them—through the eyes of love. Amen.

If you really know me, you will know my Father as well. From now on, you do know him and have seen him. —John 14:7 (NIV)

Following surgery, I felt weak as a newborn. I needed assistance. My friends rallied to my side, taking turns sitting with me. I was never left by myself. They nurtured me, sharing their hearts and joining me in prayer.

As time passed, I gained strength and needed less help. One morning after my husband left for work, I waved my final goodbye to a helper. Alone for the first time in a while, I shut the door and turned to face the deserted house. I shuddered. The quiet seemed to close in around me, magnifying my isolation. I collapsed onto the sofa, as confusing thoughts rushed through my mind. I had expected to be fine. But an inexplicable emptiness overtook me, and I began to cry. Covering my face with my hands, I closed my eyes.

In that moment, Jesus chose to remind me I'm not alone—and never will be. With a silent whisper and unseen arms, our Lord wrapped His love around me and held me until I felt secure again and safe in the knowledge that, whatever I faced, He'd be there. He'd already forgiven my sins. He'd guided the surgeon's hands as they worked to heal my body. And that day, sitting beside me on the couch, Jesus went further—He let me see God's glory as He healed my soul.

—*Heidi Gaul*

"There is a God-shaped vacuum in the heart of every man which cannot be filled by any created thing, but only by God, the Creator, made known by Jesus."
—*Blaise Pascal*

 LORD JESUS, thank You for letting me know God through Your mercy and filling my desolate heart with Your love. Amen.

This is my command: Love each other. —John 15:17 (NIV)

Being newly married and in love didn't guarantee peace on the home front. Though my pastor husband was respected at church, his role as head of household met with resistance from my children. Countless eye rolls had me threatening to call the optometrist to check for vision damage.

At bedtime, I prayed, "Jesus, is it even possible to unite as a loving family?" As I was on the edge of sleep, *Colossians 2* popped into my mind.

My biblical knowledge wasn't up to par for a pastor's wife, but that sounded like Scripture. I said a drowsy prayer that if it were, I'd recall it when I woke.

The next morning, *Colossians 2* was stuck in my mind like a repetitious commercial jingle. I beelined to the coffee table, paged through the Bible, found it, and read, *"My goal is that they may be encouraged in heart and united in love, so that they may have the full riches of complete understanding, in order that they may know the mystery of God, namely, Christ, in whom are hidden all the treasures of wisdom and knowledge."*

It was Valentine's Day, and tears stung my eyes. Jesus had given me a love letter. He wanted my family to be encouraged in heart, united in love and in Him, and to discover and cherish His wisdom and knowledge.

Even if our struggle is disunity within our families, Jesus's command to love one another is easy when we ask for His help. He is perfect love.

—*Holly Michael*

"Faith makes all things possible…love makes all things easy."
—*Dwight L. Moody*

JESUS, help us to remember that You are the third person in our marriages, the true head of our households, and the uniting force in our families. Amen.

> Jesus said to him, "Today salvation has come to this house, since he also is a son of Abraham. For the Son of Man came to seek and to save the lost." —Luke 19:9–10 (ESV)

Jesus had invited Himself over to the home of little Zacchaeus, an unlikely and unpopular candidate for the Savior's VIP attention. Luke's account seems to depict the widely reviled tax collector Zacchaeus as pretty pitiful and desperate to climb that tree to see this Jesus everyone is talking about.

As the crowds clamor, Jesus eagerly pursues Zacchaeus, who, by the world's measure, is the least likely to deserve His affection. After fleeing for a lifetime of sin, Zacchaeus is so moved by Jesus's overture that he immediately gives half his goods to the poor and repays his victims fourfold.

I have been at times unlikely, unpopular, reviled, pitiful, and least likely, yet the God-Man Jesus came looking for me and called me His own. Like little Zacchaeus, after a lifetime of vain pursuits, finally driven to desperately seek Him, I found that He'd always been lovingly seeking me. As He does, even now.

—Isabella Yosuico

"Is my gloom, after all,
Shade of His hand, outstretched caressingly?
'Ah, fondest, blindest, weakest,
I am He Whom thou seekest!'"
—Francis Thompson

DEAR JESUS, thank You for seeking me so faithfully, even when I am pitiful and unlikely, even now. Amen.

> Love the Lord your God with all your heart, with all your soul, with all your mind, and with all your strength. The second is: Love your neighbor as yourself. There is no other command greater than these. —Mark 12:30–31 (HCSB)

Pierre-Auguste Renoir was one of the most famous Impressionist painters, whose work spanned the late nineteenth and early twentieth centuries. Known for his lovely portraits of children and beautiful landscapes of Paris, Renoir was considered a master. Painting was his passion. And although he was crippled by rheumatoid arthritis near the end of his life, Renoir managed to tape his paintbrush to his hand so he could continue doing what he loved.

Like the famous artist, we're all passionate about something. When I was a young mom, I was passionate about my two daughters. But caring for them and doing the work were at times spiritually crippling. I would literally collapse into bed from sheer exhaustion. It was a nonstop race from the time I fixed breakfast, made sure homework was done, and attempted to semi-clean our home. Each night, I kicked off my shoes, thinking, *I don't know if I can keep doing this.* Praying to Jesus for strength and wisdom sustained me then and now. I knew His loving nature would help me in caring for those I love. So seeking Him first became my number-one priority.

Jesus explained to the scribe which commandment is the most important, and we must remind ourselves to heed that instruction every day. Jesus wants us to love Him with all our heart, soul, mind, and strength. And once we make this a priority in our lives, we cannot help but love others. A life lived for Jesus is the greatest masterpiece we can ever hope to create.

—*Angie Spady*

"God actually delights in exalting our inability. He intentionally puts his people in situations where they come face to face with their need for him." —David Platt

JESUS, thank You for telling me clearly how to live and to love others. Help me make You a priority in my life and to rest in knowing that Your commandments will lead me to peace. Amen.

> **Do you not believe that I am in the Father, and the Father is in Me? The words that I say to you I do not speak on My own initiative, but the Father abiding in Me does His works. —John 14:10 (NASB)**

As I walked through the dusty paths of one of the poorest places on earth, my heart ached with a cry too deep for tears. In a remote village in Uganda, I met a young man who has since earned a place in my heart. His name is Daniel, and he lived alone in a mud hut with barely enough to survive. Nasty parasites called jiggers crawled into his feet, making it difficult for him to move about freely. And his food supply was so scarce I could see every rib jutting out of his raglike shirt.

He was shy and quiet when we first met, but after our ministry rescued him and put him into a good school, his countenance changed and he blossomed into a funny teenage boy. When we ask him what changed him, he says, "Jesus," and I know that's true. When we love and help others, as Jesus did, we are doing the work of the Father. Sometimes it's encouraging our one child who exasperates us. It might be a gentle word to a coworker or friend who is too embarrassed to say he or she needs support. It could be working in areas where the poorest and most forgotten people live. The power of God works within us when we love.

—*Gari Meacham*

"God loves you as you unconditionally as you are and
not as you should be, because nobody is as they should be."
—*Max Lucado*

 JESUS, I pour myself out for You to fill me and work within. Today my only agenda is Your agenda. Amen.

> But love your enemies, do good to them, and lend to them without expecting to get anything back. Then your reward will be great, and you will be children of the Most High, because he is kind to the ungrateful and wicked. —Luke 6:35 (NIV)

My ex-husband was out of work and couldn't send the money he'd promised for our son's band trip. He said he'd send it later, but I knew that might not happen. We'd gotten used to broken promises and financial letdowns.

"Hold him to it," a friend said.

Instead, I decided to let him off the hook. I could always draw money from savings. I knew some people close to me would not agree with my decision, but when I read verses such as Luke 6:35, I felt confident I was behaving as Jesus wanted me to. He had shown me that, when I chose to be gracious to my ex-husband, He provided what I needed plus more.

In this case, the balance for my son's trip came through a kind couple. They even sent extra for spending.

Jesus told His followers to love their enemies, to lend without expecting repayment and to let the Father's rewards be enough. His advice goes against every "don't be a doormat" principle the world teaches. But when we have the courage to obey, we get to see His promise of rewards fulfilled. Sometimes the rewards come as immediate yet unexpected provision; other rewards He saves for eternity. Either way, we can experience the peace of knowing we live what our Savior modeled.

—Jeanette Hanscome

"To be a Christian means to forgive the inexcusable,
because God has forgiven the inexcusable in you."
—C. S. Lewis

LORD, thank You for showing me the rewards of obeying even when Your instructions don't seem to make sense. Amen.

> Yet I hold this against you: You have forsaken the love you had at first. Consider how far you have fallen! Repent and do the things you did at first. If you do not repent, I will come to you and remove your lampstand from its place. —Revelation 2:4–5 (NIV)

My friend is an antique collector, as am I. We've enjoyed many treasure-hunting trips to towns known for their great antique stores. Our exploits have been delights, and successful, as my vintage-laden shelves will attest.

Before one such trip, I spoke to her husband, pledging extra care of his lady. After all, he'd entrusted me with his most precious cargo. He gave us his blessing, telling us to have fun. Our time was full of laughter, chatter, yard sales, snacks, and the victory of finding the perfect antique.

When our adventure drew to a close, my friend seemed anxious to return to her love waiting at home. She confided she didn't want to be gone too long, lest it diminish her need of him. I found her observation inspiring and very wise.

It is no coincidence the Word likens the marriage of a husband and wife to Jesus's relationship to His church. As the Bride of Christ, we owe Him our deepest love and loyalty, hurrying home and keeping Him first in our hearts.

—*Cathy Elliot*

"Until we are able to truly make Him our first love … we will never know the fullness of Him who fills all in all. We will always be looking to a mere man to meet the desires of our heart, rather than to the One who created us, who knows us better than we know ourselves, and who gave His very life's blood to rescue us."
—*Leslie Ludy*

 LORD, change me so I might always put You first in my heart. Amen.

> **Jesus knew their thoughts and said to them: "Any kingdom divided against itself will be ruined, and a house divided against itself will fall."**
> **—Luke 11:17 (NIV)**

I often disagree with other Christians about a range of issues. Sometimes we have differing opinions about doctrine, social issues, or the best way to administer communion. My first instinct is to distance myself from those with different opinions, dismiss their beliefs, and assume I alone know what is right.

Christians have been doing this since the beginning. Jesus was with His disciples when He had to warn them not to be divided over their differences!

And it's not only Christians who struggle this way. Abraham Lincoln famously quoted Luke 11:17 in his effort to try to keep this country—deeply divided over slavery—united. I recently stood inside the edifice of the Lincoln Memorial, gazing up at the words of the Gettysburg Address carved next to his statue.

Inside this memorial to one of our nation's great leaders, I was reminded that even after the bloodiest battle in U.S. history, Lincoln did not give up on trying to unite our country. The Civil War made the president believe even more that we had to come together. He knew if the country didn't come together, it would collapse.

I need to remember this when I see the news, feel hurt by other Christians' actions, or simply look across the aisle at my church and see those whose opinions differ from mine. What unites us is so much bigger than what divides us. Together, we can make God's house stronger.

—*Elizabeth Adams*

"I know that the Lord is always on the side of the right. But it is my constant anxiety and prayer that I and this nation should be on the Lord's side."
—*Abraham Lincoln*

LORD, please help me to seek unity with other believers today. Where we disagree, help us to find common ground in You. Amen.

> I am the gate; whoever enters through me will be saved. They will come in and go out, and find pasture. —John 10:9 (NIV)

Everyone should have a relative like my great-aunt Ethel! She was a social worker by trade and, boy, did she embrace that calling. She was deeply involved in many people's lives, including and especially mine. When I was young, we had many illuminating chats, discussing every topic under the sun, including the Son. She was a beautiful, kind soul.

When it came time for the Lord to call her home, I didn't want her to be alone. I visited more frequently. The day before she passed, I was at her bedside. She tried to enter heaven's gates. She miraculously sat up in bed, though paralyzed from a stroke, and dreamily looked heavenward. She spoke of the light and of Jesus. She even named some people who were there! What a phenomenal moment that was—being on the "stairway to heaven" with Aunt Ethel. A nurse in the room suggested I tell Aunt Ethel to let go, to go back to the light, to be with Jesus, so I did. This experience confirmed for me where Aunt Ethel was spending eternity.

The next morning, Aunt Ethel met our Savior, smiling with love, while the TV aired the Crystal Cathedral Choir singing, "Mine eyes have seen the glory of the coming of the Lord."

—*Mary E. Williams*

"There's nothing like seeking greener pastures...and finding them."
—*Carlos Salinas*

 PRECIOUS JESUS, thank You for the reassurance that I will one day meet You at heaven's gate. Amen.

If you love those who love you, what credit is that to you? Even sinners love those who love them. —Luke 6:32 (NIV)

When my stepfather passed away unexpectedly, I took a good, long look at his life. My relationship with my mom was a struggle, so I had a hard time understanding why he loved her. But his love was persistent and beautifully evident, while I continued to harbor a grudge toward my mom, whom I viewed as an enemy in my life.

I had to face the sad fact that I didn't always love my mom well because in the past she had neglected me. I spent long hours alone as a child, having to fend for myself. Her three divorces, particularly the last one, left me reeling when I was in the throes of adolescence. She lived her life for herself, and I felt like an unwanted appendage. I didn't hate her exactly, but I certainly didn't pursue her, and that means I didn't obey Jesus. I didn't love my "enemy."

But her husband? He didn't share the same history. I had chosen to focus solely on her very-long-ago sins, and that prevented me from loving her for who she'd become. In light of my loss, I realized true love learns to forgive—not just because we're commanded to, but also because it helps wipe the slate clean between you and the person you feel has hurt you.

After my stepfather's funeral, something in my heart shifted. I chose to see my mom's neglect and selfishness as part of a forgiven past. This, coupled with the strength of Jesus, enabled me to do something new: pursue a new relationship with my mom.

It's been an amazing journey of reconciliation, one that started from a choice I made to love my "enemy."

—*Mary DeMuth*

"Love is the only force capable of transforming an enemy into a friend."
—*Martin Luther King Jr.*

JESUS, it seems impossible to love those who don't love me back. Help me forgive and love my enemies. Amen.

Very truly I tell you, you will weep and mourn while the world rejoices. You will grieve, but your grief will turn to joy. —John 16:20 (NIV)

I received an email a couple of years ago that sent me to my knees crying out to Jesus. Christian children on the other side of the world had just been beheaded for their beliefs, and their parents were made to witness the atrocity. How would I have reacted as a parent of one of those wee ones? What would I have felt? Amazingly, those devastated parents—through a veil of tears—gloried in the victory of their children's strong faith to the end.

Why does Jesus allow such horror and grief in this world? I don't understand, but I trust in His sovereignty and His promise to turn grief into joy even when I cannot figure Him out. He says, "My thoughts are not your thoughts, neither are your ways My ways" (Isaiah 55:8). His plans are to give us hope and a future (Jeremiah 29:11).

While the Christian life on this side of heaven is not always easy or comfortable, rest assured God will one day wipe away every tear (Revelation 21:4) and turn our sorrows into joy (Isaiah 35:10). And between now and then, He offers grace and spiritual victory for each difficult moment—and a promise of joy we can hold onto!

—*Nancy Sebastian Kuch*

"So let's look away from the circumstances that confront us, look to Christ, look to the promises, and hold fast to them."
—John Piper

JESUS, even when I cannot see Your hand, I choose to trust Your heart. I believe; help me in my unbelief. Give my soul great joy amid great difficulty. Amen.

**When Jesus saw their faith, he said, "Friend, your sins are forgiven."
—Luke 5:20 (NIV)**

The scene is vivid: in the sizzling desert sun, a group of men have lifted a friend from the ground up to the roof of a public building. The man is deadweight—he's paralyzed. They are going to lower him on his bed through a skylight to the floor right in front of Jesus, Who is there for many who need healing. The men had planned to carry their friend into the building, but the crowds were already so huge that they weren't going to be able to get close to Jesus.

What amazing friends they were. There must have been something they'd rather be doing than risking life and limb with little chance of success for their friend. But they did it! They lowered the paralyzed man maybe twenty or thirty feet to a place where Jesus saw him.

And when Jesus saw their faith, he said, "Friend, your sins are forgiven." He healed the man, who walked out with his friends.

We're told that Jesus was so moved when He "saw their faith" that He didn't just heal the man's physical ailment; He healed his spirit, too.

I don't think it's an accident that Jesus addressed the man as "friend."

I think Jesus was moved not so much by the man's disability—crowds were there to be healed—but by the deep friendship that group of men exhibited. I think He saw faith and identified them as true friends.

—*Michelle Rapkin*

"They are rich who have true friends."
—*Thomas Fuller*

 JESUS, thank You for friends. Thank You for my friends. Help me to be a good friend and to be there for my friends who need a helping hand. Amen.

> Once when Jesus was praying in private and his disciples were with him, he asked them, "Who do the crowds say I am?" —Luke 9:18 (NIV)

Everyone needs a few close friends who are willing to speak the truth. The disciples were that for Jesus. In a private moment, He asked them not what the crowds thought about Him but Whom they understood Him to be. When most of us think people are talking about us, we get defensive, wanting to clear our names. When Jesus asks, He does so out of love. He is measuring how His message is getting across and whether people are missing the boat. Perhaps He's wondering what more He can do to reveal Himself as the Christ.

Jesus is still asking the question today. Some people think it's anti-intellectual to believe in Christ. They acknowledge that Jesus was a real person, a prophet— maybe even a holy man. But the Son of God? Hardly! Their arguments can be very persuasive. But if Jesus were to sidle up to me today, I hope I would be within His closest circle and not among the crowd. When I prayerfully put myself in private conversation with Him and in the company of trusted friends, I feel my soul restored. And if He were to turn to me and ask, "Who do you say that I am?" I hope I would answer with my whole heart, "You are the Christ."

—*Andrea Raynor*

"A Christian is one who points at Christ and says, 'I can't prove a thing, but there's something about his eyes and his voice. There's something about the way he carries his head, his hands, the way he carries his cross—the way he carries me.'"
—*Frederick Buechner*

 DEAR JESUS, I want to know You. Erase any doubt, and silence the noise of the crowd. Count me as one of Your own. I put my trust in You. Amen.

You hypocrite, first take the log out of your own eye, and then you will see clearly to take the speck out of your brother's eye. —Matthew 7:5 (ESV)

When I got married, I was hoping my husband's encouragement would immediately make me more like Jesus. I thought being vulnerable and honest in marriage would be a kind of shortcut to spiritual growth.

But I remember that I could not fall asleep one night in that first year because I was so angry. My face was flushed with emotion, while my mind's gears were grinding as I tried to explain why my husband had offended me. I could not believe how insensitive and shortsighted he had been. I refused his apology and his offer to pray together. I couldn't see past his offense, nor could I see that I had offended him.

The next day, I felt convicted. All the ways my husband's encouragement, vulnerability, and honesty were helping me toward holiness were blocked by the log-sized anger blurring my vision.

Nothing is magical about my transformation toward holiness. Jesus actually used different words to give the same warning three separate times in Matthew 7. We all need to hear truth repeated, and it feels like a special grace to be reminded so gently through the Word.

Maybe the most painful part of this lesson in marriage was what it revealed about my character. I am tempted to anger and self-righteousness in a way that prevents me from seeing another human in love as Jesus would.

—Caroline Kolts

"The Bible tells us to love our neighbors, and also to love our enemies;
probably because generally they are the same people."
—G. K. Chesterton

JESUS, help me to learn a posture of humility. Amen.

> **My prayer is not for them alone. I pray also for those who will believe in me through their message. —John 17:20** (NIV)

In my novel, *And Angels Hovered*, there is a moment when a group of teenage friends, who are trapped in an abandoned shed in the middle of a raging forest fire, decide to pray. While some are reluctant, they all finally sit in a circle, and Crystal, the book's main character, asks God, "Please protect my friends in this desperate hour. Please turn back the raging fire that has brought fear to their hearts. Let them know that you will keep them from harm..."

Crystal's prayer touches them deeply and gives the group fierce resolve to meet the coming danger. But it is only much later that the group recalls Crystal's prayer and realizes she never prayed for herself. The effect of this revelation—and the selfless love it reveals—is transformative and powerful.

Jesus embodies such selfless love. His life and sacrifice prove He loves all of us—without exception—more than life itself. He prays for us always. And he prays not only for those who believe but also for those who may yet believe.

The heavens must rejoice every time we heed His selfless prayer. It makes Jesus pretty happy, too, don't you think?

—*J. Mason Williams*

"It's that wonderful old-fashioned idea that others come first and
you come second. This was the whole ethic by which I was brought up.
Others matter more than you do, so 'don't fuss, dear; get on with it.'"
—*Audrey Hepburn*

 JESUS, help me when I pray to ignore that nagging voice that says "me, me, me," and change it to "You, You, You." Amen.

> A new command I give you: Love one another. As I have loved you, so you must love one another. By this everyone will know that you are my disciples, if you love one another. —John 13:34–35 (NIV)

Jesus affirms over and over that love is the cornerstone of our faith, yet we Christians don't always seem to exemplify this cardinal trait, starting with me.

I was raised in a deeply dysfunctional home, so my ability to give and receive love was impaired and often performance-based.

On the surface, my Italian-immigrant parents were attractive, well-educated, upwardly mobile, and charming people. Yet beyond the appealing façade was a family plagued by mental illness, substance abuse, misguided ambition, and broken relationships. Home was never a safe place to love and be loved.

The unique hallmark of Christ's love is that it's entirely unconditional. Christ's love is not dependent on my performance nor on my ability to love well. He loves me just as I am and commands me to extend that same love to others. The clear implication is that loving is a choice.

Like so many other things in my Christian walk, my ability to fulfill this commandment rests squarely on my dependence on Him. My full acceptance of Christ's perfect love for me and surrender to His divine power allow His love to reach others through me.

The degree to which I can embrace His unconditional love for imperfect me equates to the very means by which I can love the many imperfect others in my life, however imperfectly.

—Isabella Yosuico

"I believe that unarmed truth and unconditional love will have the final word in reality. This is why right, temporarily defeated, is stronger than evil triumphant."
—Martin Luther King Jr.

JESUS, forgive my lack of love for myself and others, and help me to tap into the bottomless well of Your true love, that it may triumph in the end. Amen.

Love Letter from Jesus
NEW BIRTH

My Dear Child,

I want you to consider spring as My personal love letter to you. In every bulb bursting forth from the dark ground, every leaf unfurling, every seed that sprouts, and every butterfly that emerges from a chrysalis, I have written the story of new birth. This is My story. It's a story of hope. And because it is Mine, it is your story as well.

Our story doesn't end with the former things. I make all things new. Remember that nothing is impossible for Me! My desire for you is to let go of the past, and allow Me to do a new thing in your life. Just as you were born from your mother's womb onto this earth, in Me you are born again into the kingdom of God. You are an heir to all of His promises. My divine power has given you everything you need for your new life. Even though birth can be painful sometimes and new things daunting, My grace is sufficient. It is always enough for you.

I hope that, as you look around at all the signs of new birth, you will be reminded of My love for you and My commitment to the good work God began in you. I will be faithful to see it through. You can trust Me. Even though you can't see Me with your physical eyes, I am working in your life every moment. I am thinking of you all the time, and My thoughts are to prosper you, never to harm you. Put all your dreams in My hands. I live to give you hope and a future.

I love you forever.

Forget the former things; do not dwell on the past. See, I am doing a new thing! Now it springs up; do you not perceive it? Isaiah 43:18–19 (NIV)

Truly I tell you, this generation will not pass away until all these things have taken place. —Matthew 24:34 (NRSV)

When it comes to time and Jesus, sometimes I get confused. If I want to connect with Him, do I have to imagine myself back in His time, or do I somehow transport Him into my time? For instance, in this passage, when He talks about "this generation," is He talking to His disciples, who were with Him when He spoke these words? Or is He talking to me now? Honestly, I get a headache when I try to reason it out. That's when I find a quiet space, take a few real breaths, and just bring my confusion to Him.

When I ask Jesus, "What do you mean by this?" I hear Him answer . . .

"It's here and now, my friend! Everything I've been talking about—the joy, the freedom, the love—it's all right here, right now. It's all around you and within you. The kingdom of God isn't located in heaven. It permeates this messy, painful, unfair world we live in. Here and now, my friend."

"Jesus, what can I do to access it today, in my generation?"

"Rest in the connection between you and life. Find a moment to let nature speak to you today. Trust that I am speaking to you through nature. Then throughout your day, remind yourself of whatever nature showed you."

—*Lizzie Berne DeGear*

"In your light I learn how to love. In your beauty, how to make poems.
You dance inside my chest where no-one sees you,
but sometimes I do, and that sight becomes this art."
—*Rumi*

JESUS, show me fulfillment today! Let me be open to whatever it looks like, feels like, and tastes like. Today, let me be part of Your vision for our world. Amen.

> **For they cannot die anymore, because they are equal to angels and are sons of God, being sons of the resurrection. Now He is not God of the dead, but of the living, for all live to Him. —Luke 20:36, 38** (ESV)

I stood next to my friend and let her weep. She bumbled out apologies for her irrational thoughts, and I bumbled out attempts to mourn with her and for the baby she will never meet. I tell her, "The baby you carried was meant to be born, to live, to play. We were not meant to die."

Creation plays a strong dissonant chord when someone dies. I've heard it play like a record on repeat behind my rib cage, a thunderstorm roaring and raging and resisting any sort of calm resolution.

In the weeks after my brother's death, a deep sadness caused all other emotions to get stuck in my throat. I was grasping—for a car-crashed body in California, for a family spread across the country, for a purpose that could shake the shock of mortality. Why couldn't the God of the living keep my brother alive?

I wrestled with anger, bitterness, and regret. I desperately needed to know Jesus felt the fullness of the storm raging in my chest. Through tears that accompanied my prayers, I crept closer to the heart of God and felt Him shake with my sadness.

I felt the sweet faithfulness of Jesus, Who knows how to grieve. I felt the sweet comfort of Jesus, Who weeps with me because He knows we were made for life. I felt the sweet hope of Jesus, Who was torn apart on the cross when He made a way for us to live forever.

—Caroline Kolts

"We strain to hear. But instead of hearing an answer we catch sight of God himself scraped and torn. Through our tears we see the tears of God." —Nicholas Wolterstorff

 JESUS, thank You for mourning with me. Show me the way to grieve as one who has hope in You. Remind me of Your promise of eternal life. Amen.

> The disciples went and woke him, saying, "Lord, save us! We're going to drown!" He replied, "You of little faith, why are you so afraid?" Then he got up and rebuked the winds and the waves, and it was completely calm. —Matthew 8:25-26 (NIV)

On a bitterly cold morning in 1986, I almost killed six people.

We were going duck hunting on Florida's St. Johns River, and we were late. In my haste, I decided to take one trip in the boat with six people instead of two trips with three. When I hit the outboard's throttle, the bow plowed under and threw us shouting into the water.

Fear filled me as the boat turned over, the shock of freezing water hitting my skin. I knew one of my friends—maybe all of them—was going to drown. And it was my fault.

We had only one chance. "Grab the boat!" I yelled. It was upside down, but we could hold on until rescue came. Everyone took hold. "Is everyone OK?" I shouted. To my intense relief, everyone answered yes.

I looked up. Above me, standing on the upturned bottom of the boat, was my golden retriever, Champ. He looked down with a quizzical look that said, "Hey, what's everyone shouting about? It's only water."

I laughed. From relief, from emotional exhaustion, from the absurdity of seeing the only one of us who loved water—Champ—standing high and dry on the bottom of the boat.

I imagine that's what it was like when Jesus calmed the waters. Relief and joyous laughter—what incredible feelings.

—*J. Mason Williams*

"There is never a moment when God is not in control. Relax! He's got you covered."
—Mandy Hale

 JESUS, teach me to trust You in all things, and thank You for Your steadfast love. Amen.

Jesus stood and said in a loud voice, "Let anyone who is thirsty come to me and drink." —John 7:37 (NIV)

The altitude in the mountains, the dry air, and the exertion of lugging a backpack over passes and into valleys can make you very, very thirsty. You can only carry a few liters of water because of its weight. Eventually you run dry. Then you come across a stream—melted snow from high above.

But you can't drink directly from the stream. There's a good chance the water is polluted with bacteria. So you have to filter it.

What the world offers is like that stream. You want it. You think you need it. It sounds beautiful, and it feels good. But drinking it will make matters worse.

I've been that thirsty for many things. Even surrounded by people, for a long time I was thirsty for the kind of friendship that can only be found with a brother who shares a commitment to Jesus. Then God brought back into my life a man who was my friend when we were teenagers. Way back then, both of us were living apart from Christ, so our love was polluted. But now we're both following Him. With the living water of Jesus flowing in us unpolluted, we can be truer friends now than ever.

Jesus has provided a friendship I thirsted for, but He has done so much more: He has provided Himself, the greatest friend of all, a quenching and superabundant flow of glorious living water—love and peace and joy—that floods up from within me to make all the everyday thirsts of this world trivial.

—*Michael Berrier*

"Perhaps our loneliness can never be filled with even the best of human love. Maybe the longing for human love is just the beginning, and the longing for God is always the end." —Susan E. Isaacs

 MAY I thirst for You above all today, Lord Jesus, to the exclusion of all the thirsts of this world. Amen.

> Jesus said to her, "I am the resurrection and the life. The one who believes in me will live, even though they die; and whoever lives by believing in me will never die. Do you believe this?" —John 11:25-26 (NIV)

When Jesus encountered the grief of Mary and Martha over the death of Lazarus, their brother—probably their protector and provider—Jesus was deeply moved. In fact, this story includes the Bible's shortest verse, which simply declares, "Jesus wept" (John 11:35). It's important to remember that Jesus's tears were a reflection of His love and compassion for His friends. Remember this the next time you weep tears of grief and sorrow. Jesus, Who experienced every human emotion, weeps with you and for you.

However, even in the midst of Mary and Martha's grief, and His own, Jesus reminded them that death is not the end. In John chapter 11, Jesus proclaimed to these grieving women that physical death is not final and absolute death for those who put their faith in Him. "I am the Resurrection and the Life," He said. "The one who believes in me will live, even though they die; and whoever lives by believing in me will never die. Do you believe this?" Martha's answer to this question was an emphatic yes, even though Lazarus was still physically dead. Let that be our answer as well. Even when things are at their lowest point and options are limited severely—even to the point of death—we can remember that in Jesus, death is not the end but rather the beginning of resurrection and life everlasting.

—*David Downs*

"Grief drives men into habits of serious reflection,
sharpens the understanding, and softens the heart."
—*John Adams*

 JESUS, when I walk through the valley of grief and sorrow, please remind me that You are the Lord of life, and that in You there is life everlasting. This changes my complete perspective regarding life…and death. Amen.

> **Even the hairs of your head have all been counted. So don't be afraid therefore; you are worth more than many sparrows. —Matthew 10:30–31 (HCSB)**

I dashed right past her—a waiflike woman in a dirty skirt, standing across the street from the supermarket. "Can you give me some money for some food?" she asked. I shook my head and headed for the store. I was on a mission. After all, I had a week's load of groceries to buy and a detailed shopping list from my wife, Carol. Not a moment to spare.

Then I stopped. Wasn't I about to buy food for a richly blessed married couple? Couldn't I buy something for that woman in need? I walked back across the street and asked, "Is there anything you'd like at the supermarket?"

"Cheese and crackers," she said.

"Sure," I said, not at all sure where I'd find slices of cheese. It turned out they were at the deli counter, not too far from a box of Wheat Thins. I finished my shopping and headed back outside, figuring the woman would probably be gone by now. But no, she was still standing on the corner. "What's your name?" I asked.

"Heather," she said.

"God bless you, Heather," I said and gave her the cheese and crackers.

Time and again I've felt God has been watching out for me in ways too numerous to count—even beyond the hairs on my head.

—*Rick Hamlin*

"When I'm worried and can't sleep, I count my blessings instead of sheep."
—*Irving Berlin*

JESUS, may I not be so proud to share with You the details of my life, where I need You, and where I can serve You. Let me never neglect the chance to give. Amen.

> It is written in the prophets, 'And they shall all be taught by God.' Therefore everyone who has heard and learned from the Father comes to Me.
> —John 6:45 (NKJV)

After a long journey, we arrived at my grandparents' home for our annual visit. As we stepped onto the front porch, Grandma Anna spoke first. "Goilie, goilie, nice goilies," she said to my sisters and me, referring in Slovak to her little girls. "Jesus loves you; read your Bible." She gave each of us a warm hug and kiss; then we hugged Grandpa and ran inside.

Grandma wore a cotton housedress, her white hair pulled back in a twisted knot and an ear-to-ear smile that revealed a sweetness in her spirit. Her thick glasses resembled the bottoms of Coca-Cola bottles, but the love from her squinted eyes shone through like rays of welcoming sunshine.

I hold fond memories of the aroma of Slovak cooking that filled the house—dumplings, bacon, and pork. But no memory surpasses Grandma's greeting at the front door.

Grandma became a mother to nine stepchildren after my mom's birth mother died. She knew what to teach her children, and she had it down to two main truths when she greeted her grandchildren, too: "Jesus loves you; read your Bible."

Now as a first-time grandmother, I hear my grandmother's spiritually rich words ring in my ears. I want to teach my grandchildren what matters most in life—just as God, in His Word, first taught us.

—*Kathleen Ruckman*

"When you have Jesus, you have all the rest."
—*A. W. Tozer*

 JESUS, thank You for teaching me You love me and to read the Bible. You are all I need. Amen.

LEARNING TO BE SALTY

> You are the salt of the earth. But what good is salt if it has lost its flavor? Can you make it salty again? It will be thrown out and trampled underfoot as worthless. —Matthew 5:13 (NLT)

As I rushed to cook my family's favorite chicken dinner, I forgot to add seasonings. The chicken tasted bland and the vegetables flat. Then, I sprinkled salt over the food and tried again. The flavors changed, and I tasted the goodness.

Jesus said we should be "salty." It isn't easy to season our world, because we are flawed humans. Even when we are sweet and genuine, we might not be loved or liked. Being salty includes kindness, generosity, and humility.

Kindness is salty. When someone's words cut deep, I try to respond with gentleness. A lady hurt my feelings, so I sent a nice gift instead of harsh words. It wasn't easy, but it was salty.

Generosity is salty. I gave a large tip to a baggage handler at the airport. The look on his face was priceless. Once, my husband bought a meal for two ladies at the next table. We left before they discovered their bill was paid.

Humility is salty. I typically think of what I'll say next, instead of listening. Lately, I've been trying not to talk about me. People think I'm a great conversationalist, but I'm just being salty.

Even a little dash of salt flavors. Let's be salty today.

—*Karen Porter*

"My friends, love is better than anger. Hope is better than fear.
Optimism is better than despair. So let us be loving, hopeful,
and optimistic. And we'll change the world."
—*Jack Layton*

 DEAR JESUS, flavor the world by making me salty. Highlight opportunities to add the salt of kindness, generosity, and humility. Amen.

Be perfect, therefore, as your heavenly Father is perfect.
—Matthew 5:48 (NIV)

Hoots and hollers stopped me in my dusty tracks. My sister and I had left a thatched hut, where we sat on mats surrounded by women and children. Now, without a translator, we strolled the brickmaking village. The woman running toward me wasn't one I recognized from the hut.

She yanked her tattered green hat, the same color as mine, from her gray hair. I removed my new green hat as we celebrated what we had in common. Tapping our chests, we exchanged names. When the translator arrived, I learned Mono Ma was calling me her sister-friend. Too soon, she had to leave. My sister-friend smothered me in hugs and then dashed down to the brickyard. My heart brimmed with blessings.

I watched a row of women haul buckets of water in a brickmaking assembly line. While Mono Ma waited for her next trip to the river, I gained permission to go give her my hat. She posed and pranced as if I'd handed her a golden crown. Her smile alone was worth my trip to Burma.

In Matthew 19:16–19, a man asked Jesus, "Teacher, what good thing must I do to get eternal life?" Jesus's reply included, "Love your neighbor as yourself." Demonstrating God's love provides an illustration of the Father's perfection alive and growing in me.

—*Mona Hodgson*

"Act as if what you do makes a difference. It does."
—*William James*

 LORD JESUS, teach me to consistently see and behave in Your perfect way. Amen.

JESUS TRANSFORMS US

> Peace I leave with you; my peace I give you. I do not give to you as the world gives. Do not let your hearts be troubled and do not be afraid.
> —John 14:27 (NIV)

My neighbor's voice drifted through the hedge that borders our properties. Ann was talking to her fourteen-month-old grandson in that high-pitched, singsong voice adults often use with little ones. I paused and listened. It seemed remarkable that she was able to embrace what was considered normal, given that two years before she had battled cancer.

That period was exhausting for Ann. The effects of chemotherapy claimed her long, wavy hair, and she was prone to weep uncontrollably and without warning. Friends and neighbors surrounded her family with encouragement and assistance. But she alone stood toe to toe with her deadly adversary, facing the very real possibility that her life on earth was coming to a close.

During her ordeal, Ann and her husband accepted an invitation from the pastor of a small local church to attend Bible-study classes. That decision led to strong relationships with a newfound church community and greater reliance on Christ. In the face of death's assault, they discovered surprising reassurance—and new life in Jesus.

As Ann's hair began to grow back in the months following chemotherapy, I noted that Ann's attitude about facing challenges had undergone a transformation. She now seemed to approach life with an increased sense of determination and joy. I heard it in her voice when I paused to listen through the hedge.

—*Barb Howe*

"The ultimate measure of a man is not where he stands in moments of comfort and convenience, but where he stands at times of challenge and controversy."
—*Martin Luther King Jr.*

 GRANT me the grace, dear Jesus, to stand firm in the face of challenges and to remember during times of comfort that You are Lord over all. Amen.

Then Jesus told them, "You are going to have the light just a little while longer. Walk while you have the light, before darkness overtakes you. Whoever walks in the dark does not know where they are going." —John 12:35 (NIV)

Maybe if I started over, I'd remember how to get to the meeting room. I turned back toward the lodge. How could I have gotten lost after attending this writers' conference annually for almost twenty years? I'd roomed in every possible location—except this one. I'm visually impaired, so I couldn't rely on reading the signs, only my memory and sense of direction. After a deep breath, I headed down the path again and prayed. When I ran into a friend, who steered me in the right direction, I felt like I'd been rescued by an angel.

I made a point to rewalk that route several times before it got dark, and still I got really confused.

Darkness changes the most familiar paths. This is true in the physical world and the spiritual. Jesus knew His followers needed to soak up His presence and fully grasp His teaching before He left this earth and the enemy's darkness distorted everything. Today, these same words—"Walk while you have the light"—can encourage us to learn all we can from Him when life is hopeful and bright, so when the darkness of crisis falls it doesn't overtake us completely.

—*Jeanette Hanscome*

*"Unless we form the habit of going to the Bible in bright moments
as well as in trouble, we cannot fully respond to its consolations
because we lack equilibrium between light and darkness."*
—*Helen Keller*

THANK YOU for the light of Your presence. Draw me to it daily, so I'll know which way to turn when it's dark. Amen.

TRUE SECURITY

> **And this is the will of him who sent me, that I shall lose none of all those he has given me, but raise them up at the last day. —John 6:39 (NIV)**

We all have our insecurities. I am certainly no exception. Pretty much ever since middle-school age, I can remember feeling self-conscious about much of my life—clothes, acne, girls, braces, you name it. I somehow figured other people were capable of staring at every undesirable aspect of my physical appearance and that they were probably doing so right then with a critical eye.

The insecurities of adulthood aren't that much different. The idea of "what will people think?" applies to just as many things in my life now, but on a larger scale and not attributed to being an overly hormonal teenager. Certainly, the risks are much higher. Most recently, the words "data security" seem to sound the loudest alarms. It's good to remember, though, that my spiritual security is as real a concern as my ever-lengthening computer passwords.

Thank God for the security of knowing Jesus! I am His, and He is mine. And His words remind me that He attentively keeps watch over us and that He will never lose us. That's all the spiritual security we need. To those on the outside, this might seem like a crutch or a religious version of Linus's blanket in the *Peanuts* cartoons, but the reality is that if we trust in Jesus, we can rest assured we won't ever be lost.

—*Wayne Adams*

"Who among you doesn't have an insecurity? Who among you doesn't depend on someone or something...to help you get through the day? Who among you can cast the first stone?" —Linus van Pelt (Peanuts cartoon)

 DEAR JESUS, thank You for the security of knowing You and knowing that You will never leave us or lose us. Amen.

> On hearing this, Jesus said, "It is not the healthy who need a doctor, but the sick. But go and learn what this means: 'I desire mercy, not sacrifice.' For I have not come to call the righteous, but sinners." —Matthew 9:12-13 (NIV)

While I was packing for a weekend work presentation, the power flickered off. Then I heard sirens.

A transformer had exploded down the street. Power would be out the rest of the day.

I hadn't showered, and my presentation was in just a few hours. After a short panic session, I remembered my new gym membership. The gym has showers!

I realized the gym was the one place I could unashamedly be a complete disaster, because everyone there is a mess and working to get better.

Too many times I've walked into church and tried to look healthy and happy, when the truth is, I was depressed, anxious, and questioning my faith. My desire was to allow others to see my mess and love me enough to help me get back to health. But I was afraid that if I showed my true self, I would get a dose of judgment and condemnation.

Jesus spent time with people outside the religious community who were unhealthy messes. He was often condemned for it. He taught us to extend mercy to one another, because we are all sick with sin. We all need His healing touch.

I want to help others find the healing nature that is His mercy and grace. Deciding to be a safe person for others and allowing Jesus's healing touch to work through us is a start.

—*Amelia Rhodes*

"God's mercy is so great that you may sooner drain the sea of its water, or deprive the sun of its light, or make space too narrow, than diminish the great mercy of God."
—*Charles Spurgeon*

JESUS, thank You for coming to heal our sickness of sin. Help me extend Your mercy and love to others. Amen.

> But to you who are listening I say: Love your enemies, do good to those who hate you, bless those who curse you, pray for those who mistreat you.
> —Luke 6:27-28 (NIV)

My husband thrived at his job until restructuring occurred. The new manager seemed to despise him, demeaning his work daily. Her goal became obvious: she wanted him out.

My heart broke for him. Every morning he left for work determined to please her, and each evening he returned more depressed. Eventually, he decided to resign.

I became anxious. Would he find new employment? Could we pay our bills?

With diminished hope and faith smaller than a mustard seed, I knew I needed to pray. In hushed tones, I relinquished my world to Him and then stilled my thoughts to listen, really listen.

The answer Jesus gave pained me: pray for your husband's former boss. I scrambled for excuses to avoid obedience. Then I remembered His submission even unto death. I bowed my head lower and prayed for her.

Moments later, the blessings began. A fluttering sensation tickled inside my chest, like a flock of tiny birds. Fear, anger, and hurt took flight from my soul, one by one. Hope filled the void, along with the peace only He can provide.

Within weeks, Jesus provided us with steady income—more than we needed—and my faith was reinforced. He'd proven His faithfulness once again.

—*Heidi Gaul*

"There's something about love that builds up and is creative. There is something about hate that tears down and is destructive. So love your enemies."
—*Martin Luther King Jr.*

 JESUS, thank You for guiding me through life's tough spots and showering me with Your peace. Amen.

> Don't be so concerned about perishable things like food. Spend your energy seeking the eternal life that the Son of Man can give you. For God the Father has given me the seal of his approval. —John 6:27 (NLT)

When I was laid off from my job several years ago, I wondered how I would handle all my living expenses. But the day after I learned of my job status, I felt God speak into my soul: I will not let you fall, He told me.

At that moment, I had a decision: I could worry about how I was going to survive, or I could focus on trusting Jesus. Jesus promised to take care of my physical needs, so I didn't need to be concerned about that (see Matthew 6:25–34). With that worry off my plate, so to speak, I knew I needed to concentrate on the truly important things—the spiritual food Jesus alone gives.

That day, I chose to believe Jesus's words and to spend my energy pursuing His ways. An amazing thing happened: Every day since then, Jesus has shown me His faithfulness. He has not only taken care of my family's physical needs but also grown our faith.

Jesus wants us to seek after His ways rather than spend energy focusing on the perishable things. I learned that, when we seek to feed our souls with the spiritual food Jesus offers, then we will experience not only filled physical stomachs but also spiritual ones, too.

—*Ginger Kolbaba*

"Labor to feast on Jesus. Satisfy yourself with his beauty
and his hope-filled fellowship."
—*John Piper*

 JESUS, thank You that You are the Bread of Life, my spiritual food. May I always hunger for You. Amen.

> **Return to your house and describe what great things God has done for you.** —Luke 8:39 (NASB)

Sometimes the difficult things in our lives become the great things. Jesus, I've learned, uses trouble and heartache to create peace and passion. That lesson came after years of praying big scary things would never touch my family or me. I don't regret those prayers one bit, but through the course of life, lots of scary things did grab us. My husband's career failed, our marriage crumbled under infidelity, both our daughters were attacked, my career tugged and toiled, and stress just about did me in. Scary stuff.

But through each of these struggles, Jesus taught me trust. He intervened at just the right times to give me hope. He infused the perfect strength to move forward—changed, full, and free of emotional baggage. When Jesus touches our problems, we are indelibly changed. Our only response to the great things God does is to describe these things to other people. Tell the stories, share the hope, and offer comfort to those who need what you've experienced at the hands of Jesus. Every scary story in your life has a good ending: God has done great things.

—*Gari Meacham*

"Fear arises when we imagine that everything depends on us."
—*Elisabeth Elliot*

 JESUS, I need You to touch the pain and fear in my life. You are the story maker Who brings great endings. Amen.

He said to them: "It is not for you to know the times or dates the Father has set by his own authority." —Acts 1:7 (NIV)

When Jesus spoke these words in the Scripture above to His disciples, I have to believe they were utterly overwhelmed. First they'd watched Him be arrested and crucified. Then Jesus's body disappeared from the tomb. Now here He was again, after His resurrection, giving them instructions on how to move forward in ministry without Him. Of course they asked Jesus questions about what would happen next. Who wouldn't be curious? But He reminded them that God had everything under control, saying, "You don't need to know. That's God's business."

I always want to know what's about to happen and what will come after that—and after that, too. Maybe that's why so many of my friends call me a control freak!

Of course, I don't think of myself that way. It's just that if I know what's going to happen, then I can prepare for it. It's so much easier than trying to think of all the possibilities and then attempting to juggle countless contingency plans.

But God says to me, "You don't need to know, Michelle. That's My business. You know I'm going to take care of you. That's enough for now." And when I'm smart, I breathe a sigh of relief.

—Michelle Rapkin

"Patience with others is love; patience with self is hope; patience with God is faith."
—Unknown

DEAR JESUS, please forgive me for always wanting to know what's going to happen next, for feeling like I'm the one who needs to fix whatever may go wrong. Help me to relax and remember that I don't need to be in charge, because You are. Amen.

> **For they loved human praise more than praise from God.**
> **—John 12:43** (NIV)

Over the years, I've heard several speakers and writers suggest that I should try to imagine what I want people to say in a eulogy about me at my funeral and to live in a way that makes it all true. I'm sure it's good advice meant to encourage me to be caring and kind and to put others first. I want to be those things, and I certainly do hope they'll be true if someone says them about me when I'm gone. But it's always struck me as strange advice.

My response is always something along the lines of, "My funeral? Who cares what they say at my funeral? I'll be dead! I won't be around to hear it!"

I am more concerned about what God will say about me when my days on earth are done. But if I'm being honest, I don't really spend as much time as I should living as if I care what will happen in the hereafter. I often wonder, *Will Jesus greet me as a good and faithful servant? Will I have really done the best I could with the gifts God has given me?* I hope so.

What would happen if I really were to live as if I care more about what Jesus will say about me than what my friends and family will say when my time on earth has passed? I think it would change how I interact with those around me. It would certainly change me.

—*Elizabeth Adams*

"Humility is not thinking less of yourself, it's thinking of yourself less."
—*C. S. Lewis*

JESUS, help me to desire praise and honor from You today. Help me to live in a way that makes You proud. Amen.

If you love those who love you, what reward will you get? Are not even the tax collectors doing that? —Matthew 5:46 (NIV)

I was thrilled when Tracy and I got assigned as roommates for the writers' conference. She was one of the few believers in my group, and we'd immediately clicked. Then I found out the hotel staff put me with Brenda by mistake. She hadn't wanted a roommate. She and I couldn't have been more opposite, especially when it came to faith. I prayed the hotel management would correct the error for both our sakes. Instead, I sensed God correcting my attitude. Perhaps He had allowed this for a purpose.

Rooming with Brenda instead of Tracy turned out to be a challenge I needed. She wasn't shy about her thoughts on Christianity, but we had other things in common that led to some great talks. I sensed that she appreciated discovering Christians are normal, nice people. The roommate mistake was discovered, but by the time it was, Brenda and I had settled into our new relationship. I left that conference with the realization of how rarely I extended friendship to nonbelievers. Who benefited from that? No one really.

Loving those who love and agree with us comes naturally. Anyone can do it, including non-Christians. But what happens when Jesus calls us to love those who don't want anything to do with us or our faith? That's when we have the opportunity to stand out as different. Sometimes the rewards remain invisible for a long time. Once we see them, we can experience the joy of loving as Jesus loved.

—*Jeanette Hanscome*

"Love is the sum of all virtue, and love disposes us to good."
—*Jonathan Edwards*

LORD, forgive me for only loving the easily lovable. Give me a heart for those who need Your love most. Amen.

> In everything I did, I showed you that by this kind of hard work we must help the weak, remembering the words the Lord Jesus himself said: "It is more blessed to give than to receive." —Acts 20:35 (NIV)

I know that it's more blessed to give than to receive, but I must admit that every now and then I forget that. After all, very few things please me more than a surprise flower delivery or an old-fashioned handwritten note or greeting card.

Two years ago, though, I experienced the utter truth of Jesus's words from the above verse. I was having a very hard time recovering from the grief at the death of my husband. I finally decided to volunteer at an orphanage in Haiti for a week, in the hopes I might get out of my pain enough to see that my lot in life wasn't the worst.

By the fourth day of my stay, I was feeling better than I had for so long.

Daily, the children made me hand-drawn pictures and love notes written in Creole. They showered me with sticky hugs and kisses. I felt pretty good about my contributions to their well-being. After all, not only had I brought gifts and hugs, but I'd also made a donation to the orphanage.

So imagine my surprise when I arrived home and started crying in the US Customs line. It turns out my generosity didn't hold a candle to the gifts of smiles, giggles, hugs, and love letters sixty girls and boys showered me with that week.

I had to truly measure the worth of our exchange. Turns out I received more than I could ever have imagined.

—*Michelle Rapkin*

"The more you give, the more comes back to you, because God is the greatest giver in the universe, and He won't let you outgive Him. Go ahead and try. See what happens." —Randy Alcorn

 JESUS, thank You for teaching us to give. Thank You for showing us that we can never outgive You, and that whatever we give, You multiply it and use it to bless us, too. Amen.

> Do not worry then, saying, "What will we eat?" or "What will we drink?" or "What will we wear for clothing?" For the Gentiles eagerly seek all these things; for your heavenly Father knows that you need all these things. But seek first His kingdom and His righteousness, and all these things will be added to you. —Matthew 6:31-33 (NASB)

I don't know about you, but I can be something of a worrier. I get anxious about any number of things during a normal day—my career, my kids, my outfit, almost anything. Two things that help calm my worries are thinking about the words of Jesus and a certain Christian punk-rock band.

When I was in college, one of my best friends was the drummer in the rock band Big Fil, and I was its number-one fan. I liked the band for its music, but the lyrics also resonated with me. One of Big Fil's best songs was about famous theologian Charles Spurgeon, who, it's said, was so confident in his salvation that he could swing out over hell on a cornstalk and still sing "Blessed Assurance." Wow. That might be the ultimate definition of confidence, but how much more should I rely on the words of Jesus Himself, when He says, "Do not worry"? After all, He reminds us that He created everything, and there are much better things for me to think about—like the kingdom of heaven.

—*Wayne Adams*

"Do not anticipate trouble, or worry about what
may never happen. Keep in the sunlight."
—*Benjamin Franklin*

DEAR JESUS, please give me the confidence to stop worrying, trust in You, and keep my eyes on Your kingdom. Amen.

> "My food," said Jesus, "is to do the will of him who sent me and to finish his work." —John 4:34 (NIV)

"Stop working," I warned my husband. "You have a fever."

"But we must finish."

My husband insisted we remain in the remote fishing village in India until we completed our mission work.

That night, on the bus back to the city, I urged him to drink water. My hand on his forehead proved fever reducers weren't helping.

My thoughts galloped to dark conclusions. *Did my spouse, a pastor and native of India, have dengue fever?* That horrible illness, contracted via mosquito, had recently claimed his sister's life.

Still hours from the city, I had no phone and didn't speak the language.

I cried, "Jesus, did You send us here only to have my husband die?"

Several hours and many prayers later, my beloved was hospitalized with severe dehydration due to dengue fever. His condition was critical, but after he was given IV fluids and constant care, he recovered.

As a pastor's wife, I struggle with putting the Lord's work first and setting aside doubt. I question why God has us struggling through difficult situations.

Jesus's passion, for the sake of humanity, gives us encouragement to do His work.

—*Holly Michael*

"Any man can work when every stroke of his hands brings down the fruit rattling from the tree…but to labor in season and out of season, under every discouragement…that requires a heroism which is transcendent."
—*Henry Ward Beecher*

 JESUS, grant us patience when our work becomes challenging and help when we grow weak, weary, and doubtful. Amen.

**Those whom I love I rebuke and discipline. So be earnest and repent.
—Revelation 3:19 (NIV)**

Several years ago, we lost our youngest son.

No, it's not what you're thinking. He didn't die, though we worried desperately that he might. No, we lost him to the world of drugs.

We tried to help him. We fed, clothed, and housed him. We offered therapy. We even got him a job, which he promptly lost. Then he stole from us. When my wife discovered her grandmother's silver was missing, she cried for hours.

It was gut-wrenching to turn him out of our home, but we had to do it. We loved him, you see, and the only way to help him was to *not* help him.

He promptly disappeared. We spent sleepless nights, expecting a call from the police or hospital. Or worse, from the morgue. We prayed and prayed for him to be healed and to come home. But we heard nothing.

Then he called. Living on the street, having no place to turn, he had checked into a treatment center. He had hit rock bottom and wanted to work his way back.

It wasn't easy. He didn't move forward without stumbling. Thankfully, he earnestly wanted to take another path, and with God's help, ultimately he did.

And we are so very proud of him.

—*J. Mason Williams*

*"What parents need to teach their children is not how to keep from falling
down but rather to understand that, no matter how many times
they fall down, they can always get up again!"*
—*Chica Umino*

JESUS, thank You for always loving us and for showing us the way, even when we stray from the path You've set for us. Amen.

> Then he said to them all: "Whoever wants to be my disciple must deny themselves and take up their cross daily and follow me." —Luke 9:23 (NIV)

A dear friend reminds me often of what a true disciple of Christ is. She works as a hospice nurse—a job that has its rewards and sorrows. She offers physical and spiritual care for the dying. Every touch is accompanied with prayer.

To my friend, a good death is one through which the patient embraces Jesus and looks forward to eternal life. The person accepts the process of concluding this life, often joyfully. The family knows the patient is going to heaven and will see the person again. The process becomes a celebration of life eternal.

A heartbreaking death is when a person refuses Jesus's gift of eternal life. My friend has witnessed patients plunge into agony as he or she faces death. My friend grieves for their souls.

One of the worst deaths is of a non-Christian who has a Christian family.

My friend is sad but not deterred when patients turn away from Jesus. She simply goes on telling them about His amazing love and how He wants them to spend life with Him forever. She keeps planting seeds.

My friend wears a shirt with the words "Celebrate Life" to encourage every patient to grasp the love of Jesus. And because of her selfless efforts, many more will spend their lives eternally with Jesus.

—*DiAnn Mills*

"Show me your hands. Do they have scars from giving? Show me your feet. Are they wounded in service? Show me your heart. Have you left a place for divine love?"
—*Fulton J. Sheen*

 DEAR JESUS, thank You for giving us the words to tell others about You. Let us not become discouraged when others turn away, but have us continue to sing Your praises. Amen.

This is the meaning of the parable: The seed is the word of God.
—Luke 8:11 (NIV)

A few months ago, I watched our Amish neighbors till their fields and hand-plant row after row of tiny, hard kernels of corn reserved from last year's crop. In no time at all, those small seeds sprouted and grew into plants taller than I am, with succulent ears of juicy deliciousness.

A tiny seed of hope. That's what I need on days I'm discouraged and nothing seems to be going quite the way I expected. A kernel of promise can help me move forward, to anticipate something good just around the corner on this crazy journey called life.

Jesus tells us His seeds of hope can be found in the Word of God. My faith grows each time I read or review Scripture. Planted deep in my heart are promises like "Never will I leave you or forsake you" (Hebrews 13:5); "I will give you rest" (Matthew 11:28); and "Ask and it will be given to you" (Matthew 7:7). Yes! Indeed, Jesus's words fill us with hope and encouragement. "Thanks be to God! He gives us the victory through our Lord Jesus Christ" (1 Corinthians 15:57). Choice food for thought!

—*Nancy Sebastian Kuch*

"The Holy Spirit can take God's word of truth and minister it to our deepest needs."
—*Billy Graham*

THANK YOU, Jesus, for the precious promises I find in Scripture, seeds of hope for my heart today. Speak to me from those promises, as we walk together in victory. Amen.

> **Hearing this, Jesus said to Jairus, "Don't be afraid; just believe, and she will be healed." —Luke 8:50** (NIV)

Remember that old cliché "where there's life, there's hope"? I remember using it to comfort a friend who feared for her son's life. His destructive lifestyle held him prisoner, and he felt he couldn't escape. Yet even on his downward spiral, I saw hope—because he lived. Perhaps he could seek counseling or salvation in Jesus. Or just decide to stop.

When Jairus sought Jesus to heal his dying daughter, our Lord set out without delay. How anguished Jairus must have felt, impatient for the Master to restore his beloved child to health. But along the way, a suffering woman placed her finger on Jesus's garment and He stopped to turn to her. Imagine Jairus crazy with worry and hating every minute taken away from his little girl.

Before Jesus finished speaking to the woman, a messenger brought word that Jairus's daughter had died. Such heartbreaking news. If only the Lord hadn't been interrupted. Now it was too late. But Jesus, full of compassion, gave Jairus a promise to sustain his faith. "Just believe, and she will be healed." Soon, she was brought back to life.

The resurrection of Jairus's daughter tells us the truth that Jesus alone is our hope. He has power over all things, even death. So we should have faith in the Faithful One. In Him is life indeed.

—*Cathy Elliott*

"It is not the strength of your faith that saves you,
but the strength of Him upon whom you rely!"
—*Charles Spurgeon*

 LORD, grow my faith that I might trust You in all things, for nothing is impossible for You. Amen.

He replied, "Isaiah was right when he prophesied about you hypocrites; as it is written: 'These people honor me with their lips, but their hearts are far from me. They worship me in vain; their teachings are merely human rules.' You have let go of the commands of God and are holding on to human traditions." —Mark 7:6–8 (NIV)

My hubby's faith in Jesus was fresh like spring grass when we married forty-four years ago. Unfortunately, he'd married a spiritual know-it-all. I thought I knew all there was to know about living the Christian life. I'd given my heart to Jesus a decade earlier and grown up attending church, memorizing Scripture, and practicing platitude-speak.

Hubby hadn't.

In my skewed perspective, true Christians carried their Bibles to church and took notes during a sermon. Prayed aloud. Were always ready to spout spiritual-sounding answers. My hubby's faith paled in comparison to my expectations.

I'd chosen to judge myself and others, using a flawed paradigm devoid of God's grace and barren of the fruit of His Spirit.

Once I realized I'd elevated human rules over a relationship with Jesus, I asked for and experienced grace anew. Grace from the hubby I had judged according to my church traditions. Grace and forgiveness from my Savior. He bridged the gap between His Father and me not because of my conformity to the law but as a gift of amazing grace.

—*Mona Hodgson*

"The prime characteristic of someone justified by faith in Jesus is love."
—*Robb Williams*

JESUS, help me release human traditions and expectations, to worship You in truth and share Your grace. Amen.

NOTHING IS IMPOSSIBLE

With people this is impossible, but with God all things are possible.
—Matthew 19:26 (NASB)

I sat on the edge of my bed, moaning in uncontrollable sobs. My life was utterly broken, and I saw no way out. I was in bondage to something so simple but unrelenting: food. For years I binged as if in a secret tryst with a cruel lover. Covert drive-through trips, stuffing food in my mouth while no one was looking, and planning my day so I could overeat were routine. After years of living in this miserable state, I began to diet like a drill sergeant, counting every calorie and beating my body into submission. Soon I withered to a bony shape, and deep in the throes of anorexia, I realized I'd simply traded one compulsion for another.

One day on my bed, I cried out to Jesus, asking Him to do the impossible: heal my body, spirit, and soul. It's challenging to describe what happened next. It felt like a prison break, as the chains of delusion fell to the floor. I reached for a Bible I'd never read and began my journey back to health.

If your life feels full of impossible obstacles—relationship heartaches, financial strains, health issues, or daunting uncertainty—remember that Jesus promises *all* things are possible with God.

—*Gari Meacham*

"Nothing is too hard for God, no sin too difficult for his love
to overcome; not a failure but He can make it a success."
—*Oswald Chambers*

 JESUS, help me to remember Your promise that nothing is impossible for You. No circumstance is bigger than Your power to change it. Amen.

Very truly I tell you, whoever hears my word and believes him who sent me has eternal life and will not be judged but has crossed over from death to life. —John 5:24 (NIV)

Jesus first called my name when I was nine years old. I was discontent with my young life, and depression walked with me as I couldn't get past the teasing of being an overweight little girl. I wanted to hide from everyone. My faith began as just a kernel of hope, because I didn't understand the concept of turning my life over to a God Who loved me unconditionally. If He were the perfect Father, then why did I feel ugly and fat? I attended church and Sunday school regularly, and I studied the Bible. Something lacked in my faith, and I had no idea what it was.

Ten years later, I had a breakthrough. I was alone and watching a Billy Graham crusade, and Jesus spoke to me. He wanted me to follow Him and leave all my doubts and fears behind. I accepted His gift of everlasting life and imagined myself walking to the front of the auditorium during the singing of "Just as I Am."

I felt the perfect love that can only come from heaven.

The moment is fixed in my mind of how Jesus never let me go even when I didn't understand what putting Him first in my life meant. And the faith born out of that experience has guided me ever since.

I know now Jesus is the God of creation and my soul. One day I will live with Him in peace and purpose, but until His return, I will show my faith in my thoughts, words, and deeds. That means loving others and myself just as Jesus said.

—DiAnn Mills

"As a Christian, Christ died so that we will have eternal life in Him in heaven.
What it looks like doesn't matter, what it smells like doesn't matter,
as long as Christ is there it will be Heaven to me."
—T. D. Jakes

DEAR JESUS, thank You for reaching out to me and all those who believe in You with Your unconditional love. You are my Lord and Savior now and forever. Amen.

NOT AN ACCIDENT

Heaven and earth will pass away, but my words will never pass away.
—Mark 13:31 (NIV)

Hubby and I sat in the front seats, me on the passenger's side. Our twelve-year-old grandson sat behind me on our way to drop him off at his dad's house. We'd driven the hour over the mountain and were making our way to the next turn when I saw a black pickup truck moving out of its lane and toward me. The impact pushed our vehicle into the left-turn median.

Words flooded my mind. *Did that just happen? Everyone OK? Is the car drivable? Why did he do that?* The other driver said, "No need to call the police. I'll take care of the damage." *Should we listen to him? The court issued a warrant on him? Two warrants? Is he dangerous? How long before the officer arrives?*

Situations arise. Circumstances change. Jobs end. People pass. Deliberate changes sometimes need to be made. Accidents will happen. When they do, no words are as bracing and comforting as Jesus's words: "Never will I leave you; never will I forsake you." This promise Jesus made, found in Hebrews 13:5, is one of the staples of faith founded in Him.

Jesus's promises will never pass away. I draw strength, wisdom, and courage from His words, come what may.

—*Mona Hodgson*

"We need to fortify ourselves with the Word of God." —Billy Graham

LORD JESUS, I'm grateful for Your words, which stand the test of time and always will. Help me rest on Your promises. Amen.

Flesh gives birth to flesh, but the Spirit gives birth to spirit. You should not be surprised at my saying, "You must be born again." —John 3:6–7 (NIV)

Some people can tell you the exact day they trusted in Jesus. Others point less to a moment and more to a process, a whole series of factors and events: "A coworker invited me to a Bible study in February of 2006...By that summer I was a believer."

I'm a member of the second group. Growing up in a Christian home, I can't recall not believing in God or not knowing Jesus came to save sinners. I also can't count the number of times during my childhood and youth when, deeply aware of my own sin, I asked Jesus to forgive me and change my life. Truth be told, I don't know exactly when I put my faith in Christ. I just know my trust is in Him today. He is my one and only hope.

All this "born again" talk leaves lots of people feeling confused. For some of them, the uncertainty is due to a popular but erroneous notion that spiritual rebirth is a reward—something we get for engaging in certain religious actions, avoiding certain sins, taking communion, or undergoing baptism.

Jesus stated, however, that being "born again" is a gift. It comes to us from above, by God's grace. We can't earn it; we can receive it only through faith in Christ.

—*Len Woods*

"Of course God does not consider you hopeless. If He did, He would not be moving you to seek Him (and He obviously is).... Continue seeking Him with seriousness. Unless He wanted you, you would not be wanting Him."
—*C. S. Lewis*

 JESUS, thank You for the free gift of new life! Fill me with Your Spirit, I pray. Amen.

Love Letter from Jesus
EASTER/FORGIVENESS OF SIN

My Dear One,

If you ever wonder how much you are loved, look to the cross. While you were still a sinner, I died for you. Each thorn in My brow, each lash, each insult, each nail, each drop of My blood is proof. The cross was the cost of your redemption, and I willingly paid it. There is nothing you could ever do that would make Me love you less, or more. Let that sink in.

Because of My blood, you can come boldly before the throne of grace. You can lay down your burdens, all of your shame. You can bring your brokenness and be made whole again in Me—I am the One Who holds everything together. And I forgive you and cleanse you from all unrighteousness. My blood covers you. Your sins are forgiven—past, present, and future. They are blotted out, remembered no more. You are free to forgive yourself and others, because I have forgiven you. I laid down My life for your freedom.

Take My hand, and walk with Me out of the tomb. Come out of darkness and into the Light. Come out of whatever sorrow or pain or disappointment or loss you might have experienced. I am the resurrection and the life. I have come to give life to you—a full and joyous life, a life of peace that passes all understanding. All that the Father has and is belongs to Me, and I long to share it with you. Let Me live My life through You.

I love you forever.

I am crucified with Christ: nevertheless I live; yet not I, but Christ liveth in me: and the life which I now live in the flesh I live by the faith of the Son of God, who loved me, and gave himself for me. —Galatians 2:20 (KJV)

> And they were all amazed at the greatness of God. While everyone was marveling at all that Jesus did, he said to his disciples, "Listen carefully to what I am about to tell you: the Son of Man is going to be delivered into the hands of men." —Luke 9:43–44 (NIV)

The worst thing you can ever imagine happening will happen. The hero in the real story of your redemption is about to be captured and crucified. Let that sink in. The hero loses. Jesus, the Messiah, the Savior of the world, dies.

This does not read like the story of the Creator of the universe, but this is the story of Jesus. "Light came into the world and the darkness could not overcome it." I memorized John 1:5 when I was nine, but I always imagined a brightness entering like the morning and banishing cold shadows to corners.

When my friend grieved a sister with a terminal-cancer diagnosis, the cold shadows felt closer than sunshine. When we mourned the bombings in Baghdad and the shootings across the United States, the darkness seemed to be winning. And when my mom called to say my brother had died, I felt my body collapse onto the hardwood floor and the bright morning disappeared altogether.

The world's deep hunger and Jesus's deep mercy met at the cross. He secured victory over pain and death and all of the worst things that can ever happen. For the joy set before Him, Jesus was delivered into the hands of men so that terminal cancer and warring regions and my brother's death are not the end.

The deepest gladness of Jesus was to take on the worst of humanity—the places that are dark and desperate—so that our hunger for life is satisfied in Him.

—*Caroline Kolts*

"The place God calls you to is the place where
your deep gladness and the world's deep hunger meet."
—*Frederick Buechner*

JESUS, I am amazed by all Your marvelous works. Draw me into Your Word. Help me understand and believe You are greater than anything opposing You. Amen.

THE FAITH OF A CHILD

For God so loved the world that he gave his one and only Son, that whoever believes in him shall not perish but have eternal life. —John 3:16 (NIV)

When I was a child, I memorized John 3:16 for my Sunday-school class. I stood in my frilly dress and patent leather shoes, and recited the words and got a sticker to hang on my chart on the wall. I remember being proud because the verse felt long. I was sure knowing this famous verse meant I was a good Christian.

At the time, I had no idea what the verse meant. I still don't really understand it. John 3:16 is, I've been told many times, the gospel in a nutshell. It's the basic outline of our faith in one handy verse. But it's one of those verses I know so well that it's hard to really see it with fresh eyes.

When I read the verse today, I'm filled with questions. *Why did God love the world so much? Why did He have to give His Son? Where did His Son come from? Why does He only have one? What does it mean when it says we won't perish?* The certainty of childhood has been replaced by the desire for understanding.

The more I try to wrap my head around the words, the less I seem to know. But I have to keep trying to understand. I will keep trying to make sense of the kind of love that would sacrifice everything for someone like me.

Perhaps we're not meant to fully understand. God is bigger than we can imagine, and I believe He is pleased when we trust Him even when we don't understand. For now, I'll focus on the things I understood even as a child: God loved the world. God loved the world so much He gave us Jesus. All we have to do is believe in Him.

—*Elizabeth Adams*

"I believe in Christianity as I believe that the sun has risen: not only because I see it, but because by it I see everything else." —C. S. Lewis

 THANK YOU, God, for loving the world enough to send Jesus. Please help me to understand that kind of love more each day. Amen.

Jesus answered, "I am the way and the truth and the life. No one comes to the Father except through me." —John 14:6 (NIV)

While visiting a friend in Colorado, my husband and I mentioned we wanted to go high up into the mountains, so we asked him how to get there. He began to give us directions, and then he offered to get into our car and go with us to show us the way.

The road was unpaved, rugged, and narrow. In many places we had a mountain wall on one side and a straight drop on the other. If it were just my husband and me, I would have been terrified, but with our guide, I felt secure. He instructed us how to maneuver the car so we wouldn't get stuck or drive over a cliff. And when we arrived at the mountaintop, we were awestruck by the view. It was well worth the dangerous trip, and I couldn't thank our expert friend enough for his guidance.

In a somewhat similar way, Jesus makes Himself available to guide us safely through this life and to our eternal life. He alone knows the way—He created the road!—and He provides us with the road map and guidance for us to arrive safely at our destination. As we ask Jesus to show us the way, He tells us, "I'll do even better than that. I am the Way, and I'll take you there Myself."

—*Ginger Kolbaba*

"Through faith in the Lord Jesus alone can we obtain forgiveness of our sins, and be at peace with God; but, believing in Jesus, we become, through this very faith, the children of God; have God as our Father, and may come to Him for all the temporal and spiritual blessings which we need."
—*George Muller*

JESUS, I acknowledge You as the way, the truth, and the life. Grant that I follow You closely each day. Amen.

Father, if you are willing, take this cup from me; yet not my will, but yours be done. —Luke 22:42 (NIV)

"This isn't fair," I whispered from the hospital bed, after the doctor confirmed I was miscarrying. This was my first pregnancy, and I loved this baby already.

My heart breaking, I surrendered the child in my womb, praying, "Jesus, this pain is more than I can bear. If I lose this baby, I'll grieve but will accept it as Your will."

What else could I do?

At my "amen," peace washed over me. To the nurses' surprise, a heartbeat was discovered.

A few months later, Jake was born. In our first moments alone, his gaze locked in on mine. His eyes seemed to carry heavenly knowledge. His coos entered my heart as a thank-you. Then, in a blink, his eyes transformed to those of a typical newborn.

A few years later, I faced another potential miscarriage. I prayed, but lost the baby. Jesus's peace softened my grief.

During my moments of despair, I learned Jesus is always the answer. We must surrender. "Take this cup from me. Not my will, but yours."

Though we can't always understand God's will, when we surrender ours, His perfect will reigns and peace prevails.

—*Holly Michael*

"Our heavenly Father understands our disappointment, suffering, pain, fear, and doubt. He is always there to encourage our hearts and help us understand that He's sufficient for all of our needs. When I accepted this as an absolute truth in my life, I found that my worrying stopped." —Charles Stanley

LORD JESUS, angels attended You during Your passion. Help us to remember to surrender all to You, and when Your perfect will means suffering, grant us Your peace through it. Amen.

> Sitting down, He called the twelve and said to them, "If anyone wants to be first, he shall be last of all and servant of all." —Mark 9:35 (NASB)

As a twenty-five-year-old head college-baseball coach, I was on the fast track. This gig was going to be a short stopover on my way to big-time professional coaching. Given that this was a Christian college, we often spoke of the Lord. We had devotion time together, and we even spoke of the higher meaning of sports in our lives as we traveled together to our first away game.

After four hours of driving, we stepped jelly-legged out of the team van, trying to shake the drone of the highway. The field was some four hundred yards away. I began packing my game bag as everyone left, and I was the last to leave the parking lot. Locking the van, I made my way to the passenger's side and jolted to a halt. All the baseball gear had been plopped on the pavement. Helmets, catcher's gear, bats, baseballs, water cooler, cups—all waited to be carried.

Indignant, I took a breath to call out to the disappearing players in the distance. No, wait, I had a better idea—one that would teach them a lesson. I would meet them in the dugout and make them all walk back as a team. I took twelve paces more from the van when the previous night's devotional struck me like a line drive. *Servant of all... really?* I thought. I turned around.

I made three long trips to the van and back. The other team snickered as they saw the coach doing the work of mules. I did indeed teach a valuable lesson to my team that day, and it had nothing to do with baseball.

—*Erik Person*

"Good leaders must first become good servants."
—*Robert K. Greenleaf*

LORD, You came to serve. Even in positions of leadership, help me to follow Your example of servant leadership. Amen.

> A slave isn't a permanent member of the household, but a son is. Therefore, if the Son makes you free, you really will be free. —John 8:35–36 (CEB)

Dad was famous for his long, rambling graces at the dinner table. Anything that occurred in the course of the day or was coming up that night was fodder for prayer—the Dodgers game, my sister's tryouts for drill team, the president's press conference, Mom's rolls heating up in the oven, my brother's spelling test, or the traffic on the 405 freeway. If we kids got fidgety, Dad blessed us, too: "I thank you, God, for our children's high spirits."

"It's the six o'clock news," one family friend declared, after hearing a particularly lengthy grace. "Anything your dad hears on the radio on the way home, he puts in his prayer." That's how Dad prayed night after night, always ending with the same words: "Bless this food to our use, and us to Thy service, and the hands that prepared it."

Dad is gone now, and we kids are grown with households of our own, but consciously or unconsciously we learned from our father's prayers what permanent guest should be housed in every room and praised at every table. The six o'clock news? More like the good news, faith lived out day to day, the food blessed to our use and us to the Son's service.

—*Rick Hamlin*

"I was not born to be free—I was born to adore and obey."
—*C. S. Lewis*

 JESUS CHRIST, set us free to do Your will as we reach out every day to welcome You into our hearts and homes. Amen.

> When Jesus saw their faith, he said, "Friend, your sins are forgiven."
> —Luke 5:20 (NIV)

When our small group gathers for weekly Bible study, we share prayer requests. One of our members might ask for prayer related to an ailment, or someone will mention a friend's health request. Sometimes we share emotional and spiritual requests, but it's difficult to focus on those when you're hurting physically.

It reminds me of the men who carried their paralyzed friend to meet Jesus. They were so determined in their healing mission that they lowered him through the roof tiles right in front of Jesus! I love the imagery of these dedicated friends carrying their loved one straight to the feet of Jesus.

Once the man was lowered down, Jesus commended their faith and forgave their sins. Can you imagine the reaction of these loyal men? They brought a man in need of physical healing, but before Jesus healed the man of paralysis, He lifted the burden of sin from their spirits.

I believe the sequence of these events is important. Before addressing the obvious physical need, Jesus granted forgiveness. He allows us to bring to Him all of our requests—physical, emotional, and spiritual. He knows what we most need.

The extension of that same privilege of carrying our friends' needs to Jesus is one of the many benefits of trusting in Him. But, I know my faith is still required along with the dedication and follow-through of prayer.

—*Allison K. Flexer*

"We never know how God will answer our prayers, but we can expect that He will get us involved in His plan for the answer. If we are true intercessors, we must be ready to take part in God's work on behalf of the people for whom we pray."
—*Corrie ten Boom*

JESUS, we're grateful that You want to hear from us. Thank You for the privilege of bringing prayer requests directly to You. Forgive us, heal us, and change us. Amen.

> But I have pleaded in prayer for you, Simon, that your faith should not fail. So when you have repented and turned to me again, strengthen your brothers.
> —Luke 22:32 (NLT)

I tend to open my mouth before I think. My foot-in-mouth disease is a chronic condition of a sanguine personality. A sanguine is an extrovert who is too loud and draws attention to herself, and I think Simon Peter, too, was sanguine. He followed Jesus with enthusiasm, beginning on the day Jesus said, "Follow me." Peter dropped his fishing nets to pursue the man who said, "I'll make you fishers of men." Peter swore he would never let the Romans take Jesus and attempted to cut off the ear of one soldier. Peter's enthusiasm didn't help him speak up. He said he would never deny Jesus was the Messiah. Later, during Jesus's trial, Peter stood in the courtyard and swore three times that he didn't know Jesus.

Jesus prayed that the three denials would not destroy Peter's faith, that he would repent and become stronger—so strong that he would be able to "strengthen his brothers." And he did!

When our failures—and yours—shake us, we need to follow Peter's example. Turn back to Jesus. When we do, we discover that overcoming troubles only makes us stronger. Our newfound power allows us to strengthen others.

—*Karen Porter*

"Only those who dare to fail greatly can ever achieve greatly."
—*Robert F. Kennedy*

 DEAR JESUS, help me when I fail. Allow my failures to make me stronger so I can help others. Amen.

**They will do such things because they have not known the Father or me.
—John 16:3 (NIV)**

I had a few hours of free time one afternoon during my week of teaching at a Christian university campus far from home. Instead of my usual downhill walk that led me to the ocean, I decided to venture farther to shop at a department store. No shuttle van was available on the campus that day, so I called for a taxi.

I'd just climbed into the taxi and shut the door when the driver started complaining about the beliefs, as he perceived them, of those affiliated with the university. My association with the school's mission and the Jesus we serve made me a target of his condemnation. Despite my attempts to redirect the conversation, the driver's rant continued and its intensity grew. So did my discomfort. I asked him to stop and let me out.

My knees quaking like aspen leaves, I closed the taxi door and mentally recharted charted my course for the ocean. The trip to the store would wait another day, when I could ride on the campus shuttle van.

The experience, though dim in comparison, brought to mind that every day brothers and sisters in the Christian faith are persecuted, even to death. That afternoon as I walked toward the ocean, I prayed for those being mistreated and asked God to give me a heart to do so regularly.

—*Mona Hodgson*

*"If you look at the world, you'll be distressed. If you look within,
you'll be depressed. If you look at God you'll be at rest."*
—*Corrie ten Boom*

 JESUS, thank You for being with me always. Thank You for the reminder to pray for those being persecuted for their faith in You. Amen.

> Therefore, I tell you, her many sins have been forgiven—as her great love has shown. But whoever has been forgiven little loves little. —Luke 7:47 (NIV)

Shame had me hiding in the corner of my bedroom and afraid to leave the room. I had lost my temper and spat hurtful words at my family. I was too embarrassed to face them. Fear told me I was unloved and unwanted. I thought maybe they would all be better off without me. My husband probably regretted marrying me, and my kids likely wished they had a different mother. With a tear-soaked face, I was certain I shouldn't even call out to Jesus.

Not only had I sinned, but now I was also listening to lies of the enemy.

In that dark moment, Jesus gently reminded me that my many sins are forgiven. I don't need to hide in shame. Instead, I can run to Him with my sin, knowing He has already forgiven me.

The woman in Luke 7 provides a beautiful example of how to respond to the forgiveness of our sins. Rather than hiding in shame, she ran to Him and publicly displayed her love through tears, kisses on His feet, and a costly bottle of perfume. When others wanted to condemn her, Jesus upheld her as an example of how to respond when we realize we are forgiven.

Whatever your sins, run to Jesus. His arms are open, and His love is plenty. We don't need to live in shame, but with a heart filled with grateful love.

—Amelia Rhodes

"Forgiveness is the final form of love."
—*Reinhold Niebuhr*

 JESUS, I am overwhelmed by Your forgiveness of my sin. Today, I desire to pour out my love for You. Amen.

> And he said to them, "Why were you looking for me? Did you not know that I must be in my Father's house?" —Luke 2:49 (ESV)

Both my little boys are prone to wandering when we're out and about. They tend to go wherever their interests lead—usually the toy aisle. More than once, one has slipped out of my sight, and so far, I've been able to find him around where I expected him to be. I'm grateful we haven't had a lost-kid-over-the-loudspeaker episode yet.

Traveling with a mass of friends and family for the Passover Feast, Mary and Joseph lost track of twelve-year-old Jesus…for three days. Yikes! Meanwhile, Jesus was engaged in heavy conversation with the Jerusalem temple rabbis, seemingly oblivious to His parents' understandably "great distress." We're never told if Mary and Joseph were given a clear schedule of Jesus's road to Calvary, but Jesus reacted as though they should have expected Him to be just where they found Him.

More often than I'd like, I find myself in "great distress," wondering where Jesus is. *Doesn't He know how anxious I am?* I wonder. *Doesn't He know how desperately I'm searching for Him?* Looking back, after I finally find Him in my circumstances, I realize He was there all along.

—*Isabella Yosuico*

"Look for Jesus and when you find him, you'll find everything else thrown in."
—*C. S. Lewis*

JESUS, help me know that even when I can't seem to find You, You are there and I need not be anxious. Amen.

> In the same way, after the supper he took the cup, saying, "This cup
> is the new covenant in my blood, which is poured out for you."
> —Luke 22:20 (NIV)

I gave blood today. I try to do so every other month. When the time comes to prick my finger for a blood sample, I look away. I do the same when the needle punctures my vein and blood starts flowing through the tube to the pint bag that collects my donation. I'm not sure why I look away. It's not because I have ever gotten faint or sick at the sight of blood.

The regular experience often prompts me to think of Jesus, and how Luke's gospel records not only that "he set his face to go to Jerusalem" (Luke 9:51, NRSV) but also that, at His last supper, He lifted a cup of wine and told them it represented His own blood, which He knew would soon be poured out in the most gruesome way imaginable. Maybe that image caused Him to pray, moments later, for "this cup" to be taken from Him (Luke 22:42), but when push came to shove, He faced His trial courageously and resolutely. He said, "I lay down my life of my own accord" (John 10:17-18, NIV). He never flinched. He never looked away.

When I take communion, I often pause an extra moment to gaze on the bread and the cup, the "body" and the "blood." While I find no benefit in watching my own blood flow, I try never to look away from the blood of Jesus, which gives me life day by day.

—*Bob Hostetler*

*"The hidden value of His blood is the spirit of self-sacrifice, and where the blood
really touches the heart, it works out in that heart, a like spirit of self-sacrifice.
We learn to give up ourselves and our lives, so as to press into the
full power of that new life, which the blood has provided."*
—*Andrew Murray*

JESUS, thank You for Your life, Your blood, and Your sacrificial love. Teach me to live in a way that honors Your great sacrifice. Amen.

I have spoken these things to you so that My joy may be in you and your joy may be complete. —John 15:11 (HCSB)

The night before His death, Jesus huddled one final time with His most loyal followers. What He said was troubling: "I am going away, and the world will hate you." And what He said was reassuring: "You are my beloved friends. I will send My Spirit and give you My peace. I will come again."

Why did Jesus feel the need to share this mixed bag of final instructions and reminders? Because He wants His followers to be filled with joy. Biblically speaking, joy is that otherworldly gladness that bubbles up in our hearts when we remember—and trust—that the lover of our souls is also the Lord of the universe.

When I was a younger Christian just getting my feet wet in ministry, a junior-high kid once asked me, "What is it about you? You smile all the time!"

The statement surprised me. I surely wasn't trying to act cheerful. Rather, in seeking by faith to live in the power of the Holy Spirit, I was experiencing the wonderful truth that "the fruit of the Spirit is joy" (Galatians 5:22).

A couple of years ago I heard different words: "You have become grim!" It was true. I was sighing, rather than smiling, my way through life. My former lighthearted faith had been replaced by a dark heaviness of soul. When faith becomes dreary—all duty and no delight—it's past time to ponder and claim Jesus's promise of joy.

—Len Woods

"A negative, joyless Christian is a contradiction in terms."
—Billy Graham

JESUS, fill me to overflowing with Your unspeakable joy. Show the world through me that You are the source of true happiness. Amen.

> **The thief comes only to steal and kill and destroy; I have come that they may have life, and have it to the full. I am the good shepherd. The good shepherd lays down his life for the sheep. —John 10:10-11 (NIV)**

The woman I'd interviewed was a great example of someone overcoming adversity. Nancy accepted Christ through prison ministry and had reentered society with new hope.

Yet my heart was troubled while writing the newspaper piece. A few nights earlier, I'd dreamed about Nancy. She appeared weary and defeated. Then, suddenly, a bold voice interrupted the dream: "Tell her I love her. Tell her not to lie down and sleep."

Joy-filled Nancy? Lord, she knows You and loves You. Still, guilt weighed like bricks on my chest. I called Nancy and shared the dream.

Silence. Then sobs.

Nancy choked out her words. "I said what you wanted to hear...what would make a good story." She explained the difficulties of life outside of prison. "I was about to take a bottle of sleeping pills," she confessed, weeping. "But now I know that Jesus really loves me."

"He laid down His life for you," I assured her. "That's how much He loves you."

I thanked the Good Shepherd for allowing me to be His instrument.

We don't always realize the depth of others' suffering. I was grateful the Good Shepherd shared this truth with me. He loves all of His sheep enough to lay down His life for them. The devil has no power over that kind of love.

—*Holly Michael*

"We must not lose hope. Hope is an anchor to the souls of men.
Satan would have us cast away that anchor."
—*Ezra Taft Benson*

 LORD, let us never forget Your great love through Your ultimate sacrifice, and may we boldly remind those who forget. Amen.

> When evening came, Jesus was reclining at the table with the Twelve. And while they were eating, he said, "Truly I tell you, one of you will betray me." —Matthew 26:20-21 (NIV)

As a pastor, I've spent many hours counseling and encouraging parishioners regarding emotional and spiritual pain. Such pain is common to the human experience. Eventually, we all deal with some form of pain—grief, depression, or low self-esteem. Perhaps the greatest cause of emotional and spiritual pain is a sense of betrayal. Few experiences can trigger a broken heart and all of its symptoms like a sense of betrayal. The reality is, the closer we are to the person who has betrayed us, the greater the sense of pain we endure once that betrayal is discovered.

Among Jesus's saddest quotations was His foretelling that one of His chosen disciples, one from His band of brothers, would willfully betray Him to His enemies. "Truly I tell you, one of you will betray me," Jesus said as they began their last supper together. These words of Jesus are recorded not just as a lasting indictment of Judas but also as an expression of Christ's humanity and emotion.

The very word "mercy" has its roots in empathy. How encouraging and healing for us to know that Jesus knew and felt our darkest experiences. When we are wounded by the harsh reality of betrayal, it is powerfully comforting to know that Jesus, to Whom we turn for healing, has walked that path before us...and He is merciful toward the betrayed.

—*David Downs*

> *"Unto a broken heart*
> *No other one may go*
> *Without the high prerogative*
> *Itself hath suffered too."*
> —*Emily Dickinson*

 THANK YOU, Jesus, for enduring betrayal. As I seek healing of my spirit and mind, it helps to know that You understand how I feel. Amen.

> **We are going up to Jerusalem, and the Son of Man will be delivered over to the chief priests and the teachers of the law. They will condemn him to death and will hand him over to the Gentiles to be mocked and flogged and crucified. On the third day he will be raised to life! —Matthew 20:18-19** (NIV)

In June 1998, my family moved out of state in hopes of benefiting from a job transfer and lower cost of living. In November 2012 I returned home, with my youngest son, as a divorced single mom. If I'd known hardship would be our constant companion during that decade and a half, I would have talked my husband out of transferring. I'm glad I didn't know. Along with job losses; cold winters; dry, hot summers; and a pitiful list of stresses and disappointments, I would have missed out on deep friendships, ministry opportunities, lessons in independence and resourcefulness, and profound spiritual growth. The painful discoveries that ended my marriage might have happened anywhere. The divorce that followed, and all that came with it, solidified my bond with Jesus in ways that no easy road could have.

Jesus told His disciples, "We are going to Jerusalem," knowing the sufferings that awaited Him. But He also knew the triumphant end of the story—that the pain, betrayal, abandonment, and death would result in drawing us to Him. Easter reminds me that closeness with Jesus requires suffering, but that suffering is followed by joy. The greatest rewards come when we are willing to follow our Savior's lead in trust that He knows what is ahead and will use every hardship for good.

—*Jeanette Hanscome*

"Any discussion of how pain and suffering fit into
God's scheme ultimately leads back to the cross."
—*Philip Yancey*

LORD, thank You for going to Jerusalem. Help me to trust You on my uncertain road, as I know You will be with me. Amen.

And forgive us our debts, as we also have forgiven our debtors.
—Matthew 6:12 (NIV)

"I'm sorry, Mom," my fifteen-year-old said, barely able to look at me. I gently lifted her chin and looked at her tear-filled eyes. "I forgive you," I whispered as I drew her into a hug.

Forgiving my daughter isn't hard. I adore her, and on the whole she's easy to love and forgive. But every relationship isn't that way. Most of us have at least one relationship that presents a "forgiveness challenge"—a person we forgive over and over, or maybe someone who left a wound so deep that we struggle to forgive even the first time.

I've experienced the freedom that comes from forgiving a wrong, and I've walked the halls of unforgiveness. I've nursed hurts and clung to anger. And I've found myself right where my daughter was—head low and heart aching, unable to look at the One from Whom I most need forgiveness.

In the same way I pulled my daughter close, Jesus has drawn me in and whispered His peace and forgiveness over me. He keeps no record of wrongs, never says, "I can't believe you did that again." No, our Savior accepts our apologies and guides us forward. With Him as an example, we too can learn to forgive those who come before us.

—*Teri Lynne Underwood*

"Everyone thinks forgiveness is a lovely idea until he has something to forgive."
—*C. S. Lewis*

 JESUS, give me the strength and desire to forgive as You do. May I follow Your example of loving forgiveness. Amen.

> He said to them, "Go into all the world and preach the gospel to all creation. Whoever believes and is baptized will be saved, but whoever does not believe will be condemned." —Mark 16:15-16 (NIV)

"I called out to Jesus," Sharma said. Raising her gaze, the Hindu girl glanced from the headmaster to my pastor husband, who is a native of South India.

We'd come to my husband's homeland for mission work and to disperse funds we'd raised after the 2004 tsunami.

Sharma's gaze returned to her teacher. "Mr. Rethinam loves Jesus, and I know that Jesus saves. He saved me when the monster wave roared into our village."

Mr. Rethinam's big smile widened as he put an arm around another child. The sandy schoolyard, filled with frightened children, was a sanctuary in a land ravaged by a violent sea. As they clamored around their teacher, it was evident Mr. Rethinam was their safe harbor.

Laws in India prevented Christians from evangelizing, especially in government schools, but a Hindu girl knew of Jesus from her teacher, and called His name when her life was threatened.

The apostle Thomas evangelized and was martyred in India. Because of him, my husband's family and many others became Christians generations later. Today, though India reports that Christians make up only about two percent of the population, Christian love reigns big in the hearts of that small percentage.

Jesus is a choice we all must make. He is the Savior of the world. Nothing should ever stand in the way of showing others Christ through us.

—Holly Michael

"Evangelism is the spontaneous overflow of a glad and free heart in Jesus Christ."
—Robert Munger

LORD, we pray that through our works and love, seeds of Christian faith will be planted in the hearts of many. Amen.

> Jesus called out with a loud voice, "Father, into your hands I commit my spirit." When he had said this, he breathed his last. —Luke 23:46 (NIV)

I have a friend who makes me crazy with jealousy. He often inserts into the middle of a conversation a comment like, "Reminds you of Proverbs 10:4, doesn't it?" I usually resist the urge to respond violently, and I swallow my pride, saying, "I don't know, Jim. What does Proverbs 10:4 say?" (If you're also wondering, the NIV translation reads, "Lazy hands make for poverty, but diligent hands bring wealth.")

I wish I had his gift for Scripture memorization and recall. It's not that I haven't tried; I have—just maybe not as diligently as he has. As I read my Bible more often, however, I am discovering that a Bible-saturated life brings many rewards—strength in weakness, light in darkness, and often clarity in otherwise confusing times.

I wonder if that is what happened in Jesus's darkest hour. I read several of His famous "seven sayings" on the cross as quotes from and references to the Hebrew scriptures. In fact, I repeat His prayer, "Father, into your hands I commit my spirit," every evening before I go to sleep. Both as David sang it in Psalm 31:5 and as Jesus spoke it on the cross, it reminds me that the Father can be trusted to hold me fast, whatever I might be going through—such as a bout of jealousy over a friend's excellent (and annoying) memory.

—*Bob Hostetler*

"All things are safe in Jehovah's hands; what we entrust to the Lord will be secure, both now and in that day of days towards which we are hastening."
—*Charles Spurgeon*

 JESUS, I commit my life to You, and my spirit now and forever into Your hands. Amen.

A REFLECTION OF MERCY

> **Blessed are the merciful, for they will be shown mercy.**
> **—Matthew 5:7 (NIV)**

I remember a time when I was surprised by mercy. My friend and I had a discussion that took a left turn. I wounded her with an unkind remark and realized shortly afterward that I needed to ask for her forgiveness. A few days had passed, and I went to her house and hesitantly knocked on her front door. Armed with cookies still warm from the oven, I raised my other hand again to knock louder. The door swung open, and there she stood with a welcoming smile.

I didn't think she'd be smiling for long, in spite of my peace offering.

"I...uh...need to apologize—"

"For what?" My friend interrupted my stream of guilt-speak. "I can't imagine."

"You don't remember?" I was flabbergasted. Of course she did. "Take a moment. You will."

"Nothing comes to mind." She hugged me and pulled me inside, leading me toward the kitchen. "I'm so glad you stopped by! Let's make some coffee to go with those cookies."

Instead of doling out the judgment I'd expected, my friend wiped my scorecard clean and showered me with mercy. With one small act of forgiveness, she painted a beautiful picture of our compassionate Lord alive in her heart. I recognized her act as one of mercy and of love. It made me love her more. And I loved even more deeply the merciful Jesus she reflected.

—*Cathy Elliott*

"I have always found that mercy bears richer fruits than strict justice."
—*Abraham Lincoln*

 LORD, teach me to be quick to forgive and extend mercy, as You do for me. Amen.

> If you forgive other people when they sin against you, your heavenly Father will also forgive you. But if you do not forgive others their sins, your Father will not forgive your sins. —Matthew 6:14–15 (NIV)

My friend's actions against me felt too painful to forgive. She'd betrayed a confidence. I said I forgave her, but deep inside, I held onto that resentment.

At church I never allowed my decision against her to enter my thoughts as I joined the congregation in reciting the Lord's Prayer: "And forgive us our debts, as we also have forgiven our debtors" (Matthew 6:12). I knew God had forgiven me. That other thing with her, I believed, didn't affect God's decision to absolve my wrongdoing.

Then one day during my devotional time, I read the Lord's Prayer and continued reading the verses following it. Jesus's words shot through me. He made it clear: Forgive or you cannot be forgiven. It must come from the heart—not just the mouth—or it is meaningless. My willingness to forgive reveals what is truly in my heart.

We must forgive in order for God to wipe our slates clean. Then we can receive God's forgiveness along with other rewards. We experience Christ's love and His freedom. To live without offering forgiveness is to place ourselves in a prison. And Christ came to set us free (Galatians 5:1). This is why we forgive—to experience true freedom both in this life and, according to Jesus, in the life to come.

—*Ginger Kolbaba*

"To forgive is to set a prisoner free and discover that the prisoner was you."
—Lewis B. Smedes

JESUS, I long to be forgiven, so grant me a forgiving heart toward those who have mistreated me. Amen.

> **"The time has come," he said. "The kingdom of God has come near. Repent and believe the good news!" —Mark 1:15 (NIV)**

I was five years old when I accepted Jesus as Savior. I remember the night I sat on my bed, and Mom led me through a prayer that I ended with, "Please write my name in Your book." When I caught on that not all families went to church, I felt sad and shocked. Why wouldn't they go?

"Not everyone believes in Jesus," Mom told me.

"Why not?" It didn't make sense.

The older I got, and the more people I met who hadn't grown up in homes where Mom and Dad introduced them to Jesus, especially after facing painful "I couldn't have gotten through this without Him" trials, the more thankful I was for my foundation of faith. God knew I needed Jesus early on before navigating a life that would include depression, crushing betrayals, and choices that seemed impossible to redeem.

More than forty years after that night when I asked Jesus to write my name in His book, I reread His statement in Mark 1:15 and marveled over the knowledge that He offers each person a "repent and believe" moment. For some of us it comes at five years old. For others it comes during the teen years or after decades of regrettable decisions. Claiming my faith was a gift I cherish to this day.

—*Jeanette Hanscome*

"This is the love of God, an alchemy that can turn enemies into children."
—Mark Buchanan

 LORD, thank You for opening my heart to repent and believe. Thank You for your gift of salvation. Amen.

> Be on your guard! If your brother sins, rebuke him; and if he repents, forgive him. And if he sins against you seven times a day, and returns to you seven times, saying, "I repent," forgive him. —Luke 17:3–4 (NASB)

I was counseling a couple that was struggling in their marriage. The wife was adamant her sins should be covered.

"He's supposed to forgive me!" she clamored. "Isn't he?"

After the session, her question stayed with me. Something wasn't quite right about this whole forgiveness thing. It seems Christians are either relegated to doormat status or elevated to a snob. What is the balance? "Be humble," I preach to myself. "Haven't you been forgiven much?"

The words of Jesus, recounted by Luke, stared at me. What was I missing? I went to sleep. The following morning a radio interview woke me. A politician publicly sought forgiveness. Something was unsettling about the apology however. Then it hit me: He sounded just like the woman I was counseling. He wanted forgiveness but was not really asking for it. It was more like an "if I have offended anyone, I'm sorry" sort of thing. Then I heard a whisper in my mind: "Forgiveness is the resolution, but the asking is what is commanded."

The next session, I asked the woman, "Have you asked for forgiveness?"

"Yes," she snapped.

"No, from God. It is He whom you have offended. Tom is just a witness."

Tears began to pool in her eyes. It occurred to me she'd probably just realized the cost of forgiveness.

—*Erik Person*

"Cheap grace is the preaching of forgiveness without requiring repentance."
—*Dietrich Bonhoeffer*

LORD JESUS, give me the wisdom to recognize Your holiness, the courage to call sin out, the mercy to forgive sin in others, and the discipline to repent of my own sin. Amen.

> Therefore, if you are offering your gift at the altar and there remember that your brother or sister has something against you, leave your gift there in front of the altar. First go and be reconciled to them; then come and offer your gift. —Matthew 5:23–24 (NIV)

A year had swept past since I'd spoken with my lifelong friend, though thoughts of her haunted me daily. *How had our argument taken root? Who'd started it?* Those things were no longer relevant. It was time to call her.

I remembered Jesus's words telling me to reconcile before going to the altar. So many times I'd knelt before Him, guilt and residual anger distancing me from Him, poisoning our closeness. Shame weighed heavily on me, the burden bowing my shoulders and weakening my spirit. I missed my friend. More than that, I missed the intimacy I'd shared with Christ.

As I picked up the phone, my heart raced, and I hesitated. What if my friend were to refuse the call? Closing my eyes, I whispered a quick prayer. Courage flooded my soul, and I punched in her number.

Our Lord had revealed one of His truths to me. Whether my friend accepted the apology wasn't important. Jesus had already forgiven me.

Placing my problems at His feet as the phone lines connected, I smiled.

"Hello? It's me."

Speaking the words, I heard a sound. I like to think it was the wall, which separated me from Christ, as it came crashing down.

—Heidi Gaul

"To love means loving the unlovable. To forgive means pardoning the unpardonable. Faith means believing the unbelievable. Hope means hoping when everything seems hopeless." —G. K. Chesterton

 DEAR JESUS, guide me as I struggle with reconciliation. Take my hand, and lead me back to Your altar. Amen.

> Sanctify them by the truth; your word is truth.
> —John 17:17 (NIV)

I received an angry call from my friend filled with false accusations, and I had no idea where the statements had come from. Stunned best described my emotions. I'd invested hours getting to know her and thought we were sisters in Christ.

Later, I learned she'd spread her accusations to business associates and friends. The betrayal stung, and I never learned why she'd done this. Unfortunately I wasn't her first victim. Anger seized me and seemed to paralyze my faith. If anyone chose to believe her, my reputation was ruined. But those who knew me also recognized the lies. Truth surfaced like rich cream.

But I had a choice to make: follow God and forgive her, or take my hurt feelings to my grave. Being a nonconfrontational person made the decision even harder. I chose forgiveness. Phoning her proved more difficult than I ever imagined. Yet the moment I uttered those three precious words—"I forgive you"—His sweet love filled my soul.

Truth always wins. If I'd walked away from the relationship without honoring Jesus, righteous pride would have one day caught up with me. Then I'd be faced with humbling myself to the One Who is Truth.

I will strive for truth and make a positive stand for Jesus, no matter the circumstances.

—DiAnn Mills

"If you shut up truth and bury it under the ground, it will but grow, and gather to itself such explosive power that the day it bursts through it will blow up everything in its way." —Émile Zola

DEAR JESUS, You are my light and my salvation. When I follow Your truth, I'm secure and happy. Hold me tight, and give me strength to hold on forever. Amen.

Therefore I tell you, whatever you ask in prayer, believe that you have received it, and it will be yours. And whenever you stand praying, forgive, if you have anything against anyone, so that your Father also who is in heaven may forgive you your trespasses. —Mark 11:24–25 (ESV)

I have always felt uncomfortable about the conversation I should be having with the Lord—the assumption being that every Christian is in mid-sentence dialogue with our Creator and Redeemer. Because, well, I'm not. My prayers are thoughts smooshed together before sleep and desperate pleas for mercy in the middle of trouble. I would love to have a continual prayer woven through the fabric of my day, but I am still very much working on threading the needle.

But Jesus meets me exactly where I am. He doesn't reject my efforts because they are imperfect. He knows I have trouble believing He is able, but still He promises that when I do pray, He will listen. He knows I struggle to forgive my offenders, but still He encourages my spirit that when I do forgive, He will also forgive me.

Jesus calmed the raging waters, healed the lepers, fed the multitudes, listened to the brokenhearted, walked toward the hurting, and endured the cross. And Jesus is saying to me, "Ask me for anything, and believe I can do it. Forgive your offenders, and receive my forgiveness." What a powerful invitation! Though I have given Jesus every reason to ignore my prayers, He persists in patience to listen, encourage, and love every conversation we have.

—*Caroline Kolts*

"God does not love some ideal person, but rather human beings
just as we are, not some ideal world, but rather the real world."
—*Dietrich Bonhoeffer*

JESUS, thank You for listening. Help me believe You are able to meet my every need. Teach me how to forgive as You have forgiven. Amen.

By myself I can do nothing; I judge only as I hear, and my judgment is just, for I seek not to please myself but him who sent me. —John 5:30 (NIV)

On April 27, 2014, while singing in the choir at church, I had a heart attack. I was forty-two years old, completely healthy, and with no risk factors. My husband rushed me to the emergency room, and from there I was sent by ambulance to a larger hospital for stent placement and angioplasty.

In the days to follow, I learned more than I ever imagined about dependence on others. Tasks I had never given thought to suddenly required assistance. From doing laundry to driving my car, my new reality meant I could do nothing by myself.

Just as I had to learn to rely on others in every way, Jesus said He was completely dependent on the Father. Many of us are repelled by the idea of dependence and want to do everything on our own. But that is not the example of Jesus. He continually submitted Himself to the Father's will and purpose, seeking the glory of God in every way.

Weeks of relying on others gave me a clearer picture of what it means to depend on Jesus entirely, to submit to His purpose, and to give Him the glory in everything. Though I am able now to do everything I could before my heart attack, I have a deeper understanding of what it is to recognize I can do nothing without Jesus.

—*Teri Lynne Underwood*

> *"Let God's promises shine on your problems."*
> —*Corrie ten Boom*

JESUS, keep my heart stayed on You so that I remember it is only through You I can do anything of value. Amen.

> I tell you that in the same way there will be more rejoicing in heaven over one sinner who repents than over ninety-nine righteous persons who do not need to repent. —Luke 15:7 (NIV)

Jesus must have loved to speak in parables, because He told a lot of them!

In the parable about the lost sheep, Jesus spoke to a group that happened to include the town's tax collectors and sinners. They were the ones the townspeople avoided. Some might have been unemployed; maybe they had no place to live; perhaps they drank or made money illegally. The leaders of the synagogue were not happy with Jesus. They grumbled, "This man welcomes sinners and eats with them." I wonder if they worried that maybe Jesus would invite this ragtag group to a temple service. Before you know it, they'd be at coffee hour taking sugar packets and putting cookies in their pockets.

Jesus heard the grumbling, and that's when He compared one sinner who repents to one lost sheep its shepherd had found. I've always considered myself to be one of the ninety-nine sheep. Sure, now and then I've rebelled and even wandered off at times. But mostly I've been a good sheep and haven't caused trouble. For those who have had trouble minding the Shepherd, I tend to say, "That other sheep is rewarded for her bad behavior. That's not fair!" Then I think of one word: mercy. Mercy isn't fair. If it were, I wouldn't be in the fold to begin with. Thank You, God.

—*Michelle Rapkin*

"God loves each of us as if there were only one of us."
—*Saint Augustine*

DEAR JESUS, thank You for Your mercy, Your forgiveness, and Your generous spirit. Please help me to remember that each of us has been a lost sheep, so that I may have a more generous spirit. Amen.

> Jesus called the crowd to him and said, "Listen and understand. What goes into someone's mouth does not defile them, but what comes out of their mouth, that is what defiles them." —Matthew 15:10-11 (NIV)

If you have little kids, you've probably identified a child or two you'd prefer they avoid as friends. It goes something like this: "Whenever my Johnny spends time with little Timmy, he comes home more _____ than before."

Likewise, I want to blame my short temper, reckless spending, and critical attitude on something or someone outside myself.

In Matthew 15, though, Jesus uses questions about Jewish dietary prohibitions of what is clean or unclean to make a point that smarts a bit. It's not "that" which is unclean, unholy, or otherwise a bad influence. "It" is inside of me: my sin nature.

Don't get me wrong. Elsewhere, Scripture speaks clearly to watching the company we keep, and guarding our hearts and minds against negative influences, but the fundamental problem is our very own hearts. So it does make good sense to avoid feeding our sin nature bad food.

Thankfully, we need not rely on our good diet for our spiritual health and fitness. Because of Jesus, we are clean inside and out, spiritually fit for His eternal kingdom.

—Isabella Yosuico

"The proof of spiritual maturity is not how pure you are but awareness of your impurity. That very awareness opens the door to grace."
—*Philip Yancey*

JESUS, I know I am unclean. Purify my heart, Lord, that what comes from my mouth might be good and true and a blessing to You and others. Amen.

> Jesus knew what they were thinking and asked, "Why are you thinking these things in your hearts? Which is easier: to say, 'Your sins are forgiven,' or to say, 'Get up and walk'? But I want you to know that the Son of Man has authority on earth to forgive sins." So he said to the paralyzed man, "I tell you, get up, take your mat and go home." —Luke 5:22-24 (NIV)

"Blessed assurance, Jesus is mine. Oh, what a foretaste of glory divine!"

I grew up singing these lines of the stalwart Baptist hymn "Blessed Assurance" by Fanny Crosby. It brought a comforting reminder of the certitude I could have in my life through Jesus—especially when so much of the rest of it seemed in flux. How much greater, it would seem, to have had Jesus actually speak to me the words, "Your sins are forgiven," as He did for the man in Luke 5. I know we are considered blessed for being "those who have not seen and yet believe" (John 20:29), yet if I'm honest, I often find myself craving the sacred assurance of that hymn. Indeed, Jesus's forgiveness is the blessed assurance we seek as Christians.

Thankfully, as an adult I can still find comfort in Jesus's words. When Jesus saw the faith of the paralytic man and his friends, He pronounced the man's sins forgiven. Then, to demonstrate His power, He healed the man's paralysis. If I believe in this same Jesus, Who can not only pardon sin but also heal paralysis and even raise people from the dead, then I can also have the "blessed assurance" that He has forgiven my sins when my faith is placed in Him.

That's truly something worth singing about!

—*Wayne Adams*

"Faith is the confidence, the assurance, the enforcing truth, the knowing."
—*Robert Collier*

DEAR JESUS, thank You for the assurance we can have—despite our fears and doubts—in Your faithfulness and forgiveness, despite our fears and doubts. Amen.

My Treasured Jewel,

As you go about mothering—whether it be your own children or any of God's other children, big or small—let me encourage you. I am the original caregiver. Like a mother hen gathers her chicks, I gather my own. I see you. I see you in the hours of seemingly endless work for your family, both intimate and extended. I see you feeding hungry mouths. I see you bandaging hurts and soothing sore feelings. I see you peacemaking. I see your nurturing spirit. I see you coupling loved ones' hearts in yours. I see you teaching, guiding, instructing, and counseling. I see you desperate sometimes for answers, for a sign that things will be OK. I see you on your knees, and I hear your prayers.

When My mother, Mary, was chosen for the task of nurturing Me, she was overwhelmed. She was young—and in the eyes of the world ill-equipped for the job—and in many ways alone. But her response to the call of God on her life was to glorify Him, to rejoice in the depths of who she was, and in those depths to find her strength and courage in Him.

Call on Me, and I will help you. I will strengthen you and uphold you. Rejoice in Me. In your deepest parts, trust Me. Remember it's in Me you live and move and have your being. Whatever you lack I will freely give you so you can carry out the sacred calling God has given you to nurture His children.

I love you forever.

Mary said, "With all my heart I glorify the Lord! In the depths of who I am I rejoice in God my savior." –Luke 1:46-47 (CEB)

> When Jesus saw his mother there, and the disciple whom he loved standing nearby, he said to her, "Woman, here is your son," and to the disciple, "Here is your mother." From that time on, this disciple took her into his home.
> —John 19:26–27 (NIV)

When my mother passed away, I was devastated. She'd been my best friend and confidante all my life. I couldn't imagine a day without chatting, and sharing laughter and an occasional tear.

My husband's mother joined mine in heaven four months later, and our grief deepened. I doubted I'd ever make it through a day without breaking down. I felt broken and empty, certain the space in my heart once occupied by their sweet souls would forever remain a jagged, raw hole.

But over years the pain lessened and the wounds healed. One day my husband and I met an older woman whose children did not live nearby. We became friends, and soon my husband started doing her yard work. I baked for her, and she bought us small gifts and called daily. In many ways she became like a mother to us, and I believe we're like children to her. She'll never replace our mothers, but I consider it a familial relationship and a cherished blessing.

I think Jesus told Mary and John to see each as mother and son because he knew the valley they'd soon walk, and how much easier it could be when shared with a loved one. Just as He did for them, He provided us someone to love, trust, and laugh with again.

—*Heidi Gaul*

"If you have a mom, there is nowhere you are likely to go
where a prayer has not already been."
—Robert Brault

 JESUS, thank You for understanding our grief and providing friends to fill the void left by loved ones who have passed. Amen.

> He said, "Whoever has ears to hear, let him hear."
> —Mark 4:9 (WEB)

These might be the humblest words Jesus ever uttered! As passionate as He is about sharing the good news, He finishes His parable-teaching with this statement. It's really about letting go. It's an acknowledgment that not everybody will receive what He's offering.

It reminds me of a precept a Zen priest once shared with me: When giving a gift, act as if you are dropping it into the middle of the ocean. It's gone. To try and hold onto the preciousness you offer to someone else, or to seek validation of its worth in his or her response, is pointless.

In my daily life with my husband and children, more times than I can count I find myself feeling misunderstood or trying to get the same message across for the umpteenth time. And what really drives me crazy is that the message I'm trying to deliver is actually for their own good! When this happens to me, I try saying it louder or differently, or conveying it more intensely. But Jesus seems so nonchalant in His approach. Can I join Jesus in speaking my full truth—with all its potential good news—and then trusting the winds of the day to carry it where it needs to go?

—*Lizzie Berne DeGear*

"Do what you feel in your heart to be right—for you'll be criticized anyway.... The purpose of life is to live it, to taste experience to the utmost, to reach out eagerly and without fear for newer and richer experience."
—*Eleanor Roosevelt*

JESUS, do I have ears to hear? Can You lay Your healing powers upon me, increasing my capacity to hear the good news? Give me a listening heart. Let me be surprised by what I hear, not only the good but also the new. Amen.

> As the Father has loved me, so have I loved you. Now remain in my love. If you keep my commands, you will remain in my love, just as I have kept my Father's commands and remain in his love. —John 15:9–10 (NIV)

When asked whether Christianity is about law or grace, I once heard a preacher answer simply, "Yes." Jesus said He was the fulfillment of the law, yet the New Testament and Jesus Himself call for obedience, even as I enjoy the freedom of His unconditional love and unearned salvation.

Here at home, I do want my kids to promptly and without argument do what I say. I'd prefer they obey out of love and respect for me rather than for fear of losing screen time. I want them to trust that I know what I'm doing and have their best interests at heart. But even when they don't obey, I don't disown them. I more or less lovingly keep inviting them to obedience, in my less-than-holy human way.

I remind myself of this when I consider what Jesus says in John chapter 15 and elsewhere.

By believing and doing what the Word says, not grudgingly but with simple trust, I demonstrate my love for Jesus.

—*Isabella Yosuico*

"Our Lord told His disciples that love and obedience were organically united. The final test of love is obedience."
—*A. W. Tozer*

 OH, LORD, help me love You and trust Your love more, that my obedience would be from my heart. Amen.

He said, "The knowledge of the secrets of the kingdom of God has been given to you, but to others I speak in parables, so that, 'though seeing, they may not see; though hearing, they may not understand.'" —Luke 8:10 (NIV)

My five-year-old grandson loves to tell riddles, jokes, and stories. He thoroughly enjoys the plays on words that have rhyming sounds or funny punch lines. But sometimes he doesn't get the joke or understand the message in a story. I explain jokes such: "What did the rabbit give his girlfriend for her birthday? A fourteen-carrot ring." It helps him to see nuances and develop his critical-thinking skills.

Once he understands the meaning, he wants to share that joy with other people. Sometimes he explains why the joke or story is funny, and he even corrects me if I don't deliver it correctly. His level of awareness shows that he is listening and has uncovered the deeper meaning of what is being said.

In this way parables are similar. They use ordinary situations or ideas to present messages that are more complex. That might be part of their charm: peeling back the covering to find a delicacy inside. But unlike childlike stories, parables have more complex insights. I often find new, different, and deeper messages each time I read an old favorite. Did Jesus intend for that to happen? I believe He did.

—Barb Howe

"Jesus of Nazareth could have chosen simply to express Himself in moral precepts; but like a great poet He chose the form of the parable, wonderful short stories that entertained and clothed the moral precept in an eternal form. It is not sufficient to catch man's mind, you must also catch the imaginative faculties of his mind."
—Dudley Nichols

JESUS, how delightful it is to find new treasures in familiar places— beautiful gems waiting to be spotted in the parables You shared. Help me to see and hear Your wisdom. Amen.

> My sheep hear My voice, and I know them, and they follow Me.
> —John 10:27 (NKJV)

When my son, Mark, was a kindergartner, he walked to school with his buddy every day as I watched from the corner. As they followed a fence along a field where sheep grazed near our house, they giggled at the *baa-baa* of the sheep.

When his teacher planned a school play, I couldn't get Mark to go to school. He cried and clung to me. I told his teacher about his fear of being onstage, and that night, I prayed a special prayer that became our bedtime ritual for years.

I said to Mark, "The Bible tells us, 'The Lord is my helper; I will not fear'" (Hebrews 13:6). Peace filled the room when I prayed those words, tucked Mark in, and turned out the lights. My son, Jesus's little lamb, came to depend on that Scripture to fall asleep every night.

Mark is all grown up now and lives out of state. I texted him the other day, "The Lord is my Helper—with a capital H!" His response of gratitude blessed me. We hear the voice of our ever-present Jesus through His word in all seasons of life.

Today I drive where sheep once grazed and apartments now stand. The sheep and a blond, curly-haired boy are like a mirage now—but Jesus my Shepherd reminds me He is my Helper and I should always follow Him.

—*Kathleen Ruckman*

"The fear of God is not to be afraid of Him—but to be terrified without Him."
—*Unknown*

JESUS, thank You for being my Shepherd Who is always near. I hear Your voice, and I am not afraid. Amen.

> Blessed are you when people hate you, when they exclude you and
> insult you and reject your name as evil, because of the Son of Man.
> —Luke 6:22 (NIV)

I think I am a generally happy person. But there are levels to my happiness. On one level, things like a fresh doughnut (or two), a television comedy, or finding money in my pants pocket can make me happy. On another level entirely, a date with my wife, a phone call from one of my children, or a hug from a grandchild can bless me deeply.

Most of us think, feel, and operate in any of those levels of happiness I describe above. But contrary to popular belief and behavior, Jesus promises a different level of happiness and blessings for those who are hated and reviled because of Him. I tend to think I need the acceptance and approval of everyone around me in order to live "the good life." But being ridiculed by a professor for my beliefs or jeered for participating in a candlelight vigil brought a deep sense of Jesus Christ's presence and a peace I hadn't previously possessed. Those rare times when people insulted or excluded me because I was a follower of Jesus blessed me and shaped me profoundly, at an altogether different level than a tasty doughnut or even a grandchild's hug.

I don't crave such experiences—after all, Jesus didn't tell His followers to invite rejection and persecution. But I am learning, little by little, to court His smile rather than the approval of others, and if that results in poor treatment, it also results in divine favor.

—Bob Hostetler

"Those who are with Jesus in suffering hear . . . music to which other men are deaf.
They dance and do not care if they are considered insane."
—Richard Wurmbrand

JESUS, thank You for enduring the worst kind of treatment imaginable—for me. Help me always to choose Your favor over anyone else's. Amen.

> **But the Advocate, the Holy Spirit, whom the Father will send in my name, will teach you all things and will remind you of everything I have said to you. —John 14:26** (NIV)

Once, when I was driving to my parents' house, which is three hours from ours, our four kids were driving me crazy, continually asking me to stop. My answer was always, "Not this time." Three miles from my folks' house, they all chimed in one more time.

"We want to see the cows!"

"Please, Mommy!"

"C'mon, Mom, for Bethany!"

And finally, "Pease, Mommy, pease," toddler Bethany said.

Why not? I heard a voice within me. So I put my foot on the brake as I entered the intersection just before the dairy farm to our right. The second after I braked, a driver raced through the intersection from my right to my left, running his stop sign. If I hadn't braked, we would have been T-boned and possibly dead.

I believe I received godly counsel just as Jesus said. Even though Jesus left this earth, His Father sent His Counselor and we are never alone. I love knowing I have a personal Counselor—the Holy Spirit—Who can coach me with the words of Jesus. Just as an earthly counselor can caution and guide and encourage, the Holy Spirit nudges or warns me—even to put my foot on my car's brake.

—*Janet Holm McHenry*

"If you are a believer, you also benefit from the Holy Spirit's ministry.
He guides you to the truth of Scripture, teaches you,
affirms the truth in your heart, and convicts you of sin."
—*John MacArthur Jr.*

 THANK YOU, Jesus, that Your Spirit reminds us of Jesus's words, teaches us all things, and guides our every step. Amen.

I tell you the truth, everyone who acknowledges me publicly here on earth, the Son of Man will also acknowledge in the presence of God's angels. But anyone who denies me here on earth will be denied before God's angels. —Luke 12:8–9 (NLT)

"My son walks a few steps in front of me or a few steps behind me, because it would be uncool to be seen with his mother." As my friend described her experience, I remembered what it was like to parent teenagers. Teens, trying to take those scary steps toward adulthood, don't know why they act the way they do. One minute they might be laughing with their parents, pulling away the next. They haven't stopped loving their parents, but they want to avoid embarrassment. When my children were teenagers, they had rules for me because I wasn't athletic. "Don't run in public, Mom." Now, those same kids are grown up and happy to show the world we are a close family.

It's great to say, "That's my son," or, "That's my daughter," and feel the joy of a mother's heart as I talk about what they've accomplished or the kind of people they have become. And I love hearing them say, "I love my mom and dad."

Jesus feels the same way about us. He is pleased when we acknowledge Him in front of others. When I say, "I am a Christ follower," or, "I love Jesus," my words bring joy to Him. And I can almost hear Him saying up in heaven, "That's my girl!"

—*Karen Porter*

"We are the Bibles the world is reading; we are the creeds
the world is needing; we are the sermons the world is heeding."
—*Billy Graham*

DEAR JESUS. I want others to know I follow You. Help me publicly acknowledge Your amazing love and peace. Amen.

Blessed are the meek, for they will inherit the earth.
—Matthew 5:5 (NIV)

It was that time of year again. The flowers were blooming, the breeze was warm, and the local doomsday preacher was shouting on his soapbox in the middle of campus. His words flung out like buckshot, aimed at any students passing by, warning of the coming judgment. As a Christian, I appreciated his conviction but was troubled by the reverse effect it seemed to be having. He was turning people off, rather than onto, the path to faith. Instead of drawing students into a dialogue about Jesus's saving grace, he was trying to scare them into believing.

A few fellow students and I went to our religion professor, begging him to confront the preacher. "You know the Bible backwards and forwards," we said. "Your knowledge and experience could wipe the floor with this guy."

The teacher just smiled. "He will not hear me," he said quietly. "Remember, faith isn't something won in an argument. It's found in opening one's heart to Jesus. If you are willing to share the love of Jesus with others, you will silence this preacher of fear." His gentle words gave us the courage to do just that—one student, one heart at a time.

—*Andrea Raynor*

"We are not called by God to do extraordinary things,
but to do ordinary things with extraordinary love."
—*Jean Vanier*

DEAR JESUS, grant me the courage to share Your message and the wisdom to know how. When I want to be "right," remind me to be loving instead. Amen.

> And whoever among you would be greatest must be servant of all. For even the Son of Man came not to be served, but to serve, and to give His life as a ransom for many. —Mark 10:44-45 (MEV)

Growing up, I spent countless hours following my mother around town as she visited housebound, elderly members of our church, played piano at local nursing homes, and delivered food for funeral dinners. She also faithfully served in countless ways that seemed to go unnoticed.

I often whined in attempt to get out of accompanying her. I used a multitude of excuses: hospitals made me queasy, or I had homework.

Yet Mom insisted this was how we showed our love for Jesus. She assured me that even when I didn't know how to serve people, Jesus would provide His help.

I am thankful she insisted I shadow her on those many visits. I saw God's presence and blessings through Mom's service. I learned serving isn't convenient and is most often done in quiet. No one sees your work, except the other person and Jesus.

Now, whenever I drive across town to deliver a meal or sit in a hospital waiting room with a loved one or repair a friend's garment, I remember my mom's example. I know these small acts of service are how I display my love for Jesus, and I know His presence guides my service.

Jesus served us by giving His whole life for us. We serve Him by giving our time and talents to help other people.

—Amelia Rhodes

"Everyone can be great, because everyone can serve."
—Martin Luther King Jr.

 JESUS, show me how I can serve someone around me today. Help me remember no act is too small. Amen.

> I tell you the truth, anyone who believes in me will do the same works I have done, and even greater works, because I am going to be with the Father. —John 14:12 (NLT)

Jesus is in the business of loving others. In the Bible, we learn about Jesus performing incredible miracles. At the heart of every miracle He performed was His love for all people. Jesus loved people regardless of their station in life and in spite of their sin. Whether man or woman, Samaritan or Jew, Jesus reached out and loved others.

How can we continue the great works of Jesus today? One way is to love others in a manner that draws them to Jesus. When it doesn't make sense to the world to show love, people will notice when we do.

Each of us has been given a unique spiritual gift. Since one of my gifts is writing, I joined the "Notes and Cards" team at my church. Each month, I write a few notes to members who are grieving or sick and also to those who are celebrating a joyful event such as the birth of a child. It's a small offering that makes a big difference for each recipient who receives a note in the mail.

The great works we perform might not be in the form of miracles as we read about in the Bible. Yet each of us has the ability to love. As we love others and pray for them, we continue the works of Jesus.

—*Allison K. Flexer*

"Today somebody is suffering, today somebody is in the street, today somebody is hungry. Our work is for today. Yesterday has gone, tomorrow has not yet come. We have only today to make Jesus known, loved, served, fed, clothed, and sheltered. Do not wait for tomorrow."
—*Mother Teresa*

JESUS, thank You for the privilege of continuing Your great works of love. Guide us as we use our gifts to love others. Amen.

> In everything I did, I showed you that by this kind of hard work we must help the weak, remembering the words the Lord Jesus himself said: "It is more blessed to give than to receive." —Acts 20:35 (NIV)

Can I play with it?" the little boy asked, shuffling his IV stand over to point at the magic kit I'd brought to the hospital. His eyes, set deep in a pale, drawn face, peered at me hopefully and my heart ached at the sight of his bald head—sure evidence of the cancer treatment that ravaged his frail form. "Of course," I said brightly. "We are going to have so much fun!"

And we did. For an hour, that little boy became a master magician. We laughed as he waved his wand and produced a brilliant bouquet of flowers. We giggled like schoolchildren when he pulled a seemingly never-ending stream of knotted scarves from a hat. His cheeks filled with color as we played, and it seemed he had forgotten where he was and the pain he must have been suffering. For a short time, we were both carried to a place full of love and happiness.

I cried when I learned Jesus had taken that little boy home, but I was so thankful for our time together. It was a gift to spend time with him.

I've heard it said, "You can't out-give God," but I'm going to always do my best to give to others wherever and whenever I can.

—*Mary E. Williams*

"We make a living by what we get, but we make a life by what we give."
—*Winston Churchill*

DEAR JESUS, please help me recognize the need and to give like You. Amen.

DO IT AFRAID

> **The following night the Lord stood near Paul and said, "Take courage! As you have testified about me in Jerusalem, so you must also testify in Rome."**
> **—Acts 23:11** (NIV)

Many times in my life, Jesus has asked me to take steps of faith way outside my comfort zone: completing my degrees while working and raising a family, starting a business, giving birth to a child with special needs, moving a long distance from the familiar...

I've almost always been initially overwhelmed at any given prospect, projecting what it might involve, wondering if I could do it or even wanted to do it. Each time, Jesus has reminded me of how He equipped me to face the same or a similar challenge before. In the end, Jesus and I always made it through. As my friend says, "There's nothing Jesus and I can't handle."

Paul faced truly life-threatening persecution in Jerusalem, surely along with the contempt and ridicule of his former companions and fellow Pharisees. Heading to Rome must have been scary, as suggested by the simple fact that Jesus urged Him to take courage.

I can take comfort and courage in knowing this illustrates that Jesus doesn't fault me for my fear. I'm able to acknowledge that He stands near me and urges me forward, knowing He will equip me to accomplish His purposes.

—*Isabella Yosuico*

"Feel the fear and do it anyway."
—*Jack Canfield*

 LORD, thank You for standing by me, and for encouraging me to step into the unknown and to trust You will provide. Amen.

Then he called the crowd to him along with his disciples and said: "Whoever wants to be my disciple must deny themselves and take up their cross and follow me. For whoever wants to save their life will lose it, but whoever loses their life for me and for the gospel will save it. What good is it for someone to gain the whole world, yet forfeit their soul? Or what can anyone give in exchange for their soul?" —Mark 8:34–37 (NIV)

It was Mother's Day again, and well before dawn I was lugging supplies to the prayer booth for the annual walk/run. Banner, check. Dozens of muffins, check. Prayer-request card, check. Attitude? Not so good.

It *was* Mother's Day—when mothers can relax and be treated to breakfast in bed with happy-face pancakes. Where was my happy face? Missing, certainly.

However, quickly after setting up prayer shop, moms in pink tutus, dads in pink shorts, and kids in pink everything headed my way—possibly drawn by the homemade muffins I'd brought, but even more possibly by their need for Jesus and His healing grace.

"Could you pray for my sister? She's in remission."

"My mom just had surgery…"

"My wife just died from cancer. I don't know what I'll without her."

By later that day, I'd decided it was the best Mother's Day ever, because giving is so much more rewarding than receiving. I realized Jesus had offered me a new perspective. Yes, following Him requires sacrifice, but He gives us great joy in return. Putting Jesus first is the best gift we can give—or receive.

—Janet Holm McHenry

"How would things change if you began to see it as 'a fragrant offering and sacrifice to God'?" —Rick Warren

JESUS, I gladly give you my time, talents, and everything I have. Use me, Jesus, to be a blessing to others. Amen.

> Then the woman, seeing that she could not go unnoticed, came trembling and fell at his feet. In the presence of all the people, she told why she had touched him and how she had been instantly healed. Then he said to her, "Daughter, your faith has healed you. Go in peace." —Luke 8:47–48 (NIV)

The woman hoped to remain unnoticed in the crowd. If she could just touch the edge of the garment Jesus wore, she believed, she would be healed. She didn't want attention, but she was desperate for relief from her condition. She reached out and touched Jesus.

I wonder if this woman felt her physical ailment made her less worthy of his attention. Jesus could have allowed her to remain hidden in the crowd. He already knew the answer when he asked, "Who touched me?" Instead, Jesus wanted this faithful woman to realize her worth. He wanted her to know she had value.

It's tempting to remain in the background, convinced others are more important to God's kingdom. Sometimes I struggle to believe Jesus delights in me, especially when I lose control of my temper and hurt someone's feelings. We are all immensely valuable to Jesus. No sin we have committed can change that. Nothing we've done in the past can disqualify us from the love of Jesus.

Jesus doesn't want us to hide in the shadows of life and wonder if we are worthy. Jesus sees us through the lens of love and forgiveness. He believes we are worth dying for.

—*Allison K. Flexer*

"Because in that moment, she believed him to be more powerful than the condition that had crippled her for over a decade of her life. She was a woman with nothing left to lose and he recognized her faith in him."
—*Angie Smith*

 LORD JESUS, thank You for recognizing my value and worth. Heal my insecurities, and calm my fears. Amen.

> These people honor me with their lips, but their hearts are far from me. They worship me in vain; their teachings are merely human rules.
> —Matthew 15:8–9 (NIV)

"**A**re you going to the membership class?" My friend Cheryl looked so hopeful. "I think so."

My heart quivered as I thought of the friends who would disapprove of the church I'd grown to love. I was certain they would label the denomination "too liberal." What would they say if they came for a visit, asked to attend church with me, and discovered two of its pastors were women and that my Bible-study leader was an elder? Actually, I knew exactly what some of them would say: "Jeanette, I'm concerned that you're attending a church that is so unbiblical." Maybe, instead of taking the membership class, I should find a church my friends would be OK with. The Lord stopped me mid-worry: *Who are you worshipping—your friends or Me?*

How many times had I gotten myself into trouble because I caved under restrictions based more on my way than Christ's way? The examples of my new church's members, including those two female pastors, were encouraging me to get to know Jesus more intimately. Isn't that what He wanted from me?

As I prayed for wisdom, I considered how often Jesus rebuked those who "honor me with their lips, but their hearts are far from me." I wanted to honor Him, whether people approved or not. In the end I chose to honor the desire He placed in my heart, and I signed up for the membership class.

—*Jeanette Hanscome*

"You can see God from anywhere if your mind is set to love and obey Him."
—*A. W. Tozer*

LORD, forgive me for making faith about pleasing people instead of You. Help me as I try to honor You in everything. Amen.

> I have revealed you to those whom you gave me out of the world.
> They were yours; you gave them to me and they have obeyed your word.
> —John 17:6 (NIV)

In May 2016, I completed four years of teaching Genesis through Revelation to a group of ladies in our church.

Every week, we met in a classroom to discuss what we'd read the week before. While some passages were familiar, I quickly found much of the Bible was unfamiliar even to those who had grown up attending Sunday school and church. We wrestled through the pages of Leviticus and struggled to remember which prophet spoke during the reign of each king.

When we reached the New Testament, everyone breathed a sigh of relief. After two and a half years of studying, we were on familiar ground. Still, we discovered the teachings of Christ seemed harder to obey than the lists of names from Numbers were to pronounce.

Jesus's lessons about forgiveness and loving our neighbors convicted and challenged us. But Jesus's words also offered grace and hope. We are not subject to the Law, because He fulfilled it. Our sacrifice isn't about pigeons and lambs—it's about ourselves. We obey not to earn salvation but as a response to the salvation He provided.

As we finished our last lesson in Revelation, my friends and I wept at the beauty of the Word of God and the hope we have in Jesus, the Word made flesh.

—*Teri Lynne Underwood*

"Faith never knows where it is being led,
but it loves and knows the One who is leading."
—*Oswald Chambers*

 JESUS, help me obey the Word as a response to Your gift of grace and promise of life. Amen.

> Give, and it will be given to you. A good measure, pressed down, shaken together and running over, will be poured into your lap. For with the measure you use, it will be measured to you. —Luke 6:38 (NIV)

I was a busy mom, volunteering at our daughter's school, working full time, and serving at church. I had family and friends who needed my attention and wanted my time. I had clothes to fold, dishes to wash, and furniture to dust.

God obviously didn't check my calendar when He gave me the crazy idea to invite my neighbors over for coffee! I didn't have time for one more thing in my life, so I shushed His voice and went on with my other little plans.

After a few months of busyness as usual, I noticed my work had become unproductive and frustrating. My family was being neglected, and my house was a mess. Worst of all, my worship felt dry—I couldn't hear Jesus anymore. The last thing I remembered Him saying was, "Hey, what about that neighborhood coffee idea?"

When I finally scheduled an open house to get to know my neighbors, an amazing thing happened: God magnified each minute! I was once again productive, resourceful, capable, energetic, and effective.

I offered tips and tools to others who wanted to share coffee, conversation, and Christ with their neighbors. This grew into a ministry called the Neighborhood Café, and there are now Neighborhood Café groups from Connecticut to California, from Australia to Great Britain and Canada!

Little did I know how God would overflow the simple cup of coffee served at my kitchen table.

—Amy Lively

"Being a good neighbor is an art which makes life richer." —Gladys Taber

JESUS, You've already given me so much, yet You promise to give me even more. Please show me what I'm selfishly holding onto and what I can give to others. Amen.

What I tell you in the dark, speak in the daylight; what is whispered in your ear, proclaim from the roofs. —Matthew 10:27 (NIV)

At the children's science museum, my daughter's six children are always like quicksilver, each heading in a different direction—especially three-year-old Temperance, who seems not to the have the slightest bit of fear.

When I lost sight of her in the crowded hallway, I remembered she loved the camping exhibit, and sure enough, there she was—cooking over a pretend fire and singing, "Jesus loves me, this I know..." Loudly. Very loudly. She was so loud, it seemed she might startle the simulated fireflies to life.

As one mother pulled her two children away, I stepped into the shadows. But then I caught myself. *Am I ashamed of my Jesus-inspired granddaughter? Shame on me!* I decided to join her in song and sample her pretend "shtew."

Jesus knew His disciples would have more of a public ministry than He did. Jesus's ministry would end after three years, while some of His disciples would travel far and testify widely, putting their lives on the line.

Jesus encourages us to courageously share our faith with those who do not know Him, those who haven't yet met Him. Just as we would introduce a friend to others we know, Jesus wants us to introduce Him. We need not be afraid about being bold, because just as He takes care of the sparrows, He will take care of those who stand for Him.

—*Janet Holm McHenry*

"The bold way is the biblical way. Testify boldly and without fear, regardless of the response, and you will know God's favor upon your witness for Christ."
—*James McDonald*

 JESUS, help me be bold about my faith, because many need Your saving grace and Your daily help and hope. Amen.

Do not let your hearts be troubled. You believe in God; believe also in me. —John 14:1 (NIV)

Sometimes I devote more energy to focusing on my failures than to trusting Jesus. I haven't lived the life I dreamed of when I was a child. Boys typically don't dream of growing up to be businessmen. In my playtime as a child, I was a secret agent, a war hero, a cowboy gunfighter—anything that could have the word "hero" attached to it. As I grew older, those imaginations became less heroic but still involved great victories and accolades. I would be a leader in thought, a man whose wisdom was well known, or a great author.

Like the disciples, my heart is troubled when I dwell on disappointments and unattained desires. However childish or naïve those imaginations might have been, I become depressed when I look at my life through the haze of childish hopes. But this viewpoint disregards all Jesus has said and done. When I turn to sit with Jesus and remember His words, He clears my vision and tells me to believe in Who He is rather than who I am. When my regrets and mistakes distract me from Him, I must remember that my past was in His hands, my present is in His hands, my future will always be in His hands, and that pursuing Him will lead to the life He has in mind for me—a life of spiritual adventure to surpass any childish imagination.

—*Michael Berrier*

*"Leave the broken, irreversible past in God's hands,
and step out into the invincible future with Him."*
—*Oswald Chambers*

LORD JESUS, when I become depressed or sorrowful, help me to remember all You've done for me, that You're with me now, and that You prepare my future. Amen.

> **Jesus said, "Let the little children come to me, and do not hinder them, for the kingdom of heaven belongs to such as these."** —Matthew 19:14 (NIV)

I had planned what I thought would be a fun sleepover for granddaughters Faith, seven, and Temperance, three: pizza and a stack of princess movies. However, their idea of fun was something else.

"Could we have a tea party, Nana?" Faith asked.

"Of course!" As it turned out, though, neither of them like tea. Ice water is their drink of choice. What they really wanted, I discovered, was to spend face-to-face time with me so they could tell me about their topics of interest: insects and reptiles (Faith) and how hard it is to be a princess (Tempe).

Jesus invited children to have face-to-face time with Him. He valued them and welcomed them. He knew every life is precious—no matter the race, gender, or age. His Father's kingdom is inclusive: all are welcomed, all belong, and all are valued. And what's so inspiring about children is that their faith is refreshingly pure and unjaded.

Jesus shows us that children can, in fact, teach us how to love our Savior. We can run to Him seeking face-to-face time. We can spill out our thoughts about our day. And we can show Him our hurts and ask for His healing touch. After all, we too are children of God.

—*Janet Holm McHenry*

"Every human being is the child of a King."
—*John Ortberg*

 JESUS, I am thankful for this face time with You. Help me embrace the childlike quality of my faith today. Amen.

Then Jesus said, "Come to me, all of you who are weary and carry heavy burdens, and I will give you rest." —Matthew 11:28 (NLT)

Zella Ruth was ten months old before I felt the completeness of motherhood, like a new and heavier skin I realized I could never shed. The emotions were complicated. The tension of a new identity and old ambitions stretched my heart, while a tiny human spent days nestled under my chin.

I marveled at the beauty of new life, but wondered how I would ever survive the seemingly endless interrupted nights and blurry, red-eyed mornings. The same Jesus Who once offered me the truth of salvation was ready to listen to my new questions and doubts.

Come to me. Jesus, Who led me into love with Him, is faithful to light a path for me today to His side. He makes it possible to get close enough to tell Him how motherhood has made me weary.

I will give you rest. Jesus, Who gave me abundant life, is not surprised by all the ways I fall short as a wife and mother and friend today. He is ready to lift the burdens that have made me weary and replace them with refreshment that will make me whole.

Jesus invites me into His presence, takes my weariness, and gives me rest. The unique beauty of Jesus is that He does not tire of this burden-bearing. His invitation to rest does not change, grow dull, or fade. He is strong enough to bear my burdens today and enduring enough to offer the same strength tomorrow.

—*Caroline Kolts*

"You don't realize Jesus is all you need until Jesus is all you have."
—*Tim Keller*

 JESUS, thank You for inviting me into Your presence. Help me believe You will give the rest You have promised. Amen.

PRECIOUS LITTLE ONES

And whoever welcomes one such child in my name welcomes me. If anyone causes one of these little ones—those who believe in me—to stumble, it would be better for them to have a large millstone hung around their neck and to be drowned in the depths of the sea. —Matthew 18:5–6 (NIV)

"Swim, baby, swim!" I cried as the little sea turtle tried to paddle through the returning tide. I stood over that tiny turtle, feeling like its grand protector, hoping to help it, and praying it would make the arduous trek into the ocean. It was not going to die on my watch!

It was so close—inches away from the incoming tide that would wash it out to sea—but it just couldn't muster the strength to swim into the waves. I used two seashells to carefully pick up the tiny body and set it inside the tide line. But he struggled. I tried again and again, until I heard those precious words from an onlooker: "He made it!" What a relief! I wanted that little one to have a chance at life. He reminded me of the young children in my spiritual care at church.

I have a soft spot for all kinds of little ones. For many years I was a children's-ministry director. I prepared each child to accept Jesus as his or her Savior. When children become believers, they are refreshingly bold and candid about their faith. Nothing gets in their way! They walk with Him, through calm or rough seas.

We are all His children. We must help one another, sincere and bold in that same fearless way, so that we spread Jesus's love throughout the world.

—*Mary E. Williams*

"God has given us two hands, one to receive with and the other to give with."
—*Billy Graham*

JESUS, I am Your child. Please help me to lift up those who stumble and bring them to You. Amen.

Then Jesus said to Simon, "Don't be afraid; from now on you will fish for people." —Luke 5:10 (NIV)

My sixth-grade son Aidan and I sat with other mission team members in the humid room. We'd traveled to Northern Region of Ghana because Aidan had single-handedly raised money for a well there. Today our task was to go into the community and share the good news of Jesus with its mostly Muslim population.

I was scared. I hadn't shared my faith that openly—door to door—in a long time. But more than that, I was afraid for my son, so I offered to have him on my two-by-two team. He looked at me, then said, "No, Mom, I want to go with him." He pointed to his new Ghanaian friend. Even though I worried, I decided he could go.

Later that afternoon, Aidan shared his faith without shame or fear. His new friend translated everything he said, and several people asked to receive Jesus into their lives. Aidan's face radiated such joy! It was the kind of joy that comes from risking, sharing, and talking about the beauty and power of Jesus.

He said, "I've never felt more alive." We were meeting people on the dusty red earth on the other side of the world, and my preteen had found his passion—being a fisher of men.

We returned from Ghana, and my son's example continues to inspire me. I've grown more comfortable boldly sharing my faith in Jesus with people who don't yet know Him. It's become a new faith practice I embrace in my daily life.

—*Mary DeMuth*

"Witnessing is not a spare-time occupation or a once-a-week activity. It must be a quality of life. You don't go witnessing, you are a witness."
—*Dan Greene*

JESUS, what a privilege it is to share Your love with others. Please open up new opportunities for me to bear witness of Your glory. Amen.

And will not God bring about justice for his chosen ones, who cry out to him day and night? Will he keep putting them off? —Luke 18:7 (NIV)

When my second daughter started to talk as a baby, she naturally imitated phrases she heard the rest of the family say often. But I was horrified when she toddled around the house, repeatedly telling us, "I'm busy."

There was no doubt in anyone's mind where she'd picked that one up.

I confess I *am* busy. We all are. Sometimes nothing is wrong with asking my daughter to wait until I finish folding the laundry before I get out a new toy. And while I feel a minor twinge of guilt about letting my daughter hear me say, "I'm busy," mostly I feel relief that Jesus is better than I am. He assures us that God is never too busy for me.

Jesus tells us in Luke 18 that God isn't like us. In this passage, Jesus shares the parable of a widow who's been wronged. She comes to an unjust judge every day, looking for justice. Eventually her persistence wears him down, and the judge helps her. The squeaky wheel gets the grease, and all that.

But God is not like this unjust manager. We don't have to cry out to Him again and again. He hears us, and He will not keep putting his children off. That's the promise Jesus wants us to hold onto.

God is never too busy to hear and answer my prayers. All I need to do is set down the laundry, take some time, and talk to Him.

—Elizabeth Adams

"Never be so busy as not to think of others."
—*Mother Teresa*

 LORD, thank You that You always hear our prayers and are never too busy to listen. Amen.

> Jesus answered, "Everyone who drinks this water will be thirsty again,
> but whoever drinks the water I give them will never thirst."
> —John 4:13-14 (NIV)

My parents used to tell a story about a family trip we took to see Niagara Falls. I was five years old and very excited to be on an adventure. Several miles from the falls, we boarded a tour bus that would take us to see that natural wonder. Apart from an occasional comment from the tour guide, the trip on the approach to the falls was quiet.

I was sitting with my sister, a few rows from my parents. In a louder voice than necessary, I said, "Mommy, is there water in Niagara Falls?"

People laughed, and my mother responded that, yes, there is.

"Good, 'cause I'm thirsty!" I announced.

Then our bus mates let out loud peals of laughter, which puzzled me. I had no idea what Niagara Falls was. It could have been an adventure park or a shopping mall.

I was just asking about a water fountain.

The woman at the well whom Jesus is speaking to in John 4 wasn't looking for the kind of water Jesus offered. She didn't even know it existed. But by the time their discussion was finished, she was a different person, nourished by the kind of water only God can provide.

—*Michelle Rapkin*

"Something of God . . . flows into us from the blue of the sky, the taste of honey, the delicious embrace of water whether cold or hot, and even from sleep itself."
—*C. S. Lewis*

DEAR JESUS, thank You for sustenance that doesn't run out. Thank You for being here for us forever, that the well of Your healing, love, and guidance will never run dry. Amen.

> **Blessed are the pure in heart, for they will see God.**
> **—Matthew 5:8** (NIV)

Why can't I see Jesus like I can see you, Mama? Why can't I hear His voice like I hear yours?"

I wasn't prepared to answer my preschool daughter's thought-provoking questions before bedtime. Throughout her early years, the desire to see Jesus consumed her.

"When He comes back, I think I will be so excited, my mouth will drop open, and I just won't even know what to say," she told me one evening.

Her pure desire to see and know Jesus like she does her family, inspired and convicted me. Sometimes I'm so consumed with the day's tasks that I don't think much about Jesus or my own desire to see Him.

Jesus reminded me through my daughter to keep a simple and pure heart—one focused not on getting things done, but on being in love with Him and in relationship with Him. He showed me how we do get to see and hear Him every day—whether in the innocence of a child's gaze, the whisper of His words to our hearts, or the beauty of answered prayers.

When life gets hectic and complicated, remember to cultivate a simple and pure heart that's focused on loving Him. He will give you the gift of seeing Him.

—*Amelia Rhodes*

"Purity and simplicity are the two wings with which man soars above
the earth and all temporary nature. Simplicity is in the intention, purity
in the affection; simplicity turns to God; purity unites with and enjoys him."
—*Thomas à Kempis*

 JESUS, in today's hustle, help me keep my heart pure for You. I desire to see and know You. Amen.

Whoever has ears, let them hear what the Spirit says to the churches. To the one who is victorious, I will give the right to eat from the tree of life, which is in the paradise of God. —Revelation 2:7 (NIV)

I spent the summer and fall of 2015 reliving the most painful years of my life. A publisher had contracted me to write a devotional book for single moms, and this required me to revisit my feelings of abandonment, loss, and grief for the sake of offering hope to others. My six-month deadline made it impossible to procrastinate. Some days I wanted to do anything but face the next chapter. I persevered, knowing I'd made a commitment. When I saw my book making a difference, the long hours, tears, and pain would be worth it.

As I reflect on those months of writing, Jesus's message in Revelation 2:7 reminds me that, from the moment He called His first disciples, believers have had to persevere through pain. The physical and emotional turmoil some people endure—horrible diseases, heartbreaking loss, persecution—makes my intense book-writing journey, and even the circumstances that inspired it, look pretty trivial. But in the end, their reward for sticking it out is "the right to eat from the tree of life."

How precious it is to know Jesus doesn't ask us to be victorious just for the sake of proving how tough we can be. He encourages us with a promise of eternal reward that is worth every hardship.

—*Jeanette Hanscome*

"It's easier to go down a hill than up it but the view is much better at the top."
—*Henry Ward Beecher*

LORD, sometimes I want to take the easy way out. Thank You for keeping me strong as I wait for Your reward. Amen.

GRACE WHEN WE NEED IT

> So if you ignore the least commandment and teach others to do the same, you will be called the least in the Kingdom of Heaven. But anyone who obeys God's laws and teaches them will be called great in the Kingdom of Heaven.
> —Matthew 5:19 (NLT)

It's one of my sweetest memories as a mother: Emma, only ten years old, woke herself before dawn on the first day of school to spend a few minutes reading a devotional very much like this one. I treasure a photograph I secretly snapped of her sweet profile bent over the Bible pages, her blond hair ruffled like a rooster tail, the sun barely brightening the sky. She sat in the same spot where she saw me sharing the first few minutes of each day with Jesus, on a yellow loveseat with a dog curled at her feet. I think I even made her a cup of tea, just like Mama! This tradition continued until the day she graduated from high school. Daily we shared breakfast and a thought from God's Word, and prayed together as a family before she left for school.

Not all of those mornings were as poignant as the moment in my photograph. Many of them were hurried; some of them were harried. Not all of them were holy. Sometimes the example I set for her was not one I'd want to capture forever on film. But over time, the portrait created in our home resembled Christ.

One of our greatest responsibilities as followers of Jesus is knowing we are always teaching, always demonstrating, and always setting an example. Showing others the way to Christ is also one of our greatest privileges. God sees when we get it right, and I'm so thankful He gives us grace when we miss the mark.

—*Amy Lively*

"Train up a child in the way he should go—but be sure you go that way yourself."
—*Charles Spurgeon*

JESUS, help me to follow all of Your ways. Remind me that others are watching all I do and listening to all I say. May they see You in me today. Amen.

However, when He, the Spirit of truth, has come, He will guide you into all truth…and He will tell you things to come. He will glorify Me, for He will take of what is Mine and declare it to you. —John 16:13–14 (NKJV)

The difficulty of saying a long goodbye to my husband's mother broke my heart. Feeble and childlike, this once-wise and once-vibrant woman grew weaker and less responsive as Alzheimer's took its toll.

Sometimes when I visited Elnora, she was agitated. But when I took her hands in mine and said, "Jesus," her spirit quieted. The eternal part of her must have been touched by the sound of His name. Her spirit and her mind were separate, and the Spirit of truth strengthened and enlightened Elnora's soul because Jesus took residence in her.

In her better days, Elnora planted a variety of flowers every spring and often referred to their beauty. "Didn't the Lord think of everything?" she'd say. "So many colors, and they smell good too!"

On one memorable day in the garden, shortly before she died, we walked along a path lined with flowers. As we passed yellow roses, I paused as Elnora touched a blossom. Her language, reduced almost to silence, now declared joyful words. "Didn't the Lord think of everything? He's a good guy!" she said.

Jesus, glorified in Elnora with a bit of humor too, warmed my heart. I took her hand in mine as we strolled, and a sweet silence returned.

—Kathleen Ruckman

"What lies in front of you or behind you is nothing
compared to what lies within you."
—Ralph Waldo Emerson

JESUS, Spirit of truth and Creator of the roses, You have put eternity in our hearts. Amen.

JESUS THE LIGHTHOUSE

The eye is the lamp of the body. If your eyes are healthy, your whole body will be full of light. But if your eyes are unhealthy, your whole body will be full of darkness. If then the light within you is darkness, how great is that darkness! —Matthew 6:22–23 (NIV)

Have you known someone who always sees the good in others? Finds the gold nugget in each challenging situation? Or speaks kindness where none is deserved? Folks of this caliber seem rare. But I know one: my mother.

When reconnecting with a long-lost friend, the first question I usually heard was, "How's your sweet mother? I love her."

I recall one gal reminiscing about visits with Mother that made her feel as important as a beloved child. Another spoke of Mother's gentle nature and how, in her presence, the world seemed at peace.

To me, the attention was justified. How many times had I seen Mother offer goodwill toward someone scorned by another? Or enjoy the fresh fragrance of a new rain when her companion saw only mud puddles? I cannot calculate how often she said, "Let's look on the bright side!"

According to the above verse, unhealthy eyes cannot discern grace, generosity, or blessings. The mind is clouded, the heart blind, plunging one's life into darkness. But my mother's eyes were healthy, a lamp to her entire body, allowing light to flood her heart and mind. Her devotion to Jesus shone as a lighthouse, through her treatment of others and in her perception of loveliness everywhere.

—*Cathy Elliott*

"It is only with the heart that one can see rightly;
what is essential is invisible to the eye."
—*Antoine de Saint-Exupéry*

LORD, enlighten the eyes of my heart that I might see through the light of Your love. Amen.

Dear Friend,

I ever live to make intercession for you, and My prayer is that our Father will reveal Himself to you in new and beautiful ways as you grow in your relationship with Me. You know the Father and I are one. So everything you know about Me, and everything we experience together is an extension of the Father.

It's important that you know the value of fathers on earth. I know what it's been like for you. I know your relationship with your father in this world, as well as I know the intimacy of your relationship with the Heavenly Father. He is good. All of the time. He is your example. He never sleeps, but is always watching and caring for you. He is slow to anger. He is full of loving kindness. He never changes. He is faithful. He knows everything about you. He loves you. He forgives and restores you. He craves your attention. He is your Comforter, your Healer, your Provider. He knows everything you need before you ask and stands ready to help you. He is always there. He takes joy in you and sings over you. He is your refuge and strength. He is merciful, generous, and wise. He is just—a God of all grace. He disciplines you for your own good, because He loves you. He longs to gather you in His arms. He promises to answer when you cry out to Him. He wants you to call Him "Daddy."

I'm so glad you're a part of the family.

I love you forever.

Grace, mercy, and peace will be with you from God the Father and from the Lord Jesus Christ, the Son of the Father, in truth and love. —2 John 1:3 (NKJV)

BLESSED FATHERHOOD

All things have been committed to me by my Father. No one knows who the Son is except the Father, and no one knows who the Father is except the Son and those to whom the Son chooses to reveal him. —Luke 10:22 (NIV)

Fatherhood is a strange and wonderful concept for me. I'm sure it is for most men, but for me, it's particular to the fact that I lost my biological father when I was less than two years old. So when the younger of my two daughters turned two recently, it gave me pause for the second time, to think I was stepping into somewhat uncharted territory—that I didn't have exactly what she is experiencing in a present and nurturing father.

Now, to be sure, I haven't exactly had a hard-knocks life. My mom remarried a wonderful man, who was a loving father to me from when I was about four years old until he passed away a few years ago. But I am reminded of a Stevie Wonder song called "Isn't She Lovely." Stevie Wonder reminds me to stop and appreciate what I have and be conscious of the present moment. In my mind, this means being aware of my daughters and what a privilege it is to be their father. What a comfort and joy to share the same loving Heavenly Father with our Savior Jesus Christ!

—*Wayne Adams*

"We have been heaven blessed
I can't believe what God has done
Through us he's given life to one
But isn't she lovely made from love"
—*Stevie Wonder*

 DEAR JESUS, thank You for showing us God the Father through Your life. Please give us the wisdom and strength to live and love as You love us and are loved by the Father. Amen.

Just say a simple, "Yes, I will," or "No, I won't." Anything beyond this is from the evil one. —Matthew 5:37 (NLT)

Recently, I watched a movie about a father who habitually disappointed his young son.

The dad would tell him, "I'll be there. I swear it. I promise." But then he never showed up. He had to go to greater lengths to get his boy to believe him when he said anything because a simple "Yes, I will" wasn't enough anymore.

When Jesus told us to let our answer be a "yes" or "no," He was teaching us a lesson in character. When I tell my children I'll pick them up from school, they don't question me. I don't need to cross my heart or pinky-promise, because I've consistently shown them they can trust me. But I have dropped the ball when asked to do something small, like send cookies to school or call a friend back. Jesus wants us to be reliable, in small and big matters. We shouldn't have to convince anyone beyond our simple "Yes, I will" or "No, I won't."

Our days can be hectic, and it's easy to forget all the things we're obligated to do, and that is why I purchased a day planner and carry it everywhere. I jot down what I've committed to, because I want people to trust that my word is good. And I do my best to be reliable, knowing they're seeing me imitate Jesus's character.

—Jessica R. Patch

"Character is much easier kept than recovered."
—*Thomas Paine*

JESUS, help me organize and keep my commitments so I can be reliable and trustworthy and honor You. Amen.

> So I say to you: Ask and it will be given to you; seek and you will find; knock and the door will be opened to you. For everyone who asks receives; the one who seeks finds; and to the one who knocks, the door will be opened.
> —Luke 11:9–10 (NIV)

When I was a little girl, my father was my source of fun, happiness, and security. He let me tag along when he did errands in town, and he took me snowmobiling on frozen lakes and wilderness paths. He wasn't a rich man, but every now and then he took me to the local toy store and told me to choose whatever I wanted. "Your wish is my command," he'd say. When I read today's verses, it's easy to think Jesus is saying, "Ask God for anything. Your wish is His command."

The point is not that the Father will give His child whatever she wants—far from it. The point is that the Father is so in love with His child that He will do whatever it takes to make sure the child's best interest is served.

This Scripture appears right after Jesus teaches the disciples to pray.

In Luke 11:2 He tells them, "Say: Our Father." In other words, "Call Him Daddy." In fact, the original Greek is *Abba,* which means "daddy." It's a much more intimate way to come to the throne of grace.

My father didn't always say "yes" to me. If he had, I would have ended up a mess, and my life today would probably be pretty miserable. Instead, my father's yes meant, "I will do the very best for you, no matter what you ask for."

I think that's what Jesus meant too.

—*Michelle Rapkin*

"I am a princess not because I have a prince,
but because my father is a king, and He is God."
—Unknown

 DEAR JESUS, thank You for telling us to call Him "Daddy" and for the assurance that God will always open the door when I knock and will always see to it that His child is cared for. Amen.

> And he said to them, "Truly I tell you, some who are standing here will not taste death before they see that the kingdom of God has come with power."
> —Mark 9:1 (NIV)

My wife and I were watching a favorite sitcom on television. Halfway into the episode, the television shut off. In fact, everything turned off. We sat in darkness. The power had gone out. We didn't know why it happened or how long it would last, and we were relieved and grateful when the power returned, and we went back to watching TV.

Jesus's earliest followers felt the power of His presence while He was with them. But they were plunged into darkness the day of His crucifixion. He had told them, however, that some of them would not die before the kingdom of God came with power. He often spoke of the kingdom of God, but only once is He recorded as referring to the kingdom of God coming with power, an apparent reference to the day of Pentecost, when His followers would "receive power when the Holy Spirit comes" (Acts 1:8).

I wasn't there at Pentecost, but I have experienced both the darkness of doubt and the power of the Holy Spirit. I have seen the kingdom of God coming with power in my life and in the lives of others. I have learned that I need the uninterrupted flow of the Spirit's power in my life—partly through daily prayer and Bible reading—to maintain and increase the kingdom's influence in my life, family, church, and community.

—*Bob Hostetler*

"Never think that you can live to God by your own power or strength; but always look to and rely on him for assistance, yea, for all strength and grace."
—*David Brainerd*

JESUS, let the kingdom of God come with power into my life, family, church, and community. Amen.

If the world hates you, keep in mind that it hated me first.
—John 15:18 (NIV)

Like so many of his generation—what many call the "greatest generation"—my dad saw hatred firsthand during World War II. He flew bombing missions over Germany in a B-24, assignments not many survived, and he was MIA for months until smuggled out by the French Resistance. He was shot down twice, and not all his fellow crewmen survived. Although he was a gentle man, he did his duty. He fought bravely against the consuming evil that was Nazi Germany. But after the war, he never flew again.

I found out about my Dad's bravery and sacrifice after his death, because he never talked about the war. I think he felt guilty to have survived when so many of his comrades died. But I can imagine he felt the cause he fought for was right, that the evil of Nazi Germany had to be opposed and defeated for the world to be safe again.

Jesus faced so much hatred in His short life. Yet He stayed steadfast, never wavering in His faith and His witness of God's enduring love for us. He knew evil had to be opposed and that the will of God was worth fighting for. And that we, His people, were worth dying for.

This day, and every day, no matter what the obstacles, I ask Jesus to give me the strength and courage to do His will and to be an ever-present witness of His love.

—*Mary E. Williams*

"Lord, make me an instrument of Thy peace. Where there is hatred, let me sow love."
—*Francis of Assisi*

 DEAR JESUS, thank You for giving me the strength to do Your will in all things. May others see Your love in me. Amen.

> Anyone who does not love me will not obey my teaching. These words you hear are not my own; they belong to the Father who sent me.
> —John 14:24 (NIV)

My thoughts went to the less fortunate, the homeless, and the suffering, as I knelt in the small chapel during prayer hour. I asked Jesus to send someone I could help. At my "amen," I heard a knock.

In the doorway stood a disheveled, ragged man.

He wasn't exactly who I had in mind. The guy smelled bad. What if he was a criminal? I glanced at my watch. I had to pick up my kids from school.

"I need help," the man said.

Burying my head in my hands, I considered recalling that prayer.

A woman closer to the doorway gave the man directions to the church office.

Groaning, I stood. Jesus's teachings were about compassion. He helped the poor, the despised, and the outcasts. If I loved Jesus, I had to be obedient.

I met the man in the church office. The busy secretary nodded approval at my offer to help. I invited the man to sit, listened to his woes, and then shared encouraging Scripture. I assured him that Jesus doesn't abandon us. Before he left, I promised to pray for him and then directed him to the receptionist for helpful resources.

Accepting Christ as our Lord and Savior, and promising to follow Him, sometimes puts us in precarious situations, but we must be obedient to His teachings. He says to love Him and also our neighbor, even those who don't appear lovable.

—*Holly Michael*

"You express love by obedience."
—*Dr. Jack Hyles*

LORD, help us to obey Your teachings and to recognize that answers to prayers don't always come in pretty packages. Amen.

> "Which is easier: to say, 'Your sins are forgiven,' or to say, 'Get up and walk'? But I want you to know that the Son of Man has authority on earth to forgive sins." So he said to the paralyzed man, "Get up, take your mat and go home."
> —Matthew 9:5–6 (NIV)

I called Mom from a pay phone.

"I thought you were at the picnic," she answered with a curious tone.

"Well, I thought I would call and just say hello," I said, quivering, "and ... to say that I just crashed the car."

Silence. I was sixteen. My remorse for speeding around that sharp curve was deep. While it was going to cost my parents financially, that was not the root of my brokenness. It was from the guilt of breaking the law, the shame of breaking my parents' trust, the humiliation of answering the police officer's questions as to why I had totaled a car, and the disgrace of facing the parents of my friends who were in my car.

My father's answer? "Is everyone OK? Well, get your things and come home." No lectures. No anger. Only forgiveness. Gratitude flooded my spirit. I felt unconditionally loved in spite of my transgressions.

As I hung up the phone, I knew I was forgiven. "Come home." Those were the sweetest I could have heard in that moment. Jesus beckoned me to tell the truth and come clean. My father's words echoed the heart of Jesus.

Thirty years later, my son came to me in anguish over something he had done. Between his hyperventilating convulsions, I simply said, "Let's call our Father."

—*Erik Person*

"Experience: that most brutal of teachers. But you learn, my God do you learn."
—*C. S. Lewis.*

 LORD JESUS, I pray that I would seek the truth ever in humility, and every time You show mercy, it is an undeserved miracle. Amen.

> Jesus shouted, "Whoever believes in me doesn't believe in me but in the one who sent me. Whoever sees me sees the one who sent me."
> —John 12:44–45 (CEB)

You don't really have that long to raise your kids, when I think about it. How much influence does a parent really have? My experience with my two boys was that we mattered a lot until they became teenagers and then, well, we tried to guide them to the right friends, hoped they went to the right places, and prayed to God that any trouble they got into would be short-lived. Parenting really is God's schoolroom.

I find it all the more remarkable when I gaze now on my twentysomething sons and see what kind, caring, smart, funny, focused, faithful, hardworking young men they have become. All the more reason I was touched when our older son, Will, recounted a conversation he had at work. At the end of a meeting, one of his colleagues said, "I'd love to meet your parents someday."

"Why?" he asked.

"Just from knowing you, I'll bet they're wonderful people."

Like father, like son? Like parents, like offspring? It might indeed be true that the apple doesn't fall far from the tree, but nothing good grows without plenty of nurturing and care from above. We know God from the Son. And by our fruits, people come to know us.

—*Rick Hamlin*

> *"It's a father's duty to give his sons a fine chance."*
> —*George Eliot*

 BRING ME CLOSER TO YOU, JESUS, each day, so that in knowing me, people may come to know You in Your goodness through me. Amen.

FRACTURED—NOT BROKEN

And Jesus answered and said to him, "It has been said, 'You shall not tempt the Lord your God.'" —Luke 4:12 (NKJV)

With Father's Day approaching, I walked to the store with my college roommate to buy a card for my dad. We strolled back to campus, feeling happy and carefree with summer break ahead.

As we stepped into the street at the crosswalk with yellow lights blinking above us, a young man sped his car into our path. My roommate jumped out of the way, but I got the brunt of it. I was thrown fifteen feet. My fractured pelvis landed me in the hospital for six weeks.

I couldn't fly home from Oregon to my family in Pennsylvania until my bones healed. While lying in my hospital bed, alone and in pain, I was tempted to feel sorry for myself in that circumstance. I knew my soul was unsettled.

I propped my Bible on the shelf of my bed. Among many Scriptures, Lamentations 3:57–58 bolstered my spirit: "You drew near on the day I called on You, and said, 'Do not fear!' O Lord, You have pleaded the case for my soul; You have redeemed my life."

When I had to lie still for hours, or awoke at night feeling alone, if I said one word, "Jesus," I knew the enemy had to flee.

The written word and the living Word saw me through my wilderness, just as Jesus resisted the enemy by the Word of God and with His powerful presence.

—*Kathleen Ruckman*

"Satan is on a short leash, chained to the Cross."
—*C. S. Lewis*

 JESUS, thank You for being the victory in my wilderness experience through Your Word and Your presence in my life. Amen.

> **Jesus answered, "I am the way and the truth and the life. No one comes to the Father except through me." —John 14:6** (NIV)

My young nephew lived with us during his mother's illness. When I needed to retrieve some information to register him in a school near us, I told him, "We are going to your old school today." He'd had a difficult time adjusting after his mom got sick, so I wasn't surprised when he began to weep. I wrapped my arms around him and held him close. He sobbed. "I don't know how to get there."

Some days I feel like my nephew did that day. I don't know the way out of my loneliness or pain—or fear. I struggle with decisions and next steps. My battle reminds me of navigating around a new city before we had GPS. Trying to manhandle bulky maps or follow the ambiguous directions of a friend often sent me to the wrong place.

Jesus not only knows the way—He is the way. As Warren Wiersbe says, "Jesus is the example of how God acts in the world." Jesus's encouraging and powerful words help me speak caring words of reassurance. I also try to put His words into action. When I read how Jesus showed kindness to a beggar or crippled person, I see the way to be kind and generous—so I pack small backpacks with nutritious snacks and toiletries to give to the homeless people at the corner. My actions follow Jesus's way—the way to truth and life.

—Karen Porter

"Good intentions and earnest effort are not enough.
Only Jesus can make an otherwise futile life productive."
—Chuck Swindoll

JESUS, I want to know Your way. Be my GPS. Help me follow Your directions and example today. Amen.

FROM HEAD TO HEART

Believe me when I say that I am in the Father and the Father is in me; or at least believe on the evidence of the works themselves. —John 14:11 (NIV)

From a young age, I believed there is a God. I believed God created the world as the Bible states, and I believed He was my Creator too. The time came, however, that I needed to examine the evidence for myself and move my mere belief in God from my head into my heart.

During Bible-story time one morning at Vacation Bible School, my teacher, Mrs. Bacon, shared the greatest love story ever told. She told of the God Who is Father, Son, and Spirit—all in one. She spoke about sin, my separation from God because of my sin, Jesus's deity and sinless nature, Jesus's death on the cross in payment for my sin, His resurrection, and my forgiveness through faith if I believe Jesus to be Who He says He is.

Knowledge alone wasn't enough. I needed to establish a personal relationship with Jesus. Seated beside Mrs. Bacon, I prayed to accept Jesus as my Savior. That sunny June day in Southern California, because of the John 3:16 evidence that Jesus died on the cross to save me from my sin and reconcile me to the Father, my belief transformed into trust. I placed my trust in Jesus because He is God.

—*Mona Hodgson*

"Talk what we will of faith, if we do not trust and
rely upon Him, we do not believe in Him."
—*Anthony Farindon*

 LORD JESUS, my Emmanuel—God with me—thank You for Who You are and for all You do! Amen.

**Honor your father and mother, and You shall love your neighbor as yourself.
—Matthew 19:19 (ESV)**

I have found, sometimes reluctantly, that nothing in Scripture is there by accident. At first glance, respecting my parents, loving others, and loving myself appear to be somewhat disconnected, but they are really very closely linked.

In an ideal world, our parents, as God's emissaries, show us how to love by loving us in word and deed. In healthy homes, kids learn to love themselves, grounded in their parents' unconditional love. This safe, early bond enables us to go out into the world to love others.

Some of us had parents whose ability to love and care for us was impaired. In turn, they weren't able to foster the kind of loving security that equips us to freely love others. Thank God for Jesus!

In Him, we are not only perfectly loved and secure but also enabled by our willing surrender to better love ourselves and, in turn, our neighbor. Moreover, by Christ's compassionate forgiveness, we can compassionately forgive others, including our parents, honoring their gift of life if not their stellar virtues or perfect sacrifice.

—*Isabella Yosuico*

"Our parents deserve our honor and respect for giving us life itself."
—*Ezra Taft Benson*

 DEAR JESUS, in Your name I pray for the ability to honor my parents for doing the best they could. Thank You that You filled the gap by loving me perfectly, as that enabled me to love my parents, myself, and others in You. Amen.

**You will testify too, because you have been with me from the beginning.
—John 15:27 (CEB)**

I love to tell people about my friend Jorge Jarrin and what a remarkable person he is. These days he and his father are broadcasters for the Los Angeles Dodgers games in Spanish, but before that he was on LA radio, alerting commuters to traffic snafus. I've always known him to be a man of his word.

But the real reason I can testify to his character is because we go way back. I was an awkward kid in fifth grade, when he showed up on the first day of school. Even then he exuded a charm and confidence beyond his years. Somehow—and this seems the miraculous part—he picked me to be his friend. We would sit on the jungle gym and talk for hours.

Over the years we did church youth group together, starred in high-school musicals and plays, lounged at the beach, and double-dated at proms and school dances. I sang at his wedding and more recently edited his story in *Guideposts* magazine, in which he wrote about his Hall of Fame broadcaster dad, Jaime Jarrin. His faith has grown over the years, but I can testify to its beginnings because I was there, as I was called to be his friend.

Jesus called the most unexpected people His friends. And they never forgot it.

—*Rick Hamlin*

*"God will not use a compromised life to reach a compromised world.
God will use a life that is given over to Him, that is a demonstration
of the message that through the power of Jesus Christ and His love
He can transform our lives and set us free."*
—*Joe Focht*

CHRIST JESUS, I give thanks for the friends who have helped me know You because they call You their Friend. Amen.

Therefore, you should pray like this: Our Father in heaven, Your name be honored as holy. Your kingdom come. Your will be done on earth as it is in heaven. Give us today our daily bread. —Matthew 6:9–11 (HCSB)

Recently I noticed how often I rush into God's presence and immediately bombard Him with all my problems and needs. Often such frantic prayer times only make me more jittery!

In teaching his followers how to pray the famous Lord's Prayer, Jesus provided a better pattern. He wasn't mandating a mantra to memorize and repeat mindlessly. He was giving an ingenious outline to follow.

Notice the components—and their order. Prayer begins with the reminder that the Almighty isn't some distant, reluctant heavenly bureaucrat. He's our heavenly Father. Next come three very God-focused requests: for Him to be revered, for His glorious rule to permeate the world, and for His will to be carried out perfectly, right here and right now. It's only after we are reminded of the great care and kingship of God that Jesus encourages us to mention our basic needs.

It's easy to get the order reversed, isn't it? How much more joy and peace I experience when I remember to preface my prayers with petitions that focus my heart on God's glorious goodness.

—*Len Woods*

"Prayer is a mighty instrument, not for getting man's will done in heaven, but for getting God's will done on earth."
—*Robert Law*

 JESUS, thank You for teaching Your disciples to pray. Give me the wisdom to take Your words to heart. Amen.

> **Which of you fathers, if your son asks for a fish, will give him a snake instead?**
> **—Luke 11:11** (NIV)

My husband doesn't talk much. He smiles, laughs, and hugs. But when it comes to sharing deep conversations, he's likely to fall asleep, or get up and find something to tinker with in the garage.

For years our daughter couldn't accept that character trait and strove to change him. From flattery to anger to reverse psychology, she used every means she could think of to alter his behavior, but nothing worked.

He remained quiet. Amused at her antics, but quiet.

Eventually, she learned to accept her father just the way he was. She realized how much he loved her because without speaking he showed it in so many ways.

He worked overtime so she could have the special things she wanted, and he taught her how to fish. Every year, he took her on long backpacking trips to beautiful places where God's touch was obvious and words weren't necessary. He showed her how to spot Jesus's silent blessings every day, and how to live faith in both good and bad times.

He couldn't grant every wish she had or be everything she asked for in a father. But he gave his all. And he gave her the best gift of all—he believed in her. And because of him, she believes in Christ.

—*Heidi Gaul*

"My father gave me the greatest gift anyone
could give another person, he believed in me."
—*Jim Valvano*

 JESUS, teach us to love and honor our fathers, both earthly and heavenly, just as You did. Amen.

> The Spirit of the Lord is on me, because he has anointed me to proclaim good news to the poor. He has sent me to proclaim freedom for the prisoners and recovery of sight for the blind, to set the oppressed free. —Luke 4:18 (NIV)

When my husband left for work at 5:00 a.m. one morning, I wanted to crawl back into bed and sleep another hour or two. But his coworker had just called out sick. I knew he would appreciate my help getting breakfast served at our city rescue mission, so I hurriedly dressed and jumped in my car to follow him.

Pulling into a parking space, I sensed Jesus's gentle prodding. *Go and proclaim My good news to the poor. Share my gift of freedom with those who feel trapped, oppressed, or down-and-out.* I climbed out of the car with a fresh sense of purpose.

For the next few hours I made connections and shared words of encouragement. I delighted in coaxing small smiles onto weathered faces and watching tiny sparks of hope ignite in tired eyes. I noticed the major difference between me and the people I served was primarily circumstantial. Similar in body, mind, and heart, it was mostly our current situation and station in life that set us apart. Jesus's good news and freedom are for us all! Are we mindfully living in the expensive and lavish freedom Jesus purchased for each of us? And are we communicating that good news with others who are poor financially in spirit? What a joy to share God's freedom!

—*Nancy Sebastian Kuch*

"God uses rescued people to rescue people."
—*Christine Caine*

 JESUS, thank You for forgiveness, freeing my soul, and helping me see Your blessings in my life. Help me open my mouth and share Your joy and liberty with others. Amen.

> **When you fast, put oil on your head and wash your face, so that it will not be obvious to others that you are fasting, but only to your Father, who is unseen; and your Father, who sees what is done in secret, will reward you.**
> **—Matthew 6:17–18** (NIV)

When my children were growing up, a wise friend advised me to expend less effort trying to catch them doing something wrong than I did trying to catch them doing something good. The positive reinforcement, he said, would be far more helpful than always trying to curtail bad behavior. It was great advice. I loved surprising my daughter in the act of helping her younger brother with his homework, or catching my son showing a friend how to conquer a new video-game level. After pointing out their good or wise behavior, I enjoyed rewarding them by extending their curfew or offering a small boost in their allowance.

There were still times, of course, when I caught one of them misbehaving or acting self-righteously. And I still had to discipline them at times. But the best moments were those when I caught them red-handed at being good.

Jesus's words suggest to me that our heavenly Father loves to see His children being good. So why would I put on a self-righteous show for people around me? Whether fasting or giving or helping or serving, I'd much rather be caught in the act by my Father, Who sees what is done in secret. I'd much rather enjoy His rewards than the fleeting favor of others.

—*Bob Hostetler*

"Know you not that a good man does nothing for
appearance sake, but for the sake of having done right?"
—Epictetus

 JESUS, open my eyes today to every opportunity to please You—especially by doing good, out of sight of others. Amen.

For whoever does the will of my Father in heaven is my brother and sister and mother. —Matthew 12:50 (NIV)

My sister Lucy was my family's heart and soul—warm, kind, compassionate, and full of love for everyone. She exuberantly welcomed everyone into her life. She was interested in everyone.

When my wife's parents died in a plane crash, I was devastated. Lucy was the first person I called. I can still hear her saying, "I love you. It's going to be all right." You see, Lucy was love, comfort, and strength in the midst of any storm.

Right after my father died, I went on the Walk to Emmaus. The candlelight ceremony was hard, but when I lifted my head, I saw Lucy's sweet face. "I love you," she said. "It's going to be all right." She had driven hours to be there, because she loved deeply and never missed an opportunity to express it.

When my mother died, it happened too quickly for all of us to get there. But Lucy was there, with love enough for all of us. Then, not long after, Lucy suddenly died of complications from knee surgery. She wasn't there to comfort me, and I cried until I had no more tears to shed. But I could still hear her voice. "I love you. It's going to be all right."

Jesus said anyone doing the Father's will is His brother and sister. His words truly reflect on the goodness of my sister Lucy.

—*J. Mason Williams*

"A sister is a gift to the heart, a friend to the spirit,
a golden thread to the meaning of life."
—*Isadora James*

JESUS, it's all about love, isn't it? Thank You for Your love, and the love of the brothers and sisters in my life. Amen.

REFLECTION OF THE FATHER

> All things have been committed to me by my Father. No one knows the Son except the Father, and no one knows the Father except the Son and those to whom the Son chooses to reveal him. —Matthew 11:27 (NIV)

My grandmother couldn't remember where she'd met the woman who was now at the next register in the grocery store. As they unloaded their carts, she was embarrassed that they seemed to make eye contact every time she stole a glance. The woman looked so familiar! Finally, she offered a smile and a timid wave.

The woman in the mirror waved back!

I inherited my grandmother's brown eyes that squint when we laugh, and the corny sense of humor she passed down through my father. I also inherited her tendency toward mistaken identity: I was once startled to see my mother in the backseat of my car when I looked in the rearview mirror. I'd always been told we look alike, but it's hard to see that for yourself until you see your mother's eyes staring back at you.

Jesus bore a striking resemblance to His Father. Everything that is true about the Father is reflected in His Son—they are both compassionate and gracious, slow to anger, and abounding in love and faithfulness (Exodus 34:6). Everything about the Son is a reflection of His Father—they are both true, noble, right, pure, lovely, admirable, excellent, and praiseworthy (Philippians 4:8). Jesus and His Father are revealed in the mirror of God's word, and even mundane trips to the grocery store.

—*Amy Lively*

"Remember that the promises Christ makes are not merely his surmises, but they are promises with the stamp of the court of heaven upon them. Their truth is guaranteed by God. It is not possible they should fail."
—*Charles Spurgeon*

JESUS, I want to know You and Your Father. Thank You for revealing Yourself and Your Father to me, and for showing me Your grace and power each day. Amen.

> For I tell you that unless your righteousness surpasses that of the Pharisees and the teachers of the law, you will certainly not enter the kingdom of heaven. —Matthew 5:20 (NIV)

Jesus seemed to rebuke religious hypocrisy more than any other sin, but He was patient with those who knew they were sinners and came to Him in humble surrender. Many of the Pharisees and teachers of the law couldn't accept Jesus's criticism. I find myself sometimes responding like a self-righteous Pharisee when I'm criticized. My first inclination is to defend myself, refute the criticism, or accuse my accuser in response—as if that would absolve me of any errors.

Several years ago a colleague accused me of unfairness. When I spoke to a friend about it, I was directed to a teaching on the topic that at first seemed upside down. It focused on humility. It taught that I should pray to understand what God wanted to do in me through the conflict. And it taught that it accomplishes little to defend myself against criticism when another person is angry or insistent, but if I listen respectfully and offer to honestly consider the accusation and make right any error, I might defuse emotion and help lead to a resolution. The fundamental message was that humility always wins.

I can't say that employing these themes resolved all my differences with that colleague. But it enabled us to get past the immediate conflict so we could work together more smoothly, and it's helped me many times since. It's true: humility always wins.

—*Michael Berrier*

"Humility in the life of the believer is the mark of greatness—
not because you shine when you are humbled, but because
when you submit to God's will, He shines through you."
—*Charles F. Stanley*

 LORD JESUS, help me to make a habit of humility. Amen.

KNOWING HIS VOICE

> **When he has brought out all his own, he goes on ahead of them, and his sheep follow him because they know his voice. —John 10:4** (NIV)

"Buddy!" I stood on the front porch, calling my wayward dog. Once again he'd seen the open gate as an invitation to a grand adventure. I walked around the house, continuing to call his name. "Buddy! Hey, boy, where are you?"

As I looked down the street, I saw the familiar wiggle of our basset hound's backside. "Buddy, come here," I shouted. And he turned his head, those long ears perked by the sound of his name.

When he reached my feet, he lay down, positioning himself for a good belly rub. I admonished him for his bad behavior, even as I scratched his stretched-out middle. Buddy knows my voice, because he's spent years in our home. He has learned to trust my voice, as he has become confident in my care for him.

I've been like Buddy, wondering what lay beyond the boundaries in my life. For a season, I wandered like the prodigal, tasting what the world had to offer. But like Buddy, I heard my name called out by the One Who knows me best.

Jesus's voice beckons me to His side. He calls me back to the safety of His care and provision. Just as my voice is trustworthy to Buddy, I know I can trust the voice of Jesus in my life.

—*Teri Lynne Underwood*

"Our failure to hear His voice when we want to is due to the fact that we do not in general want to hear it, that we want it only when we think we need it."
—*Dallas Willard*

 JESUS, may I always be sensitive to hear Your voice, and trust Your care and love for me. Amen.

> I am the vine; you are the branches. If you remain in me and I in you, you will bear much fruit; apart from me you can do nothing. —John 15:5 (NIV)

Two rosebushes grow in my yard. They bloom all summer, beautiful and profuse, their fragrance scenting the air. One of my favorite puttering pastimes is to trim the wilted flowers or browned foliage down to the five-leaf leaflet below. Tossing the rose and stem to the ground, I continue until the bush is refreshed and only rosebuds remain.

By the time I've finished, the tossed blossoms and stems are withered, the leaves paperlike. How quickly they begin to die, apart from the bush.

The verse reveals we are as closely attached to Jesus as branches are attached to a vine. He promises that if we abide in Him, He will be in us, and we will bear much fruit. When one sees a vine, one expects to find branches teeming with grapes. And if someone observes the life of a Christian abiding in Jesus, he should recognize the fruit of the Holy Spirit—love, joy, peace, patience, goodness, kindness, gentleness, faithfulness, and self-control. Evidence of His life manifested in us.

Like my tossed roses, dying without their connection to the bush, we cannot produce anything of spiritual value apart from the true Vine. When we are united with Jesus, His life flows into and through us, transforming our lives into a greater blessing.

—*Cathy Elliott*

"As we learn better to abide, the fruit becomes 'more fruit.' But Christ is satisfied only when the 'more' becomes the abounding 'much fruit.'"
—*Norman B. Harrison*

LORD, stir in me the need for communion with You, that I may remain fully dependent on the Vine. Amen.

UNTOUCHABLE

> Jesus reached out his hand and touched the man. "I am willing," he said. "Be clean!" And immediately the leprosy left him. —Luke 5:13 (NIV)

In biblical days, lepers were required to stay away from healthy people. They were supposed to shout, "Unclean! Unclean!" if someone drew near. Jewish law mandated that anyone who touched a person with leprosy would become unclean. Due to their terrible disease, lepers were physical and social outcasts.

Have you felt excluded by a certain group of people? Even though we don't know the pain of leprosy, most of us have felt the pain of being left out and ignored. I've experienced the hurt of isolation and exclusion. Years ago, I tried unsuccessfully to fit in with my church's young-adults group. They were polite but never accepted me into their group or included me in their weekend plans. I always felt like an intruder in their close group.

When the outcast man fell to the ground in front of Jesus and begged for healing, Jesus reached out in love and touched him. Jesus could have simply spoken healing over the man. However, the man with leprosy probably hadn't been touched by anyone in years. Jesus knew that deep source of pain and reached out to physically touch him.

Jesus knows about our pain too. He sees the scars we hide and the burdens we carry. When life feels too heavy, Jesus is within our reach. He's a loving Savior, and He is willing to touch those who feel untouchable. Jesus is love.

—*Allison K. Flexer*

"Jesus tends to his people individually. He personally sees to our needs.
We all receive Jesus's touch. We experience his care."
—*Max Lucado*

 JESUS, we can cast our burdens on You. You are willing to cleanse us from whatever weighs us down. Thank You for loving us. Amen.

> And everyone who has left houses or brothers or sisters or father or mother or wife or children or fields for my sake will receive a hundred times as much and will inherit eternal life. —Matthew 19:29 (NIV)

A few months ago, I left a good job, not because I had somewhere to go but because I felt I was following Jesus's leading. Several well-meaning friends wanted to know if I was running away from anything, since I was not moving on to something better. Yet I knew my decision was soundly based on verses Jesus revealed to me, His whispered affirmation, and the voices of wise mentors. As difficult as it was, I resigned.

One of my favorite hymns says, "Trust and obey, for there's no other way to be happy in Jesus, but to trust and obey" (John H. Sammis). I was not happy at first. In fact, depression set in. I was blindsided by shame, doubts, and negative thoughts brought on by an accomplishment-driven society. But Jesus was patiently leading me toward His goal, even when I could not see it.

Right now I am working for my elderly parents, spending precious time with them in their twilight years. My mother's gardens are flourishing, their home is becoming organized, and my father and I are working on his memoir. Furthermore, Jesus is meeting my financial needs—He always makes abundant provision for His plans.

—*Nancy Sebastian Kuch*

"Whatever God is urging you to clear away cannot begin to be compared to what He ultimately wants to bring you."
—*Beth Moore*

JESUS, please confirm what it is You want me to forsake for Your sake. Then help me to obey and trust You for Your blessing. Amen.

> Be merciful, just as your Father is merciful.
> —Luke 6:36 (NIV)

Sometimes in life we don't suffer the punishment we deserve. We might get caught cheating on a test or speeding as we drive, but instead of getting an F, or a ticket, we get off. Rather than feeling the painful blow of justice, we are kissed by mercy.

When one of my sons was quite young (but old enough to know better), he took a hammer and pounded to pieces my Swiss Army knife—a beloved souvenir from a childhood trip to Geneva, Switzerland. I was mystified, appalled, and saddened all at once. As I considered various consequences—making him pay me back, taking away privileges, and so on—I thought of all the times and ways I have broken and marred that which belongs to my Father in heaven. Consequently, I decided to offer my son what God has given me in Christ: pardon instead of punishment.

According to Jesus, this is the heart of our heavenly Father. He is merciful (i.e., full of mercy). Our hearts are full of rebellion, so God has every right to drop the proverbial hammer on us. After all, doling out deserved punishment is the job description of a just judge. But instead of making us pay, God sent Christ to satisfy justice's demands. Because of Jesus's sacrifice for us, God is able to extend compassion and offer forgiveness to us.

—*Len Woods*

"The Gospel is good news of mercy to the undeserving.
The symbol of the religion of Jesus is the cross, not the scales."
—*John Stott*

LORD JESUS, thank You for making it possible for me to both receive and bestow mercy. Amen.

Not all who sound religious are really godly people. They may refer to me as "Lord," but still won't get to heaven. For the decisive question is whether they obey my Father in heaven. —Matthew 7:21 (TLB)

When I was newly married, my husband got the promotion of his dreams—a call-up to the most prestigious team in baseball, the New York Yankees. His first year at shortstop brought many highs and lows, including cheering fans on nights he performed well, and boos and taunts on nights he didn't. One night I overheard fans crushing my husband with their words. When they found out I was his wife, they smothered him with compliments and accolades I knew were fake. I left the game that night, thinking about the fickle nature of fans and how easy it is to act a certain way while secretly believing something else.

Jesus isn't impressed with fake accolades; he's more concerned with real obedience. He wants us to do right, not just say right-sounding words. After thirty-five years in professional baseball, my husband and I have learned to weed out the fake from the authentic. It's refreshing to know Jesus does too.

—*Gari Meacham*

"If you read history you will find that the Christians who did the most for the present world were precisely those who thought most of the next. It is since Christians have largely ceased to think of the other world that they have become so ineffective in this world."
—*C. S. Lewis*

JESUS, help me to live authentically and not be fickle in my faith. Strengthen me to cut through words and actions that don't reflect true obedience. Amen.

> For I have not spoken on my own authority, but the Father who sent me has himself given me a commandment—what to say and what to speak. And I know that his commandment is eternal life. What I say, therefore, I say as the Father has told me. —John 12:49–50 (ESV)

As a parent, I want my daughter to find me trustworthy. I want her to believe that what I say is true. For her safety and flourishing, I need her to trust my authority when I say stovetops and street crossings are dangerous. I need her to nod in agreement when I say Jesus loves her more than I do.

She doesn't know it, but she is teaching me to live more truthfully. Because, in order for her to trust the authority in my words, I have to speak truth. I have to rightly place words of warning and words of wisdom, gentle encouragement and tender rebuke. She is only a toddler, but she has already seen me fail plenty.

Jesus knew the importance of being truthful. The Father, in fact, sent Him to be the very expression of truth. The God Who spoke creation into existence sent Jesus into that creation to proclaim eternal life. In Jesus, God sent His Son and His glory down to be Truth in human form.

Jesus spoke with authority when He explained eternal life, and He speaks with grace as we seek truth here on earth. I know I can never be perfectly trustworthy, but I can point my family to the One Who never fails at being true.

—*Caroline Kolts*

"I am not a saint. I am, however, beginning to learn that I am a small character in a story that is always fundamentally about God."
—*Lauren Winner*

JESUS, thank You for being trustworthy, for being Truth. Thank You for speaking the commandment of eternal life and having patience as I try to follow Your example. Amen.

> But I tell you, do not resist an evil person. If anyone slaps you on the right cheek, turn to them the other cheek also. —Matthew 5:39 (NIV)

Watching the evening news, I am heartbroken by the amount of injustice in our world. I see stories about innocent people being murdered. I hear about a guilty party receiving a lenient sentence from the courts. Children are hungry, thirsty, and mistreated. The recent headlines are troubling, and it's tempting to succumb to despair.

Our human nature craves revenge or retaliation when we witness or experience injustice. We seek someone to blame. If someone hurts me, my initial reaction is to want to hurt them back. But Jesus gives us another way, a different solution. Do not resist, but instead turn the other cheek.

On this side of heaven, evil will always be present. The good news is that Jesus has already overcome evil, and every injustice will come into the light one day. When I try to take matters into my own hands, I assume I have the right to judge.

I want to learn to leave it in the hands of Jesus. He's the One Who led a perfect life and unjustly died on a cross for our sakes. He has the right to judge. But instead, He forgives. Our job is to trust Him, love Him and others, and leave justice in His capable hands.

—*Allison K. Flexer*

"Judging requires that you think yourself superior to the one you judge."
—*William Paul Young*

 JESUS, You are the only one Who has earned the right to judge. When we encounter injustice, remind us to respond in love. Amen.

Truly I tell you, today you will be with me in Paradise.
—Luke 23:43 (NRSV)

Sometimes anxiety descends upon me, even as everything around me seems just fine. One time I was on retreat, spending time by the ocean, praying, and catching up on some much-needed rest. It was paradise! On the second night, I couldn't go to sleep. I felt tortured by my own worries, and I was disappointed in myself that I couldn't pray my way out of the anxiety. If I really believed in Christ, how could my anxiety get to me like that? When daylight came I found inner stillness again, calmed by the gentle ocean breeze and soothed by the rhythm of the surf.

On the last night of this retreat, I again found myself awake and anxious. But this time, something was different. It was as if I heard Christ telling me, "Today you will be with me in Paradise." My anxiety didn't suddenly vanish, but I understood it would pass and that I could know paradise as it exists in His peace. Instead of wishing for a faith that would rid me of anxiety, that night I accepted that those bouts of anxiety will probably always be with me but that Jesus provides relief. Deep anxieties of the night give way to experiences of grace and peace that can feel like real Paradise—all within one twenty-four-hour period. Neither experience is ever going to be permanent. But Jesus reminds me that He's with me through both.

—*Lizzie Berne DeGear*

"Difficult as it is really to listen to someone in affliction,
it is just as difficult for him to know that compassion is listening to him."
—*Simone Weil*

THANK YOU, Jesus, for reminding me that I can look forward to the moments ahead when I feel secure in the kingdom of God. Please help me feel Your compassionate presence in the tough moments, too. Amen.

Now that I, your Lord and Teacher, have washed your feet, you also should wash one another's feet. —John 13:14 (NIV)

I've always imagined how dumbstruck the disciples must have been when Jesus knelt before them to wash their feet. What an incredible act of humility that was.

But it was more than that. It was about love.

My father was bedridden the last years of his life. He could not dress or feed himself, and he wore adult undergarments. To assist his caretakers, my siblings and I cared for him on alternating weekends, but his caretakers still came by to change his undergarments. I have to admit I was relieved I did not have to perform that particular task.

One afternoon, though, I stepped into Dad's room to find he had soiled himself. With no caregivers around, I was compelled to wash him and change his linens and undergarments. It was heartbreaking to have to do this for the man who had been such a pillar of strength in my life, but I felt only love as I made Dad as comfortable as I could. I was amazed to find the physical reality of what I was doing mattered not one iota.

By washing the disciples' feet, Jesus was telling them He loved them. He took them as they were—dirty and worn—and made them clean again.

What an incredible example of love for all of us.

—*J. Mason Williams*

"My wife, my family, my friends—they've all taught me things
about love and what that emotion really means. In a nutshell,
loving someone is about giving, not receiving."
—*Nicholas Sparks*

 JESUS, Your love is the purest of all. Thank You so much for washing me clean. Amen.

Love Letter from Jesus
FORTY DAYS IN THE DESERT

My Sweet Love,

When you find yourself in a desert, a place that feels spiritually dry, take heart. You are not alone. I have been there, too, and because I emerged victorious, so will you. I walk with you through the wilderness.

I make streams flow through the desert, because I am your Living Water. Drink deeply of My love—it never runs dry. I set a table for you in the wilderness. Let Me be your Bread of Life—taste and see that I am good. Let Me lead you like a Shepherd. Be comforted by My presence, My rod, and My staff. I'll restore your soul. Let Me carry you in My arms. Come to Me when you are weary, and I will give you rest.

I am the Lily of the Valley. Let Me help you bloom. Walk with Me, guided by true Light. I will show you the way. I will advocate for you, so the enemy will not have the last word. I bring beauty out of ashes, life out of death. This is My way.

I have been called a Man of Sorrows, acquainted with grief. I wept when I experienced loss, and I weep with you. Learn from Me, for I am gentle and humble of heart. Let the Spirit do His work through the pain and the hunger. Follow My example. Press in close to God. Trust that you will come out on the other side of the desert into a beautiful place with Me at your side, because I am your Redeemer. I am the Messiah. I have promised, and I will deliver you.

I love you forever.

Then the Spirit led Jesus into the desert to be tempted by the devil.
—Matthew 4:1 (NCV)

> "Have faith in God," Jesus answered.
> —Mark 11:22 (NIV)

Every year, I ask Jesus for a word that will help me grow deeper with Him. This year, the word was "subtraction." I didn't like subtraction. I worried what that word might mean for my family, but I also welcomed the idea of trimming a few things from my life. And I sincerely believed Jesus meant the word for my own good.

A few weeks later, my husband took a phone call. The tone of his voice alarmed me. He paced while on the phone, hands gesturing. I met him in the hallway.

"What happened?" I asked.

"I was just laid off. No severance." The shock on his face mirrored my own. His income paid our bills; my writing income could not sustain us.

We made our way back to the living room and sat on the couch. "We need to pray," he said.

"Jesus," I prayed, "we don't understand what just happened, but we are choosing not to panic. We choose to have faith in You today."

Peace filled me. The panic I once nursed now grew smaller. When Jesus gave me the subtraction, I had a sense it would be for our ultimate good. And even though I wouldn't choose joblessness and financial insecurity, I wanted to trust Jesus and to have faith in His ability to provide. And He has—through anonymous contributions, a new health plan that wasn't too costly, and friends who have rallied around us.

—*Mary DeMuth*

"Faith is taking the first step even when you don't see the whole staircase."
—*Martin Luther King Jr.*

 JESUS, I choose to have faith in Your ability to provide. Teach me to trust You when things I desire are subtracted from my life. Amen.

> **Pray that you may not come into the time of trial.**
> **—Luke 22:40** (NRSV)

I try to approach challenges as opportunities to deepen my faith, expand my awareness, and grow in my relationship to Christ and life. It sounds rewarding, doesn't it? It is. But you know what? It's also exhausting! And today with the eleven words spoken in Luke 22:40, Jesus encourages me to pray that my faith isn't tested. Here's Jesus, suggesting that maybe part of my contemplative life should be to pray for an easy path. Wow! Who knew? Talk about good news!

I love this kind of advice. It reminds me of the words of wisdom I got from women friends who became mothers before I did. They showed me ways to make the tasks of motherhood less burdensome, and to consider easy solutions along with the "best" thing to do in any situation. Can I apply this to my family life and my faith life? Can I trust that taking the easy road sometimes means I'm more available to Christ and to those I love? Can I find a way to be merciful to myself, so that I may share this mercy with others? Life always tests our strength and endurance and faith and capacity for love. Thank You, Jesus, for reminding me to pray for more of those merciful moments when life isn't trying at all.

—*Lizzie Berne DeGear*

"Here I was taught by the grace of God…that all manner of thing shall be well."
—*Julian of Norwich*

 OK! Today I pray that I may not come into the time of trial. Jesus, help me recognize all the moments today that do not try me at all. Let me receive these simple mercies in gratitude and joy. And let my connection to You be refreshed by these moments. Amen.

> Why do you call me, "Lord, Lord," and do not do what I say?
> —Luke 6:46 (NIV)

Over more than thirty years of marriage, my wife has learned how to get me to do things. Sometimes she comes to me and asks how to do something herself, to give me an opportunity to offer to do it for her. Sometimes she begins a task herself, knowing I think of myself as too chivalrous to sit by and watch. Sometimes she just asks politely. But she knows that if a request comes across as an order, I don't respond well.

Jesus does not treat me so gently concerning His commands. He insists on obedience. If I call Him my Lord, obedience is my duty. And His commands are not always easy to obey. He commands me to love. He initiated the great love exchange by loving us before we loved Him. Our response is to love Him in return, and He then goes further: He tells us to love others.

It's a simple command, but it's so hard. It's hard for me to love the unlovely, and those who are different from me or who don't value things I do. It's hard for me to love those whose appearances or manners I don't like, or those who I think are arrogant or proud. It's even hard for me to love those who are like me. The problem is not with others; it's with me. If I call Jesus my Lord, I need to do what He says, and that means loving people—even if they sin against me. That's how God loves me.

—*Michael Berrier*

"God teaches us to love by putting some unlovely people around us."
—*Rick Warren*

LORD JESUS, soften my heart toward all those I come into contact with today. Remind me to love the way You love me. Amen.

GRATITUDE INSTEAD OF GREED

> Yes, a person is a fool to store up earthly wealth but not have a rich relationship with God. —Luke 12:21 (NLT)

In 2013, my friends, Sonya and Don, made a bold life change. They sold their house and possessions, and started an adventure with only a few suitcases loaded in their sport-utility vehicle. They rented homes in various cities, worked remotely, and homeschooled their three children on the road. Each of the children started a blog, and I enjoyed reading about their many life experiences.

As I have watched my friends live out this unconventional approach, my admiration and respect for them has grown. I think about them a lot, especially when I get caught up in the cycle of wanting to buy new things or complaining that I don't have enough space in my kitchen. Life on the road with minimal possessions is not the right solution for every family. But this extreme example reminds me to avoid becoming preoccupied with earthly wealth.

Jesus warns us about greed. He says in Luke 12:15, "Life is not measured by how much you own." Life is about relationships and experiences, not how much stuff we accumulate. It's easy to allow possessions to take precedence over people or our relationship with God.

Jesus modeled a simple approach to life, one that highlights the difference between gratitude and greed.

—*Allison K. Flexer*

"The grateful heart is not developed in a single moment;
it is the result of a thousand choices."
—*Pete Wilson*

JESUS, forgive us for being greedy. Teach us to focus on relationships instead of possessions. Amen.

> "Martha, Martha," the Lord answered, "you are worried and upset about many things, but few things are needed—or indeed only one. Mary has chosen what is better, and it will not be taken away from her." —Luke 10:41-42 (NIV)

I lay in bed, my body weakened following surgery to remove a cancerous tumor. For some time I required bed rest, and loved ones gathered to help.

One woman chauffeured me back and forth to radiation treatments. Her contagious optimism brightened my perspective. A group of friends and neighbors provided meals for me. These women served with selflessness, seeing a need and filling it. Their actions reminded me of Martha as she worked to make Jesus more comfortable in her home, and their kindness blessed me.

But more than the meals, I craved the time my companions shared with me in quiet conversation and thoughtful prayer. I needed someone to listen to my concerns and talk me through them. Though the time we spent visiting was brief, their caring spirits proved as effective toward the healing of my soul as any medication or therapy. Like Mary, they understood what was most important and then acted on it.

Martin Luther, in a letter to Ulrich Zwingli, wrote, "God is hidden in the soup." I believe He was there during my recovery as well as in the other selfless acts performed for my well-being. I saw Jesus reflected in the eyes of friends as they listened, and I knew He too listened as we prayed.

—Heidi Gaul

"The hardest thing on earth is choosing what matters."
—Sue Monk Kidd

 LORD, help me focus on the important things in life, things that bring me closer to You. Amen.

> He did the same thing with the cup, after they had eaten, saying, "This cup is the new covenant in my blood. Every time you drink it, do this to remember me." —1 Corinthians 11:25 (CEB)

I'll remember that moment forever. My old college friend, Charley, was struggling with ALS—or Lou Gehrig's disease, as it's often called—and I was visiting him in Maine, where he was vacationing with his family. The last time I'd seen him, he could still walk, but now he was in a wheelchair and couldn't feed himself.

"Would you like to give Charley his dinner?" his wife, Lynn, asked. She would be busy enough getting dinner for their four young ones.

"Sure," I said. We sat outside on the deck, and I put his bib on him. I filled the spoon with what looked like creamed spinach and fed my contemporary. Charley dribbled a bit, and I dribbled some more, and soon we both were laughing. It could have been heartbreaking—after all, ALS is merciless. Charley was dying; in fact, he would die a year and a half later. But the memory that lasts is one of life and love.

Shortly before He died, Jesus took a cup of wine and shared it with those He loved—a ritual that has been repeated through the centuries. His death was violent and tragic, His resurrection a cause for joy. But it is through eating and drinking that He asked us to remember Him.

—*Rick Hamlin*

"I always have a funny story at communion time that underscores that no one is perfect, and that communion is not for perfect people but for hungry people."
—*Greg Boyle*

 JESUS, it is because You feed me that I am able to feed Your loved ones. Amen.

The kingdom of heaven is like a merchant seeking beautiful pearls, who, when he had found one pearl of great price, went and sold all that he had and bought it. —Matthew 13:45-46 (NKJV)

The tabernacle where I attended camp growing up resembled a barn. It was a place where members of my Slovak-American church gathered yearly. When summer lightning storms flashed outside the windows and thunder rolled through the tabernacle, the choir sang. Their voices lifted far above the raucous noise. "O happy day," some sang in English, "when Jesus saved this soul of mine."

My grandmother knelt and prayed at the pew, her Slovak Bible at her side. Grandma's babushka framed her sweet face, the scarf ready to wipe away her tears.

The dinner bell tolled, and we gathered outside the kitchen. Waiting in line, we found this time rich in fellowship and just as precious as the sermons.

The saints at camp meetings represented Jesus, as they lived out His glory. Together they became like a string of pearls, an adornment of Christ, inspiring my life. When the bell tolls at Jesus's second coming, their souls will gather together to adorn our beautiful Savior.

Like pearls in oysters, some gems are hidden in obscure places. I found mine at an old-fashioned church-camp meeting tucked away in a grove beside a small Ohio town.

—*Kathleen Ruckman*

"God does not love us because we are valuable;
we are valuable because God loves us."
—*Martin Luther*

JESUS, thank You for leaving heaven to purchase me, so I can become a pearl in the family of God. Amen.

> Jesus told them, "This is the only work God wants from you: Believe in the one he has sent." —John 6:29 (NLT)

My husband stood in waist-deep water, calling out to our toddler son: "Jump! I'll catch you." A look of fear spread across our son's face. He could walk away, or he could trust his father. The little boy knew his father was strong enough to catch him, but knowing that didn't seem to calm his anxiety nor push him into the water. The little boy bit his lip.

Finally, belief overcame fear and he jumped. Joy erupted into giggles as he shouted, "Let's do it again."

Two synonyms for "belief" are "faith" and "confidence." The Bible defines faith as being sure of what you cannot see. And so I rely on God. No matter how bad my situation, I am sure He will intervene and replace my misery with His unspeakable joy.

I trust He has good plans for my life. And by believing in Him, I'm also discovering how trustworthy He is. That's when I think, *Let's do it again.*

—*Karen Porter*

"Our belief in God is not blind faith. Belief is having a firm conviction something is true, not hoping it's true."
—*Max Lucado*

 DEAR JESUS, I believe in You. I trust You and have full confidence in Your good plans for my life. Amen.

> But everyone who hears these words of mine and does not put them into practice is like a foolish man who built his house on sand. The rain came down, the streams rose, and the winds blew and beat against that house, and it fell with a great crash. —Matthew 7:26–27 (NIV)

More than five years ago, a specialist officially diagnosed my mom with frontotemporal dementia and Alzheimer's disease. The mom I remember from my childhood was about baking boysenberry pies and dressing flannel boards with paper cutouts of Esther in King Xerxes's palace. Mom's psyche changed drastically with the disease, and so did her interests. Sitting out on the courtyard patio, silent, watching sparrows flit from tree to fountain and from pansies to the perch on the bird feeder, became her favorite pastime.

Huddled beside Mom on a cushioned wicker love seat, I'd hold her hand as we tracked her birds from branch to bloom. Contentment adorned Mom's face. Disease had nearly erased her verbal communication skills, and I wondered whether Jesus was gracing her failing memory with His words: "I am the Way." "I am the Good Shepherd." "Peace be with you."

The path you're walking might be strewn with challenging situations— chronic pain, loneliness, or the loss of a loved one.

Every day I face the choice to hear the words of Jesus and put them into practice, to exercise my faith, trusting Him to meet my every need regardless of the challenges that crowd my path.

—*Mona Hodgson*

"The strength of patience hangs on our capacity to believe that God is up to something good for us in all our delays and detours."
—John Piper

 DEAR JESUS, thank You for speaking words out of a heart I can trust, words I can live by. Amen.

> **Unless you people see signs and wonders, you simply will not believe.
> —John 4:48** (NASB)

Some scriptures make us wonder if Jesus is rolling his eyes and wondering if we'll ever get it together. John 4:48 is one of those Scriptures.

Jesus knows human nature is bent toward seeing great, grand things that blow our minds. The other day I was with my family at the swimming pool, and the lifeguards caught my eye. I was a lifeguard for many years, so I have a weird love for those boys and girls, who sit in the sun for hours and look bored!

During their breaks they were hunched over their phones, and the only time they talked was to share a funny or amazing video from YouTube. "Look at this…" "No—this is even better!" Instead of meaningful conversation or screen-free interaction, they were trying to outdo each other with signs and wonders on the videos.

I've done the same thing in my faith. I pray and long to be amazed with dramatic signs and answers to prayer, skipping right past the reality of the touch of Jesus all around me—loving relationships, the beauty of a lofty tree, the taste of food and smell of coffee, the eyes to see hope when I offer my attention to others. Perhaps we need to redefine what signs and wonders are. They're happening all around us, if we choose to open our eyes.

—Gari Meacham

"God is most glorified in us when we are most satisfied in Him."
—John Piper

 JESUS, open my eyes to mature belief that isn't dependent on miracles. Amen.

> The one who conquers, I will grant him to sit with me on my throne, as I also conquered and sat down with my Father on his throne.
> —Revelation 3:21 (ESV)

I don't have occasion in my daily life to claim a medal on a podium. The closest I've come to the winners' stand, where victory is especially celebrated, is simply running the occasional 5K or 10K race with others who've claimed those prizes.

There was that one time I made third place in my very tiny age class, but for the most part I have never come close to victory—at least not that kind. Like others, I celebrate victories of champions, but there are smaller ones I can certainly cheer. For instance, completing a race that takes a lot out of me is something special. There is a sweet feeling of victory in just making it to the finish line, and maybe even gaining a little ground in my own time. Crossing the finish line with crowds cheering is exhilarating, even from the middle or back of the pack. Because it means I did it. It is complete.

I think this must be the kind of victory Jesus speaks of in Revelation 3:21. We are to run the race, a metaphor used often in Scripture, with an eye on the prize. But we shouldn't focus on where we are in the pack. We can look to the final resting place with the resurrected Jesus, and that is where we can claim the ultimate victory.

—Isabella Yosuico

"Effort, weakness, trust, victory: that's my biography."
—*Jack Hyles*

LORD, like the apostle Paul said, please help me fight the good fight and finish the race while keeping the faith. Amen.

> See that you do not despise one of these little ones. For I tell you that their angels in heaven always see the face of my Father in heaven.
> —Matthew 18:10 (NIV)

On a recent visit to Disneyland, my wife and my oldest granddaughter discovered two costumed characters in an alcove: Alice and the Mad Hatter of *Alice in Wonderland* fame. After a short wait, seven-year-old Mia was greeted by the pair.

"Are you royalty?" the Mad Hatter asked.

Mia was stymied, so my wife answered, "Well, yes. She's a princess."

"Oh!" They bowed extravagantly, without taking their eyes off Mia. "We bow to royalty!"

Mia blushed, but she was delighted. And so were her grandmother and I.

Jesus treated children like royalty. He valued them. He spent time with them. He prioritized them. Reflecting an ancient Jewish belief that every person has a guardian angel, He said children's angels are especially close to the throne of God—not because the angels are special but because children are.

It is easy to overlook, dismiss, or devalue the smallest and youngest among us. But Jesus tells me to do the opposite and reflect the values of heaven—to notice children, value them as He does, spend time with them, prioritize them, learn from them, and reflect more of the qualities that make children "precious in His sight."

—Bob Hostetler

"Children are the hands by which we take hold of heaven."
—Henry Ward Beecher

 JESUS, let me never overlook, dismiss, or devalue any child. Make me always ready to spend time with them, prioritize them, learn from them, and reflect more of the qualities that make them precious in Your sight. Amen.

> You will leave me all alone. Yet I am not alone, for my Father is with me. I have told you these things, so that in me you may have peace. In this world you will have trouble. But take heart! I have overcome the world. —John 16:32–33 (NIV)

I grew up confident of Jesus. I believed Him for the promises of eternal life in the future and purpose in the present. I filled journals with prayers, doubts, and songs about struggling with sin. I faithfully attended summer camps, went on mission trips, and volunteered at food shelters. And somewhere along the way, I felt comfortable—sure, even—that I would not be a deserter. I thought I had been sanctified past the point of serious straying.

Jesus is speaking to the disciples in the Scripture above, after they think they finally understand what He is about. They finally believe He came from God, that He could discern a human heart, and that He knows all things. Yet Jesus says they will desert Him.

So often in my adult life, my heart strays from the conviction I had at thirteen. Though I know Jesus is the way, the truth, and the life, I am shaken by the trouble Jesus foretold. I struggle to make sense of the violence, injustice, and depravity of mankind and my own heart.

But Jesus does not encourage the disciples to rely on their own knowledge or resolve. Instead, He says peace can be found in Him because whatever trouble we meet in the world He has already overcome. Thankfully, the enduring peace of Jesus does not depend on the faithfulness of the follower.

—*Caroline Kolts*

"The awful thing is that beauty is mysterious as well as terrible.
God and the devil are fighting there and the battlefield is the heart of man."
—*Fyodor Dostoyevsky*

JESUS, I deserted You in the face of trouble. Forgive me. Grant me the peace that is only found in You. Help me to believe that You have overcome the world. Amen.

> **And these signs will accompany those who believe: In my name they will drive out demons; they will speak in new tongues. —Mark 16:17** (NIV)

Lord, I can't do this. It's impossible. My husband had left after twenty two and a half years of marriage, making me a single mom of two sons. I earned a freelancer's income, and poor vision prevented me from driving. Thanks to a loving church family, I had plenty of support, but there were some things friends couldn't do.

They couldn't shield me from the overwhelming legal process.

They couldn't give me the wisdom and strength to face bankruptcy and foreclosure.

They couldn't provide a home.

My friends weren't the ones who had to grant child visitation to a man who'd shattered my trust.

Only the Lord could help me battle depression and move forward with my life. And He did.

So when a woman at church told me, "You are a reflection of God's grace," I knew I had Jesus to thank.

In Scripture, Jesus equipped His followers to do impossible, scary, "is this for real?" things. While it's unlikely we'll be called upon to cast out demons, at some point we all face something that feels just as daunting. These are the tests that have the power to solidify our faith and cause others to marvel at His grace.

—*Jeanette Hanscome*

"It is not my ability, but my response to God's ability that counts."
—*Corrie ten Boom*

 WITH YOUR help I have not only survived the impossible but also grown stronger and better through it. Thank You! Amen.

For those who exalt themselves will be humbled, and those who humble themselves will be exalted. —Matthew 23:12 (NIV)

I lay on the couch, watching my kids play. I had just enough energy to fix bottles, change diapers, and maybe prepare lunch before I had to recline on the couch again.

I didn't know what was wrong. For weeks I had lain on the couch, begging God to help me feel better. It was a humbling experience for a perfectionist who was always on the go.

Most of my life I'd spent trying to make myself look good, focusing on my appearance. Sometimes I was more concerned about having the right Bible answer in public than humbly obeying Jesus in private.

Now I was forced to get my insides together. When I got sick, Jesus showed me how misplaced my priorities had been. I'd wasted too much time exalting myself through all the things I could do, rather than asking Jesus to exalt Himself through me. Now I could barely fulfill my duties at home, and I had no choice but to sit humbly and quietly before Him.

Eventually I was diagnosed with a thyroid disorder. But even as my physical health was restored, I continued to ask Jesus to keep my priorities in check. My hope is that whatever I do would be for His glory, not mine.

—*Amelia Rhodes*

"Humility is to make a right estimate of oneself."
—*Charles Spurgeon*

JESUS, forgive me for attempting to exalt myself. I humbly ask that You would exalt Yourself through my life. Amen.

STRENGTH TO ENDURE

> I know your affliction and poverty, yet you are rich. I know the slander of those who say they are Jews and are not, but are a synagogue of Satan.
> —Revelation 2:9 (HCSB)

The worst religious persecution I've endured has been an occasional derogatory comment, a few cold shoulders, and being unfollowed on social media. But anti-Christian sentiment is spreading all over the world. In many countries, loving Jesus means losing a job, a family, even one's life.

None of these events should surprise us. Jesus declared His followers would be hated (John 15:18–20). And yet we Western believers act shocked—even irate. In America, for example, when a judge issues an unfavorable ruling, Christians get up in arms. In the Middle East, when believers are martyred, the surviving saints get down on their knees. Their prayer is not for an end to suffering but for the strength to endure.

Late in life, the Apostle John was exiled to the island of Patmos. While there he was given a breathtaking vision of Jesus and of things to come. As instructed, he recorded what he saw and heard, and sent it to some nearby churches.

One of those congregations, the church at Smyrna, was under fire. Jesus's message to them? I know. I see. Remain faithful. Great reward awaits.

Jesus could say this, because He lived it Himself.

—*Len Woods*

"We are not to retaliate like an unbeliever, nor to sulk like a child,
nor to lick our wounds in self-pity like a dog, nor just to grin and bear
it like a Stoic, still less pretend we enjoy it like a masochist. What then?
We are to rejoice as a Christian should rejoice and even to 'leap for joy.'"
—*John Stott*

JESUS, give strength to my persecuted brothers and sisters. And if I suffer, may it be for the sake of righteousness. Amen.

So you also have sorrow now. But I will see you again. Your hearts will rejoice, and no one will rob you of your joy. —John 16:22 (HCSB)

Confusion. Anxiety. Bewilderment. The disciples were overwhelmed with such feelings upon hearing Jesus would be leaving them soon. Aware the time of crucifixion was close at hand, Jesus knew they'd need assurance since their world would soon seem turned upside down. Such is the sympathy of Christ for His beloved children. Even a few hours of sorrow He desires to eliminate.

These words in the gospel of John also ring in our ears when we're faced with the death of a loved one. Knowing the time of her passing was near, my best friend urged me to remain strong even during those moments of overwhelming grief. Her faith was unwavering. And although she whispered words similar to those Jesus said to His disciples, I knew not to be overwhelmed and confused. Thanks to His birth, crucifixion, and resurrection, I have faith that I will see both my Savior and my best friend again.

We all experience disappointment and disillusionment at some point in our lives. And in those days when we feel as if we cannot find the light at the end of the tunnel, we must hold onto the words of Jesus. With confident faith in the power of the Holy Spirit, we are assured He will not only comfort us in perilous times but also see us through each trial until the day we rejoice with Him!

—*Angie Spady*

"Faith is the process of adapting your behavior, your decisions and,
ultimately, your whole lifestyle so it aligns with what God has asked
you to do—without needing to see the evidence it will all work out in the end."
—*Priscilla Shirer*

JESUS, thank You for blessed assurance. Thank You for loving me so much that You wish to eliminate all my sorrow! Help me turn to You in both times of grief and times of rejoicing. How I love You! Amen.

Jesus replied, "Foxes have dens and birds have nests, but the Son of Man has no place to lay his head." —Luke 9:58 (NIV)

Years ago my boss approached me about doing something that went against my faith. If I agreed, I'd be guaranteed an easier path to promotion. If I disagreed, I could be ridiculed and lose opportunities to advance in my field. Although I knew the right decision, I also knew the potential cost. As much as I wanted my colleagues' approval, I wanted my Savior's approval more. So I refused.

Following Jesus seems to come at a cost. One man discovered this truth when he approached Jesus and told Him, "I will follow you wherever you go" (Luke 9:57). Jesus responded that if he wanted to be His disciple, he could expect the same hardships Jesus Himself endured.

While Jesus might not ask us to give up our homes, He will ask us to give up some things that may be dear to us in order to follow Him completely. His words to the man leave us with these questions: What position does Jesus hold in our lives? Does Jesus ask too much of us by insisting we value Him above anything else the world has to offer?

Jesus knows the cost of following Him, and He doesn't ask anything of us that He hasn't already experienced Himself. With that knowledge, we can find strength to follow Him.

—*Ginger Kolbaba*

"The decision to grow always involves a choice between risk and comfort.
This means that to be a follower of Jesus you must renounce
comfort as the ultimate value of your life."
—*John Ortberg*

JESUS, You understand the hardship that comes from following You. Strengthen me for the privileges and responsibilities that discipleship brings. Amen.

> If you then, though you are evil, know how to give good gifts to your children, how much more will your Father in heaven give the Holy Spirit to those who ask him! —Luke 11:13 (NIV)

A few years ago, I lost sight of the Lord's presence and care. In the middle of several difficult situations, I spent more nights crying than sleeping. My husband was facing a life-threatening medical condition, and our extended families lived several hours away. I often felt overwhelmed by the demands of caring for our young daughter, managing our home, and keeping up with our ministry obligations at church.

During one of those sleepless nights, I read Jesus's words: "How much more will your Father in heaven give the Holy Spirit to those who ask him!" My eyes filled with tears at the reminder I wasn't alone.

The burdens we carry and the weight of our responsibilities can leave us weary, exhausted, and lonely. Jesus offers us a simple promise that He is with us and we never have to rely on our own power.

That night, my eyes swollen from tears, I saw my situation with new hope. Jesus was with me, guiding me and giving me strength to meet each day with His power and wisdom.

As I look back on that season, I recognize the countless ways Jesus held me. I see how He was faithful even when I was too distracted or exhausted to recognize His presence. What a beautiful truth!

—*Teri Lynne Underwood*

"God sometimes washes the eyes of His children with tears in order that they may read aright His providence and His commandments."
—*Theodore L. Cuyler*

JESUS, thank You for Your faithfulness to me, even when I can't see or grasp Your presence. Amen.

> **And besides, what's the use of worrying? What good does it do? Will it add a single day to your life? Of course not! And if worry can't even do such little things as that, what's the use of worrying over bigger things?** —Luke 12:25–26 (TLB)

When my husband lost his job as third-base coach for the New York Yankees, it looked like we would collapse into financial rubble. It had taken years to achieve his dream. He had toiled away in the minor leagues, while I worked full time to make ends meet—so his job with the Yankees looked like the golden ticket. I quit my job and pursued full-time writing, while he relished a year of living out an answer to his sixteen-year prayer to coach in the big leagues.

When circumstances out of our control stripped him of that position, we were left with no jobs, bills mounting, and two kids in college. That's when I noticed my habit of worrying. "We're going to lose the house! We can't pay our bills! Will we ever find good jobs again?" It seemed my new language was worry rather than trust.

One day I sat on the floor and cried as Jesus reminded me that worry doesn't help one bit. He said to ask, seek, and knock—not worry, fret, and fear. Whenever I feel myself slipping into a pattern of worry, I remember that Jesus says worry is a waste of time and energy. Prayer and faith change things. Worry just stirs the pot.

—*Gari Meacham*

"It's not only wrong to worry, it is infidelity, because worrying means that we don't think God can look after the practical details of our lives, and it's never anything else that worries us."
—*Oswald Chambers*

 JESUS, worry is actually a habit of forgetting Who You are and what You promise. Show me my patterns of worry, so I can release them. Amen.

He said to another man, "Follow me." But he replied, "Lord, first let me go and bury my father." —Luke 9:59 (NIV)

I looked at my read-through-the-Bible schedule. I was supposed to be reading Proverbs 4–6 by this point, but the marker in my Bible showed the last chapter I had read was Psalm 107. How could a whole week have slipped by?

I mentally flipped through my to-do lists from the past week. The yard work was done on schedule. My family and I had cleaned out the basement and attic. I'd taught school all week and coordinated the senior banquet without too many blips. My priorities seemed pretty focused and appropriate.

But then I remembered: I had also mindlessly watched baseball games and home-improvement shows well into the evenings after my long teaching days. While it may be understandable that television can act as the cooldown after overpacked and sometimes overheated days, there are other godly priorities on which Jesus expects us to focus.

He shows us that, when we choose to follow Him, we need to rethink our to-do lists. Our lives should look different than the lives of those who do not know Him. Simply proclaiming we are Jesus's followers isn't enough, because following implies movement—actually doing something like reading His Word. We go with Jesus as we arise in the mornings and move throughout our days—no detours, no delays, and no distractions. We fix our eyes on Him and walk in His steps.

—*Janet Holm McHenry*

"When people make changes in their lives like this, it carries greater impact than when they merely make impassioned declarations. The world needs Christians who don't tolerate the complacency of their own lives."
—*Francis Chan*

JESUS, because I want others to see You in me, I will go and do as You lead me. Amen.

> **So do not worry about tomorrow, for tomorrow will bring worries of its own. Today's trouble is enough for today.** —Matthew 6:34 (NRSV)

If there were an Olympic competition for worrying, I'd probably have a gold medal. I've always struggled with worry. Even as a little girl, I'd lie in bed at night and worry about everything from burglars breaking in to who would care for my mother in her old age.

Fast-forward a few decades (OK, more than a few). I'd been married for ten years, and perhaps because I'd married at forty-five, I still felt like a bride. But shortly after our tenth anniversary, my husband became gravely ill. Just a month later, he died. Of all the things I'd worried about, it had never occurred to me to worry about that.

I've given that a lot of thought since his death.

What if I'd spent those ten years worrying Bob would get sick and die rather than enjoying the time I had with him? The outcome wouldn't have changed one bit, but I would have damaged our relationship and squandered much of my marriage by spending my time worrying rather than enjoying my amazing husband. On top of that, I'd have deprived myself of a decade's worth of memories that still make me smile.

I'm pretty sure Jesus was trying to spare us that kind of loss when He said not to worry about tomorrow. Thank You, Jesus.

—*Michelle Rapkin*

"Hold everything in your hands lightly, otherwise it hurts
when God pries your fingers open."
—*Corrie ten Boom*

DEAR JESUS, thank You for wanting me not to worry. You know how oppressive worry is and that it doesn't do me any good. Today please help me to hand over my worries to You. I know You can handle them better than I. Amen.

> Jesus answered, "It is written: 'worship the Lord your God and serve him only.'" —Luke 4:8 (NIV)

A dear woman in our church wore beautiful midi skirts on all occasions. They were of fine quality—wool, linen, and cotton—lasting many years after other ladies' fashions. She carried a cowhide purse and wore leather shoes, and polyester never touched her skin. This discerning saint even chose butter and cream in a dairy-substitute world.

"I like the real thing," she said, when asked about her preference for natural materials. "That's why I love Jesus! He's the real thing."

When the Spirit led Christ into the wilderness, Satan tested Him for forty days and nights. Then he tempted Jesus, displaying all the kingdoms across the earth and offering them to the Lord in return for His worship. But Jesus knew of Satan's deceit. He also understood His own destiny as Savior of the world. Through great suffering and sacrifice, Jesus would conquer all for Himself and for His own. And one day, every knee would bow and every heart confess Him as Lord. He rejected Satan's offer, answering with authority, "Worship the Lord your God and serve him only."

If I have Jesus, I don't need anything more. When tempted to put other things in His place, I must remember—Jesus alone is the real thing.

—*Cathy Elliott*

"My life and my whole eternity belong to God. All this stuff is temporary. Money, fame, success... temporary. Even life is temporary. Jesus... that's eternal."
—*Willie Robertson*

 LORD, help me hear Your voice over the world's loud allure. Let me worship and serve only You. Amen.

> Again the high priest asked him, "Are you the Messiah, the Son of the Blessed One?"
>
> "I am," said Jesus. "And you will see the Son of Man sitting at the right hand of the Mighty One and coming on the clouds of heaven." —Mark 14:61–62 (NIV)

While reading the above passage, I questioned would I have been a follower, a doubter, or a curious onlooker? How might I have answered the question "Who are you?"

The possibilities of a negative response to Jesus shake my faith. I fear my relationship with Him might not have been as strong as I'd like. While some believe the magnificence of hearing and seeing Jesus face to face would have rooted their relationship, I don't know if I'd have felt as secure. I want to give myself the benefit of the doubt...but what if I'd not honored my Lord and Savior?

Most priests and Levites approached Jesus with their own agendas. When they flung questions at Him, their tone seemed to turn arrogant.

I pray I would have been a follower of Jesus. Centuries later some still ridicule and mock us for our faith. Whether the one asking the question is a family member, coworker, or stranger, we seek to respond in a way that glorifies our Lord.

I rely on affirmations about my faith to guide my answers:

I am a child of God. I'm saved by the blood of Jesus Christ.

I'm a follower of Jesus Christ, and that makes me a Christian.

I don't know how God made the world, but I know He did. God is love.

And, I will live in eternity with my Lord and Savior Jesus Christ.

—*DiAnn Mills*

*"Faith isn't the ability to believe long and far into the misty future.
It's simply taking God at His Word and taking the next step."*
—*Joni Eareckson Tada*

 DEAR JESUS, I thank You for loving me so much to die for me. One day You will return to earth for all Your followers, and I'm so excited to see You face to face. I love You, Jesus. Amen.

If you try to hang on to your life, you will lose it. But if you give up your life for my sake, you will save it. —Luke 9:24 (NLT)

"Fly by the seat of my pants" isn't in my vocabulary. Each day, I have a set schedule, and I'm ashamed to admit I ignore phone calls and texts just so I don't have to deal with people. My scheduled tasks won't accomplish themselves.

But one morning a friend I hadn't heard from in months texted me about something I'd posted on social media. My post had ministered to her. I was blessed by that and popped her a little line that I missed her—which was true—and to come by any time—not as true. She replied, "How about today on my lunch?"

Everything I had planned flashed through my mind. I had deadlines to meet and household chores to tend to, and I wanted time to read in the afternoon. Admittedly, one area I excel in is selfishness. The day goes according to my plan. My schedule. My time.

But really it all belongs to Jesus. Each day is one He has made. And if He's Lord of my life, He has the authority to interrupt it at any moment. I might not die a martyr, but I must die to myself daily so Jesus lives through me. That afternoon, God's will was done as I prayed with a hurting friend. And that was worth more than accomplishing any earthly to-do list.

—*Jessica R. Patch*

"Let God have your life; He can do more with it than you can."
—*Dwight L. Moody*

LORD, forgive me for selfishness. My days belong to You. Help me to surrender each moment to Your will. Amen.

For everyone who does wicked things hates the light and does not come to the light, lest his works should be exposed. But whoever does what is true comes to the light, so that it may be clearly seen that his works have been carried out in God. —John 3:20–21 (ESV)

In the dark, my sins seem to look less sinful. Lying to my husband might look like a different version of the story. Desire for lattes and vacations might look like wanting good things. Boasting in my abilities might look like confidence.

I don't like (read: hate) to parade my failures and faults around in the light, because they suddenly look vulgar and I look foolish. I tell myself this: if I can manage to keep my sins hidden in the darkness, I can pretend they might not be sins or, maybe, they never happened at all.

But sins are never actually secrets. Jesus knows my heart. He clearly sees all my wickedness—everything I would like to keep in the shadows or pretend I never thought or felt.

Still, in His mercy, Jesus calls me into the light to claim the truth that I am His. I am rescued from wickedness and restored to live truthfully. In Christ, I am able to be in the light—exposed but not ashamed—and carry out good works.

—*Caroline Kolts*

"If you live in the dark a long time and the sun comes out, you do not cross into it whistling. There's an initial uprush of relief at first, then—for me, anyway—a profound dislocation. My old assumptions about how the world works are buried, yet my new ones aren't yet operational. There's been a death of sorts, but without a few days in hell, no resurrection is possible."
—*Mary Karr*

JESUS, I know my sins won't stay hidden in darkness. Please give me the courage to come into the light and the strength to do what is true. Amen.

> Remain in me, as I also remain in you. No branch can bear fruit by itself; it must remain in the vine. Neither can you bear fruit unless you remain in me. —John 15:4 (NIV)

As a gardener from the Pacific Northwest, I was anxious to garden in my newfound home, Texas. I envisioned giant watermelons, tomatoes aplenty, and a hardy peach tree—all crops that weren't easy to grow in Seattle.

But I stumbled on a big problem in my new garden. I still couldn't seem to grow watermelons. The plant emerged from the ground, followed by the big leaves falling off at the soil level. Later I learned this unfortunate gardening mishap has a name: root rot, a fungus that weakens the plant at its base.

The only solution was to kill the fungus. Otherwise, I'd have to admit garden defeat.

Jesus tells us we must remain rooted in Him. Problems come when we don't fight against spiritual fungus—the distractions of the world, sin that so easily entangles us, bitterness, life hurts, and excessive worry over money. All these threaten to sever us from the life-giving nourishment of Jesus.

If we want to be fruitful in the kingdom of God, we must protect the roots that connect us to Jesus. A plant disconnected from the soil and its nutrients simply withers and dies. It's unable to bear fruit. The solution is to cling to the vine and guard it well. Then, watch for those watermelons!

—*Mary DeMuth*

"The branch of the vine does not worry, and toil, and rush here to seek for sunshine, and there to find rain. No; it rests in union and communion with the vine; and at the right time, and in the right way, is the right fruit found on it. Let us so abide in the Lord Jesus."
—*Hudson Taylor*

 JESUS, help me guard against anything that keeps me from You, so I can be fruitful in Your kingdom. Amen.

And if anyone gives even a cup of cold water to one of these little ones who is my disciple, truly I tell you, that person will certainly not lose their reward.
—Matthew 10:42 (NIV)

I had just crossed the finish line of the half-marathon, and when I reached the table where a volunteer was handing out cups of water, I almost threw my arms around her. Instead, I took the cup she held out, drank it down, and then took two more. Nothing had ever tasted as refreshing as water did just then. It was just a cup of water, but it was exactly what I needed.

Sometimes, a cup of water is not just a cup of water. Sometimes, it's a symbol of something more. In the passage above, Jesus warns His disciples that if they are serious about following Him, things are going to be difficult. They're going to have to love Him more than they do their own families. They're going to find themselves unwelcome in many villages. But He promises that anyone who gives them even the smallest thing—a cup of water—will be blessed.

Remember, Jesus and His disciples were walking around in a desert. Water was necessary, and it didn't come from just turning on the tap. A cup of water in those days was the result of a whole lot of effort. But, Jesus says, anyone who welcomed them with a drink was doing God's work.

I might not be able to support my church the way I wish I could. I don't have money to give to all the worthy charities out there. But I can welcome into my life and home those who serve God. Jesus told us to look out for one another, to care for others. What a refreshing piece of advice.

—*Elizabeth Adams*

"No one is useless in this world who lightens the burdens of another."
—*Charles Dickens*

 LORD, please help me to see the needs of those around me and meet them. Amen.

> And Jesus came and said to them, "All authority in heaven and on earth has been given to me." —Matthew 28:18 (ESV)

Having had parents whose loving care was undermined by alcoholism and mental illness, I confess a deep wariness of those in authority—a wariness I only came to fully recognize later in life.

This guardedness really amounts to a simple lack of trust. It's a feeling that those in authority over me—teachers, employers, politicians, and members of assorted institutions—are not trustworthy in one way or another.

Let's face it, though—human authorities are indeed fallible, sometimes self-interested, even abusive. We all have true tales about how authorities have failed us.

But not Jesus. He is the only completely trustworthy authority we will ever know. And better still, He is all-powerful, all-loving, and perfectly just.

Do I truly trust Him enough to recognize and surrender to His perfect authority in my life?

—Isabella Yosuico

"Until the will and the affections are brought under the authority of Christ,
we have not begun to understand, let alone to accept, His lordship."
—Elisabeth Elliot

LORD JESUS, You are the sovereign authority of the universe, even when I hold tight to my rights. Please help me trust You as the loving authority over my entire life. Amen.

> But when you pray, go into your room, close the door and pray to your Father, who is unseen. Then your Father, who sees what is done in secret, will reward you. —Matthew 6:6 (NIV)

When we lived in France, I battled loneliness. I was thousands of miles away from close friends and family, and I felt invisible. Instead of processing my pain by talking with others, I poured out my feelings onto the pages of my journal and shared them with Jesus.

Jesus knew my pain and bewilderment. He took note of my struggles with the language barrier, my inability to understand the culture, and my overworked schedule.

Jesus met me between the pages of my written prayers. Slowly, I began to realize that affirmation for a job well done didn't have to come from other people. In some ways, serving quietly, diligently, and without fanfare became a secret delight to me—something to cherish between Jesus and me.

A decade later, I look back on my journal and smile. Why? Because He not only answered every prayer in surprising ways but also grew me up. My reward for all that wrangling was long-lasting spiritual growth in Him.

Your prayer closet might not be a room or special chair or specific place. It could be the confines of your car on a frustrating commute. Or, as with me, it might be a well-worn journal in which you pour out your heart to Jesus. No matter. The point is that we are invited to let out our concerns through prayer. Jesus knows us. He notices us. And He rewards us.

—*Mary DeMuth*

"Prayer does not fit us for the greater work. Prayer is the greater work."
—*Oswald Chambers*

 JESUS, help me find time every day to share my worries with You. Thank You ahead of time for blessing me. Amen.

Jesus answered [Satan], "It is also written: 'do not put the Lord your God to the test.'" —Matthew 4:7 (NIV)

Whenever difficulty comes, my inclination is to pray, "God, get me out of this!" That was the case when I struggled with a toxic coworker. I wanted Him to make the problem disappear. After all, Scripture says He will fight and care for us. Because He didn't handle it quickly, though, I was tempted to doubt His promises.

How often we are tempted to think that way! We want God to provide an easy escape, so we test Him—we demand that He prove His promises.

That's what Satan tempted Jesus to do. He told Jesus to throw Himself off the highest point of the temple and God would save Him (a promise from Psalm 91:11–12). Everyone would see that Jesus was the Messiah, and He could avoid the hardships to come.

Jesus responded that we should not test God—for when we do, we show our lack of trust. Jesus's trust in God the Father was so complete He didn't need to demand proof.

Satan presented to Jesus a basic life question we all must face: do I trust God?

God has a plan for us—one that will consist of struggles. For me, it was learning to respond with grace to a difficult coworker. For Jesus, it included the cross. But just as Jesus did, we can trust God the Father and His plan for us, even when we don't see the reward from where we stand now.

—Ginger Kolbaba

*"I have learned that faith means trusting in advance
what will only make sense in reverse."*
—Philip Yancey

JESUS, help me remember God's promises when I want an easy out. Give me peace that comes by trusting You. Amen.

My Faithful Follower,

When you encounter a storm in life, it might feel like I'm asleep or I don't care what happens to you. But nothing could be further from the truth. Just as I was on the boat that night with My disciples, I am always aware. I care more than you can imagine. I promise I will never fail you. Nothing escapes My notice. I am intimately acquainted with every detail of your life.

"Fear not" is the most oft-repeated phrase in the Bible. That's because I want you to take that command to heart. When your feelings lead you to fear, hold fast to the truth I have told you. I love you, and My perfect love casts out fear. I am with you. I will strengthen and uphold you. I will not allow you to fall. Nothing—not even the worst storm—can separate us. I am your Protector, your Provider, your Prince of Peace.

Trust Me. I see the big picture, the beginning and the end, and I will do what is best. I alone have the power to speak peace into the storm. And in My perfect timing, My perfect way, I will calm the storm. The wind and waves obey My voice. I am in control. I am in the boat with you—I never leave you alone—and you can count on Me to see you through.

I love you forever.

He rebuked the wind and said to the waves, "Silence! Be still!" Suddenly the wind stopped, and there was a great calm. "Who is this man?" they asked each other. "Even the wind and waves obey Him!" —Mark 4:39, 41 (NLT)

> For everyone who asks, receives. Everyone who seeks, finds. And to everyone who knocks, the door will be opened. —Matthew 7:8 (NLT)

Have you prayed about it?"

My friend sat still, waiting for me to say something. Then I shook my head just enough for her to see that I had failed at that, too. My shoulders slumped as I tried to sigh out some of the grief weight. Praying seemed like spiritual resignation to the pain God had allowed in our lives.

I was beaten down by sadness, anger, and doubt. Though my brother's death was reaching dreadful milestones of six months, one year, and two years, there was no progress to my grief. I wanted to slow every day, week, and month that passed, because it drew me further away from the last time he was my brother on earth.

I stopped believing God listened to my petitions, cared about what I sought, or was capable of opening doors when I knocked. I felt helpless because, if I could rewind everything, I would just ask for my brother to stay alive.

As the grief weight grew too much to bear, Jesus reminded me that God wanted my prayers, no matter how desperate or disordered, because He has promised to withhold no good thing from me. Matthew 7:8 is the prayer of someone who is so convinced of the Giver's goodness that he or she would petition in every possible way.

Jesus gave me the only prayer I could possibly muster in the middle of my grief and assured me my prayer would be heard.

—*Caroline Kolts*

"There is nothing that moves a loving father's soul quite like his child's cry."
—*Joni Eareckson Tada*

 JESUS, thank You for hearing my desperate prayers. Help me to be persistent in my conversation with You and in belief that You desire to give good gifts. Amen.

> "Where is your faith?" he asked his disciples. In fear and amazement they asked one another, "Who is this? He commands even the winds and the water, and they obey him." —Luke 8:25 (NIV)

After teaching much of the day, Jesus and His disciples climbed into a boat and sailed to the other side of the lake. Jesus fell asleep. A squall came down on the lake, swamping the boat. In a panic, the disciples woke Jesus, saying, "Master, Master, we're going to drown!"

Jesus rebuked the wind and raging waters. The storm subsided. All was calm.

Until my road trip into Phoenix one particular day, I would have said being paralyzed by fear wasn't an issue for me. The electronic message on the signboard overhead prompted me to lift my foot from the gas pedal. I'd heard the news reports about the freeway shooter. As I drove one of those freeways and read the warning about the driver taking random shots into passing cars, the threat became personal.

My shoulders tensed. *Is he on this freeway?* My palms got sweaty. *Is he in one of the cars in the lane beside me? Behind me?* My chest cramped. *Dare I even look around? Should I speed up? Slow down? Take an off-ramp? Go home?*

When fright threatens to topple my faith, like Jesus's disciples I can choose fear or faith. That day on the freeway, I chose to lean into my faith in Jesus and let Him dispel my fear.

—*Mona Hodgson*

"There is no pit so deep, that God's love is not deeper still."
—*Corrie ten Boom*

 JESUS, You are my hope, my strong tower. I can rebuke fear and trust You in any and all circumstances, with confidence. Thank You! Amen.

> Do not store up for yourselves treasures on earth, where moths and vermin destroy, and where thieves break in and steal. But store up for yourselves treasures in heaven, where moths and vermin do not destroy, and where thieves do not break in and steal. For where your treasure is, there your heart will be also. —Matthew 6:19-21 (NIV)

In the early nineties, I lost my job at a time when my wife and I had a newborn son. For months I prayed for a way to support them. One night, stressed and desperate, I went for a walk alone and poured out my heart in prayer to God. I told Him the date I needed work, after which we might have had to surrender our home. A few weeks later, Jesus met my deadline. I found a job at a local bank, and that led to a better job and then to a real opportunity.

Now our son has grown into a man, and my wife and I are still in the home that was saved by His grace so long ago. The Lord has provided for us through it all and blessed us abundantly. But nothing we've accumulated here is lasting. All our possessions pale in comparison to the presence of Jesus, Whose treasures are eternal.

I've come to recognize my identity is not measured by any material thing or in any position, status, or accomplishment, but only in belonging to Jesus. The identity I have in Him—and the work I do out of my love for Him—is my only lasting legacy. True treasure exists in heaven, with Jesus, and it is there that I will get my eternal reward.

—*Michael Berrier*

"Yes, in all material things we dare to be utterly independent of men, because we dare to believe utterly in God. We have cast away all other hope, because we have unbounded hope in Him."
—*Watchman Nee*

LORD JESUS, all You've given me I hold out with open hands for Your use to produce heavenly treasures that are lasting. Amen.

A SOLID FOUNDATION

The rain came down, the streams rose, and the winds blew and beat against that house; yet it did not fall, because it had its foundation on the rock. —Matthew 7:25 (NIV)

A few years ago, my husband and I visited Yosemite National Park and camped in Yosemite Valley. I stared in awe at the majestic granite cliffs, mountains, and waterfalls surrounding our campsite. While gazing at those natural wonders, I considered how many thousands of years those rock formations had stood. It's obvious neither rain nor wind has been able to move them.

In Matthew 7, Jesus mentions a house battered by rain, wind, and floods. Have you ever felt like that house? I certainly have. During my single years, I felt hopeless and lonely after a relationship ended. My dreams were crushed. I remember saying, "This isn't how I planned my life to turn out!" In spite of our best plans, life won't always be sunny and peaceful.

At times, it seems all the storms of life come rushing in at once. The metaphorical rains and winds come and beat against us.

These unplanned events can shake our faith and make us question whether our heavenly Father has forgotten about us. When the storms come, how can we cling to our faith in Jesus?

He is our Rock, and He is stronger than any majestic mountain range. We might not understand our circumstances, but we know our foundation is solid if we put our trust in Jesus. He is unmovable and unwavering. We can trust Him.

—*Allison K. Flexer*

"The secret is Christ in me, not me in a different set of circumstances."
—*Elisabeth Elliot*

 JESUS, You are our Rock. Carry us through the storms of life. Even in tough circumstances, we want to build our faith on Your solid foundation. Amen.

> **But first he must suffer many things and be rejected by this generation.**
> **—Luke 17:25 (NIV)**

"Please get out of bed, Betsy."

"I can't, Mom. My life is over. I've been rejected in every way."

Lord, you haven't rejected my child. Help her see the future You have for her.

My daughter, a college graduate, had applied for hundreds of jobs to no avail. Her last hope was a minimum-wage job at a local retail giant. She never got an interview. Then, a breakup pushed her over the edge.

"Sometimes rejection leads to better things," I offered as she sobbed.

Betsy finally got out of bed and discovered a master's program that paid tuition.

Another breakup on the heels of earning her master's degree handed her another rejection. Moving forward, she was granted entry into a Ph.D. program with a teaching assistantship at one of the country's best colleges.

"Everything has led me here, Mom," she recently said. "Jesus will bring the right person at the right time. And if I hadn't faced those rejections, I might not have looked to the better things God had for me."

Sometimes rejection seems like the end of the world. Jesus's suffering on the cross was the greatest rejection known to mankind. But through His sacrifice, we gained new, everlasting life. Sometimes rejection is not an end but a gateway to new beginnings.

—*Holly Michael*

> *"Through salvation our past has been forgiven,*
> *our present is given meaning, and our future is secured."*
> —*Rick Warren*

 JESUS, grant us courage to pick ourselves up after rejection to look forward to the perfect plan You have for us. Amen.

**Blessed are the peacemakers, for they will be called children of God.
—Matthew 5:9** (NIV)

I grew up surrounded by peaceful Amish neighbors. These passive people overlooked every offense. I struggled with Jesus's words about peacemaking, because looking calm on the outside when battling frustration on the inside made me feel hypocritical. Could routinely turning the other cheek really be His definition of peacemaking?

Then a friend shared an explanation of Matthew 5:9 that transformed my thinking. He said, "Jesus does not want you to lie down and be a doormat—nor sweep sin under the carpet." He went on to clarify that being a peacemaker can sometimes mean getting an issue out in the open, confronting it with truth, and helping bring about resolution.

I mulled over the thought that an actual peacemaker may be someone who can make others uncomfortable until a problem is settled. That sounded a lot like Jesus.

While He was here on earth, Jesus made people squirm. He asked hard questions. He got to the heart of the matter. And He brought peace to those in the world who were ready for it.

—*Nancy Sebastian Kuch*

"So we pray and we take whatever practical initiatives we can to make peace beginning with something as simple as a greeting. But we do not always succeed. And I want to make sure you don't equate peacemaking with peace-achieving. A peacemaker longs for peace, and works for peace, and sacrifices for peace. But the attainment of peace may not come."
—*John Piper*

JESUS, help me follow Your example of true peacemaking. Give me the insight and courage to wisely and lovingly confront others and open the door to Your blessed peace. Amen.

> Your eye is the lamp of your body. When your eye is healthy, your whole body is full of light. But when your eye is bad, your whole body is full of darkness. Therefore, see to it that the light in you isn't darkness. —Luke 11:34–35 (CEB)

I scrambled down the stairs, racing to catch the subway train. The doors opened, and I stepped on. I sat down, took out my book, and started reading.

Something was terribly wrong. The words on the page looked so dim. Had they lowered the lights on this subway train? Was there something wrong with the electricity? Had I picked a dark corner to sit in?

I looked around. No one else seemed to notice. Maybe my eyes were going seriously bad. I'd been putting off going to the eye doctor. Perhaps it was too late. What I needed was more than a change in prescription. I probably had the beginnings of some dreadful eye disease.

I took off my glasses to rub my eyes. Suddenly the lights went back up. Everything seemed bathed in the usual fluorescent glow. Nothing was wrong. Then I glanced down and saw the problem in my lap: my prescription sunglasses.

Everything is perception, isn't it? Cling to the wrong pair of glasses or the wrong attitude, and things can go completely awry. Let it all go, and things look sunnier, don't they?

—*Rick Hamlin*

"If the doors of perception were cleansed everything would appear to man as it is, Infinite. For man has closed himself up, till he sees all things thro' narrow chinks of his cavern."
—*William Blake*

LET ME see the world, Jesus, with the eyes of faith and hope and love, and not shrouded by my own worldly fears. Amen.

> Whoever comes to Me, and hears My sayings and does them, I will show you whom he is like: He is like a man building a house, who dug deep and laid the foundation on the rock. And when the flood arose, the stream beat vehemently against that house, and could not shake it, for it was founded on the rock.
> —Luke 6:47–48 (NKJV)

About five years ago, my husband, Tom, took me on a hike I will never forget. The trek led to Carpenter Mountain, a high peak in the low-lying Western Cascades of Oregon.

The trail, bordered by wildflowers and lush trees, wove through steep, rocky terrain. The deep greens kept us in an alcove of coolness and serenity. Then, all of a sudden, as we turned a corner, we beheld a spectacular surprise.

Jutting straight to the sky, the vertical columns in the basaltic rock emphasized the splendor of this towering mountain. King David's words in Psalm 61 immediately came to mind: "Lead me to the rock that is higher than I."

Tom took my hand and pulled me up the last six hundred feet to the top of the steep volcanic pinnacle. A fire-lookout structure covered much of the summit at 5,353 feet, giving way to dramatic views of snowcapped peaks in the High Cascades.

I now ponder the symbolism at Carpenter Mountain. When my life is built on the solid rock of Christ, He helps me see dangers from the lookout tower and anchors me in the storms. I see through an eternal lens, and I am secure.

—Kathleen Ruckman

"The loftier the building, the deeper must the foundation be laid."
—Thomas à Kempis

 JESUS, thank You for being my Rock and high tower grounded in Your everlasting love. Amen.

> Then he said to the disciples, "Anyone who accepts your message is also accepting me. And anyone who rejects you is rejecting me. And anyone who rejects me is rejecting God, who sent me." —Luke 10:16 (NLT)

The coach in the movie *Facing the Giants* has a quote that's stuck with me: "And if we win, we praise Him; and if we lose, we praise Him. Either way, we honor Him with our actions and our attitudes." The coach wanted the football team to focus on God, not on winning or losing. I try to apply that philosophy to my everyday life.

When I talk about Jesus, not everyone loves what I say. Some reject, mock, and even hate me. Rejection and resistance were often the reactions in Jesus's day, too. Indifference to religion is prevalent. Some people have quit believing in God and stopped paying attention to the gospel.

Jesus said to tell the good news about Him and not to measure the results. We tend to keep score, but approval isn't a valid measuring stick. True success comes from obeying His, command to go and tell. Acceptance is up to Him. Jesus reminds me not to take the rejection personally. When someone refuses to hear the good news of Jesus Christ, that person is not rejecting me—he or she is rejecting Christ.

Jesus loves for us to obey even if we don't know the outcome. We need not worry about the responses of others. Honoring Jesus is about pleasing Him. And that's an action I can accept.

—*Karen Porter*

"One act of obedience is better than one hundred sermons."
—*Dietrich Bonhoeffer*

 DEAR JESUS, You are responsible for results. My job is obedience. I will trust You, and I will follow You. Amen.

> Jesus said, "I tell you, Peter, the rooster will not crow this day, until you deny three times that you know me." —Luke 22:34 (ESV)

"*Jee-zus*," I hear at least once a day. "Christ!" is often yelled at my place of employment. I used to ignore it. But Jesus's words to Peter penetrated my heart. If I didn't identify with Him in public, how dare I worship Him in private?

So, with full conviction and confidence, I began addressing these offhand comments with a few of my own. "*Jee-zus*," I would hear, and then respond with an alert "Where do you see Him?" To the blasphemous use of "Christ!", I responded, "Yes, He is the Christ. Thanks for that proclamation." And to the reflexive "Oh my God," I quipped, "Is He your God, too?"

I was God's number-one, self-appointed public defender. Or so I thought.

I had a lot to say in defense of Jesus, but like Peter I was inconsistent.

Years ago I was sitting at a town fair, where an underaged man who'd had a few too many drinks started causing a scene. Two of his classmates sitting nearby ridiculed him. Little did they know the younger brother of the drunkard was sitting an arm's length away: me.

Regret, shame, and guilt covered me like a tent. How could I stand up for the name of Jesus but then deny my own brother? I had become like Peter.

Like the disciple, I've been granted grace and another chance to get it right. So now, before I put on my public defender's robe I know my duty is to do as He instructed in John chapter 21: "Feed my sheep."

—*Erik Person*

"For eighty-six years have I served Jesus Christ and He has never abandoned me. How could I now curse my blessed King and Savior?"
—*Polycarp*

DEAR JESUS, in my passion to serve You, let me not become Your public defender at the expense of excluding the sheep within the fold. Amen.

> I give them eternal life, and they shall never perish; no one will snatch them out of my hand. My Father, who has given them to me, is greater than all; no one can snatch them out of my Father's hand. I and the Father are one.
> —John 10:28–30 (NIV)

Jesus spoke these words to Jews waiting for deliverance from their Roman oppressors and hoping Jesus was their liberator. Jesus indeed freed them spiritually, but His followers remained subject to the Romans. Freedom in Christ was never intended as the practical remedy for all that ails us every day.

Ultimate deliverance—from our trials, defects, and bondage of all kinds—is so often more spiritual and eternal than practical and immediate. The latter, for some, is the expectation. But that's not my experience.

I wish I could tell you life has gotten easier since I became a Christian. I wish I could tell you I am a much better person than before. But I can't.

Since I've given my life to Christ, I've faced some difficult challenges. The death of my mother, the birth of a child with special needs, and a failed career are just a few trials I've endured.

But I can tell you with inexplicable hope that my perspective has changed, and I'm being transformed from the inside out. I can tell you I have been able to bear all things with an abundance of joy, an ever-deepening faith, and a peace that surpasses understanding. Finally, I can tell you I know that a new freedom rests in eternity.

—*Isabella Yosuico*

"Where does your security lie? Is God your refuge, your hiding place, your stronghold, your shepherd, your counselor, your friend, your redeemer, your savior, your guide? If He is, you don't need to search any further for security."
—*Elisabeth Elliot*

JESUS, please help me to know that my security, now and forever, rests solely in You. Amen.

> I have other sheep that are not of this sheep pen. I must bring them also. They too will listen to my voice, and there shall be one flock and one shepherd. —John 10:16 (NIV)

When my friend first led me to Christ, my interest was insatiable. Like a person falling in love, I thought about Jesus all the time and wanted to know everything about Him. Christ's love for me, so deep and unconditional, healed wounds I'd nursed since childhood. His words calmed my anxious soul, and His righteousness guided me to a better way to live.

While I was still early in my faith, my friend invited me to a Bible study she attended, and I was thrilled to accept. The nondenominational study was large, its branches spread worldwide. Members as varied as flowers in a garden showed mutual respect by keeping differences to ourselves. What mattered more was what we shared in common—Jesus Christ.

Years later, I still attend, not because of the kaleidoscope of individuals with whom I've made friends or because of the interesting lessons. Though compelling, they aren't the magnet pulling me in. The voice of the One calling keeps me coming back, the One uniting Christians everywhere—our Lord Jesus.

My love for Jesus has mellowed since those early days, the way a happy marriage grows softer and sweeter over the years. I know Him better now, just as He's always known me. I understand His faithfulness, power, and mercy. He is my Shepherd, showing me the way now and forever.

—Heidi Gaul

"Amid the thousands of shrill voices screaming for our attention, there is but one voice we need to hear. The voice of the Lord Jesus Christ."
—David Jeremiah

JESUS, I'm grateful to be part of Your flock. Shepherd me in the direction You would have me go. Amen.

**Then he asked them, "Why are you afraid? Do you still have no faith?"
—Mark 4:40 (NLT)**

When my boys were little, they battled the scary fantasy of monsters under their beds. My wife, meanwhile, has been a long-term sucker for far-fetched health crises. She contracted—and survived—every disease known to man, until I finally banned her from WebMD.

I'm no stranger to fear. As a self-employed writer in an uncertain economy, I confess I'm never far from the temptation to cave in to the fear of poverty. *Will God provide? Will He bring enough work my way for me to support my family?*

This is why I love the story of Jesus with His disciples in the boat. "Let's cross over to the other side of the sea," He told them. He did not say, "How about we embark on one final boat ride to Davy Jones's locker?" If only the disciples had taken Christ's words to heart...and taken comfort in His presence...and taken their cues from Him (i.e., as the storm kicked up, Jesus snoozed peacefully in the back of the boat).

Whenever I start to panic at the storm of bills piling up on our kitchen counter, it's helpful to reread the two great questions of Jesus in the verse above. Better than that, it's reassuring to realize He's with me and whispering the questions to me!

—*Len Woods*

"If the Lord be with us, we have no cause of fear. His eye is upon us. His arm over us,
His ear open to our prayer—His grace sufficient, His promise unchangeable."
—*John Newton*

JESUS, I praise You that You are Lord over every storm of life—and with me through them all. Amen.

ONE BAD DAY

**You are already clean because of the word I have spoken to you.
—John 15:3 (NIV)**

I was barely holding it together. During what felt like the longest day, the mechanic had found more expensive car problems, the orthodontist said one kid needed thousands of dollars of work done, and my husband's job took an uncertain turn.

That night, I began to return to my old habits of fear, anxiety, and anger. My anger turned toward God. We had been trying to be obedient in our finances, and this was the result? I felt myself slipping into darkness and despair.

I was studying John 15 at the time, and Jesus stopped me amid my mental tirade to remind me, "You are already clean because of My words." Peace washed over me. I realized that as I abide in Jesus and His words, He empowers me to turn away from the darkness trying to overwhelm me. I shifted my focus to Him and Scripture, and away from our financial challenges.

Our actions often follow our thoughts (see Proverbs 23:7). As we dwell on His teachings and live by them in the midst of every stress, He changes our thoughts and then our actions.

Every time old patterns of thinking and sinful habits try to overrun my mind, I remember that through Jesus I'm already clean because I abide in Him.

—Amelia Rhodes

"Purge me from every sinful blot;
My idols all be cast aside:
Cleanse me from every evil thought,
From all the filth of self and pride."
—John Wesley

 JESUS, thank You for making me clean through Your teaching. Keep my mind steady on You today. Amen.

> "You unbelieving and perverse generation," Jesus replied, "how long shall I stay with you and put up with you? Bring your son here." —Luke 9:41 (NIV)

One week I used an entire pen's worth of ink for my prayer journal, as I pleaded for God to respond to an unanswered request. It felt as if I'd been rejected and forgotten. Later, I wanted to tear those embarrassing pages out. No wonder I'd once labeled a box of old journals "Burn these when I die" (code for "Read me"). God fulfilled my desire, but the level of whining involved would've gotten my thirteen-year-old sent to his room. I didn't tear out the pages; I kept them as evidence of my failure to trust even after seeing Him provide, open doors, and work miracles in my life.

Lord, it's a wonder You still put up with me.

When I read Luke 9:41, it reminds me that Jesus got frustrated with His own followers. In their midst was the Son of God performing signs and wonders daily, and still they doubted. And what did He do? He healed anyway. He continued to perform miracle after miracle, just as He answers my whiny prayers.

I wonder if He really does get frustrated with us, or if He understands that our doubts and begging are part of our human imperfection. Either way, He cares enough to see our needs and answer our prayers.

—*Jeanette Hanscome*

"Is not the gospel its own sign and wonder?"
—*Charles Spurgeon*

LORD, forgive my unbelief after so much faithfulness. Help me to trust You whether I get what I want or not. Amen.

> "Abba, Father," he said, "everything is possible for you. Take this cup from me. Yet not what I will, but what you will." —Mark 14:36 (NIV)

"All rise," the bailiff intoned.

I rose to my feet as the judge and jury solemnly filed into the courtroom. I waited until they were seated to take my seat.

But sitting didn't help. My stomach roiled as I broke into a cold sweat. My first jury trial as a young lawyer, and if the judge asked me to make my opening statement, I couldn't. What would I say? That I needed a recess because I was so nervous I was about to throw up?

But the judge didn't turn to me. Instead, he thanked the jury for their service and reminded them of the importance of what they were about to do. He pointed out the parties and told the jury they would soon hear from the lawyers. He reminded the jury that although the lawyers would represent their clients to the best of their ability, they—the jury—would make the ultimate decision.

To the best of their ability. I focused on those six simple words. I'd spent years preparing for this moment, and months on this particular case. I'd worked diligently and left no stone unturned. My client was counting on me. There was no way I could let him down.

I lifted my eyes heavenward. *Give me strength, Lord,* I prayed. *Your will, not mine.*

The judge chose that moment to nod at me. Like warm summer rain, resolve flowed into me, and I confidently stood and delivered my opening statement.

—J. Mason Williams

"I do the very best I know how, the very best I can, and
I mean to keep on doing so until the end."
—Abraham Lincoln

 JESUS, please help me to always serve You to the best of my ability and to know that is all You will ever ask of me. Amen.

> Take my yoke upon you and learn from me, for I am gentle and humble in heart, and you will find rest for your souls. For my yoke is easy and my burden is light. —Matthew 11:29–30 (NIV)

As a child, I could never figure out how the yellow part of an egg, even if it belonged to Jesus, could help me. Eventually I learned Jesus was speaking of an animal yoke, not an egg yolk. A yoke is a wooden double collar that fastens over the necks of two beasts of burden. Once I learned that, this became one of my favorite scriptures.

If we're supposed to take Jesus's yoke, that means He'll be right beside us all the time, wherever we go. And if I read this scripture correctly, He does the heavy lifting. Our job is simply to stay with Him. If we do that, He promises, we will find rest for our souls. For His yoke is easy, His burden light.

Nobody I know exemplifies this idea of shouldering another's burdens better than Pastor Ronald Lefranc in Haiti. He pastors a large church, runs an orphanage, and mentors forty-nine congregations in remote Haitian villages. There doesn't seem to be a moment when he isn't being asked to handle a problem. And Haitian problems are big, often matters of life and death. But Pastor Ronald is always serene. Once, I asked him how he handles all that stress. He gently told me, "Jesus is handling the stress. I'm just walking beside Him."

—*Michelle Rapkin*

"The will of God will not take us where the grace of God cannot sustain us."
—*Billy Graham*

DEAR JESUS, thank You for taking the heavy part of the burden. Please help me to remember that all I need to do to find comfort and relief is to walk beside You. Amen.

"Why are you troubled?" He asked them. "And why do doubts arise in your hearts?" —Luke 24:38 (HCSB)

Aside from going to the dentist, the least favorite thing I do is board a plane. The older I get, the less I enjoy it. Whether it's waiting at the gate, squeezing into my seat (usually in the back near the bathroom), or the gut-wrenching dread of takeoff, I simply don't enjoy it like I used to. I always second-guess the entire experience, asking myself, *What if?*

After the resurrection, Jesus asked why the disciples were filled with so much doubt. Skeptical that He had risen, they looked upon their Savior in total confusion. Jesus had to go so far as to show them the holes in His hands and feet.

It was clearly a lesson in faith.

When I fly I need to remain calm. The flight attendants have gone over every scenario before takeoff, and I need to trust the people in the cockpit. They wouldn't be flying a commercial jet if they didn't have years of experience. Quite simply, I need to trust the pilots.

Just like the disciples did, we need to trust Him. Jesus assures us through His actions and words that we are always safe and secure in the hands of the Father. But we first must believe, and then He will cast away all doubt. If we remain calm and trust in our Savior, our doubts will simply be cast away into the wind.

—*Angie Spady*

"Peace is like that elusive butterfly. Even Christians chase after it and find it just out of reach. Perhaps the rarest of all virtues, real peace comes only when you decide to take God at His word."
—*Chuck Swindoll*

JESUS, thank You for assuring me of Your love. Help me to remember the countless examples of proof that I am safe and secure in Your loving arms. Amen.

> Jesus replied, "Truly I tell you, if you have faith and do not doubt, not only can you do what was done to the fig tree, but also you can say to this mountain, 'Go, throw yourself into the sea,' and it will be done." —Matthew 21:21 (NIV)

Jesus makes what might seem a pretty impossible promise in Matthew 21. His disciples have just seen Him wither a fig tree because it did not bear fruit. Jesus tells them that if they have enough faith, they will be able to do that and more. They will be able tell the mountain to fall into the sea and it will happen.

It's a nice thought, but I sometimes wonder if the disciples ever actually tried it. I know I have. I once stood on the beach, waves pounding away at the shore, and looked up at the craggy cliffs over the Pacific Ocean and commanded them to fall into the sea. It didn't happen.

Did this mean I didn't have enough faith? Maybe.

But maybe not. After all, each wave that pounded against those cliffs was breaking the rocks down bit by bit, depositing tiny pieces of newly formed sand along the shore. I couldn't see it, but that didn't mean it wasn't happening.

In this passage, I don't think Jesus is saying these people don't have enough faith.

What if this passage is less about believing I can literally move a mountain and more about teaching me to believe enough to ask for impossible things? Maybe it's less about having enough faith to do the impossible, and more about learning to have the kind of faith that believes anything truly can happen.

—Elizabeth Adams

"All I have seen teaches me to trust the Creator for all I have not seen."
—*Ralph Waldo Emerson*

 LORD, help me to have the kind of faith that can move mountains and to still believe even when things don't go the way I expect. Amen.

Therefore, whoever takes the lowly position of this child is the greatest in the kingdom of heaven. —Matthew 18:4 (NIV)

It had been a tough month. Three of our home's big-ticket items had broken down. I tried to focus on the bright side—owning new appliances—but a moment later, my stomach muscles tightened: new debt on top of our usual bills.

Finances always challenged our family. I'd learned to juggle my time and money, but I couldn't make either just appear. Anticipating the high cost of replacing the machines, I dreaded checking our bank account. After calling the bank, I learned my fears were well-founded. The balance had dropped below zero. If I couldn't deposit enough in three hours, there would be added fees.

Transferring my savings and gathering the cash from our wallets wasn't enough. I eyed the piggy bank, emptied it, then counted. Still in the red.

I fought tears as my husband and I talked together, our voices low. We prayed to Jesus, admitting our helplessness, pledging our trust in Him.

He'd guided us through every tight spot in the past. He wouldn't abandon us now. Depending on Him was the best choice—the only choice—we had. After we prayed, hope overtook the space in our hearts once occupied by panic.

Combing through the closet and drawers for old wallets and change purses, we discovered more than enough to cover our financial needs. The Lord not only had filled our pockets but He'd also replenished our faith.

—*Heidi Gaul*

"Which would you prefer? To be king of the mountain for a day?
Or to be a child of God for eternity?"
—*Max Lucado*

 JESUS, I depend on and trust You for all my needs. Thank You for Your loving care. Amen.

I have brought you glory on earth by finishing the work you gave me to do. And now, Father, glorify me in your presence with the glory I had with you before the world began. —John 17:4–5 (NIV)

Sending our children off to college was an exciting, joyful, and painful experience for my wife and me. Our daughter attended a college just ten minutes away, but our son chose a school nearly a thousand miles from our home.

Though they began their collegiate studies in different years, their graduations were only five months apart. We were so proud and happy—for them and for us. They had finished what they had set out to do. They had excelled. They had made us proud.

I hope some day my heavenly Father will think and feel that way about the work He has given me to do. I want to be able to say, in the words of Jesus, as recorded in John's gospel, "I have brought you glory on earth." I want to be able to say, "I have finished the work you gave me to do." I want my efforts to make Him proud and bring Him glory. I want to find myself someday in God's presence, knowing I did my best, was faithful, and not only began well but also finished well. I can do that, but only by reliance on Jesus, and His presence and power through the Holy Spirit working in my life.

—*Bob Hostetler*

"How happy would it be if [people] would imitate [Jesus's] example,
and not leave their great work of life to be done on a dying bed?"
—*Albert Barnes*

LORD JESUS, I need You. I long to please the Father as You did. I want to do my best, to be faithful, and to finish well. Amen.

> Pilate replied, "But you are a king then?" "Yes," Jesus said. "I was born for that purpose. And I came to bring truth to the world. All who love the truth are my followers." —John 18:37 (TLB)

Standing in the line at the grocery store, I'm bombarded with headlines that scream truth. The truth about so-and-so's failed marriage.... The truth about weight loss and health.... The truth about life and its purposes.... It's enough to make my head spin, and for the life of me I can't figure out why sometimes I still pick up those magazines to find truth. I know real truth isn't in there, but that version of it can be entertaining.

When my marriage failed due to infidelity and the lure of secrecy professional athletes get sucked into, people all around me tried to give me truth. One woman told me marriages like mine can never heal. Another told me this is what men do—women shop, and men cheat. Some of the advice I was given during that dark time was shocking.

I felt like a ship bashing into rocks at every gust of wind—until I got the real truth. Jesus said, "Come to me and I'll give you rest; I am the way, the truth, and the life." I clung to those words like a lifeboat, and so did my husband. Soon we found our own truth and rebuilt our marriage on fidelity, love, and respect. Maybe that's what Jesus means when He says, "You'll know the truth, and the truth will set you free." We can't be free until we know His truth.

—*Gari Meacham*

*"I can't depend on my own strength; I rely on him twenty-four hours a day.
If the day had even more hours, then I would need His help
and grace during those hours as well."*
—*Mother Teresa*

 JESUS, you offer real truth. Train our minds to believe nothing but Your words and whispers. Amen.

**I came to send fire on the earth, and how I wish it were already kindled!
—Luke 12:49 (NKJV)**

I sat in Prague's Old Town Square with my daughter and aunt as we waited for the tour bus. My eyes were drawn to a statue of Jan Hus, one of my heroes of the Christian faith. My intrigue in this man inspired me to study him long before my trip to the Czech Republic and Slovakia.

Hus, a reformer from Prague, preached the gospel in the late 1300s and early 1400s. His soul, lit by holy fire, knew its purpose, including translating the Bible into the language of the common people. Accused of being a heretic, Hus died at the stake by the fire of persecution, and he died singing the Psalms.

I loved the castles, music halls, and old cathedrals in Prague. The unforgettable beauty of the architecture captured my heart. But knowing I walked on the same cobblestones where Hus walked, and viewed the countryside where he galloped on horseback with fiery passion to spread the gospel, remains a deeper blessing.

The embers of truth declared by Jan Hus still burn centuries later and wait for others to fan the flame. Whether a blazing torch or glowing candle, my life can make a difference, as the Holy Spirit continues to light my soul for the glory of Christ.

—*Kathleen Ruckman*

"There is no wood better to kindle the fire of holy love than the wood of the Cross, which Christ used for His own great sacrifice of boundless charity."
—*Ignatius of Loyola*

JESUS, may Your love burn in my heart for the lost, no matter the cost. Amen.

Whoever serves me must follow me; and where I am, my servant also will be. My Father will honor the one who serves me. —John 12:26 (NIV)

The code in front of me might as well have been written in Greek, but it was actually HTML—a language used in website design. I would rather have been reading a Greek study Bible instead of building websites. My passion was teaching at church, but my place seemed to be helping customers at a job that was frustrating and overwhelming. Did I mention I was working with my husband in our family's consulting business?

Each morning I prayed, "Lord, this is not where I want to be. Until You move me, You are going to have to show me what to do and teach me how to do it." And He did! I learned how to build websites, and God blessed our company.

When the perfect job was posted at church, I thought my prayers were answered! I prepared a resume and applied...and was so quickly rejected it made my head spin. My spirit was broken, and I was so discouraged. Why would God deny my heart's desire to serve Him—and create tension at home and at church in the process?

Jesus gently reminded me to seek His honor instead of my happiness.

Eventually, God did release me to work at a church. I've also built dozens of websites that bless religious organizations as well as businesses. I've since learned every place is sacred and every job is a ministry when we follow Jesus there!

—*Amy Lively*

"The main end of our lives is to serve God in the serving
of men in the works of our callings."
—*William Perkins*

JESUS, I want to go where You are instead of forging my own way. Help me to serve and honor You wherever You lead me today. Amen.

> **But Jesus immediately said to them: "Take courage! It is I. Don't be afraid."**
> **—Matthew 14:27** (NIV)

While visiting my grandgems, four-year-old Nicholas grabbed my hand and pulled me toward the back door. "Let's make a movie, Gramsey!" I grabbed my smartphone on the way outside, asking if he had anything to tell me for our movie.

"Sure." He climbed atop a wooden chair, pointed his finger heavenward, and said, "Jesus is my Helper." Then he brought his little arms down emphatically with the words, "I will not be afraid!"

How precious were the words and this child's voice, speaking powerful truth to my heart. Back at home, if I worried about things like speaking in front of a group or driving alone on a long journey, I'd watch his video. The sweet reminder of Who my ever-present help is melted anxiety away.

In Matthew 14, Jesus sends His disciples on to the Sea of Galilee during a storm, while He remains ashore. The wind beats against their boat. The waves grow higher. Their fright turns to terror when a ghostlike figure walking on the water approaches. But Jesus tells them, "It is I. Don't be afraid." How glad they must have been to hear His calming voice. To realize the waves they feared were under His feet.

I'm thankful He is in control over every event, power, or force that frightens us. And when we remember Who He is—the great I Am—what need we fear?

—*Cathy Elliott*

"Turn your eyes upon Jesus, look full in His wonderful face. And the things of earth will grow strangely dim, in the light of His glory and grace."
—*Helen H. Lemmel*

LORD, remind me that because even the winds and the seas obey You, I can be courageous. Amen.

> Consider the ravens: They do not sow or reap, they have no storeroom or barn; yet God feeds them. And how much more valuable you are than birds!
> —Luke 12:24 (NIV)

"I'm just so tired," I responded to my friend's text asking how I was doing.

"What kind of tired? Physically?" she texted back.

"Physically, emotionally, spiritually—all of it." I had finished an exhausting but good season of ministry, and my family was in the midst of a big and uncertain move.

I'm not always the best at taking care of my own physical and emotional needs. I'm better at helping others. All too often my needs can be overwhelming. The season I was in when my friend texted swept me up in a storm of worry and fatigue. In the midst of it all, I forgot to ask God for help. Sometimes I feel as if I shouldn't even bother God with my concerns.

Jesus provided a beautiful example throughout His life of how to care for oneself. He often retreated alone to pray and sleep. Jesus reminds us in this passage that God sees our value and wants us to be cared and provided for.

Jesus understands our physical and emotional needs. As I trust Him, He removes the tension of my anxiety. When I come to Him, He provides rest despite wearying uncertainties. He releases me from fear, giving me a mind focused on His provision. I'm learning that nothing is too small or insignificant to bring to Him.

—*Amelia Rhodes*

"You are valuable because you exist. Not because of what you do or have done, but simply because you are."
—*Max Lucado*

JESUS, please help me remember how valuable I am to You and how You care for all my needs. Amen.

> On hearing this, Jesus said to them, "It is not the healthy who need a doctor, but the sick. I have not come to call the righteous, but sinners."
> —Mark 2:17 (NIV)

The pain was sudden and excruciating—like a dagger thrust into my back. I motioned for my husband to please hurry. I needed to get to a hospital, stat. In the waiting area, the pain was so intense. I rolled into a ball on the antiseptic floor, trying desperately not to groan or scare my children.

After administering tests, the ER physician gave me the diagnosis: kidney stones. There were ways to intervene, but he said it would be best to deal with the pain and wait for the stones to pass. After several days, the stones passed, much to my extreme relief.

That experience made me realize one thing: I needed a doctor. It was my only goal. This kind of utter need is what Jesus addresses here. He has come for the sole purpose of finding those in dire spiritual need.

When we're desperate for Him, He diagnoses our problem and then walks alongside us as we heal. But He cannot enter into that healing relationship with us if we deny our need. If I had pretended my pain didn't matter and never gone to the hospital, I would not have known my diagnosis nor received the proper care. Sin has made us gravely ill. The only way to spiritual health is through Jesus, our Great Physician.

—*Mary DeMuth*

"Christ is the Good Physician. There is no disease He cannot heal;
no sin He cannot remove; no trouble He cannot help. He is the
Balm of Gilead, the Great Physician who has never yet failed to heal all the
spiritual maladies of every soul that has come unto Him in faith and prayer."
—James H. Aughey

JESUS, I desperately need Your healing presence. Please walk alongside me today. You truly are my Great Physician. Amen.

> **"If you have faith the size of a mustard seed," the Lord said, "you can say to this mulberry tree, 'Be uprooted and planted in the sea,' and it will obey you."**
> **—Luke 17:6** (HCSB)

Did you ever plan a vacation down to the tiniest detail, only to feel let down once you finally experienced it? If there were an OPA group—Over Planners Anonymous—I could be a founding member. Regardless of where our family goes on vacation, I plan things months in advance. Hotel? Check. Something educational for the kids? Check. Dinner reservations? Check. My husband says it's because I'm a control freak, and perhaps he's correct. But I have to admit I think it comes down to a trust and faith problem. I'm so afraid things won't turn out as I envision that I micromanage everything. It's exhausting.

I would have driven George Müller bonkers. He was a nineteenth-century prayer warrior who felt missionaries should be supported not by a denomination but by individuals and churches. Quite simply, he had faith.

In his lifetime, Müller's orphanage in England cared for more than ten thousand children. He wasn't a control freak; he was a faith freak.

I want to be like that.

Christians throughout history displayed incredible faith when faced with tough circumstances. Many even lost their lives in the process. What if we were to heed Jesus's advice when challenged. Whether it concerns our health, a family vacation, or praying for that job interview, by displaying faith the size of a mustard seed, we are assured Jesus has got this.

—*Angie Spady*

"With faith, God will always provide."
—*George Müller*

 JESUS, thank You for reminding us how powerful faith can be. Help me to remember Your words when uncertainty arises in my life. Give me peace in knowing that in You all things are possible. Amen.

There is nothing concealed that will not be disclosed, or hidden that will not be made known. —Luke 12:2 (NIV)

One of my sons is a rule-breaker. When he was a teen, I had a ritual. When he left the house, I always told him I'd prayed that if he did anything wrong, he'd be caught. I loved him enough to see him face the consequences for his behavior, a tough call for a mother.

He was caught several times. The repercussions of breaking home rules as well as the law weren't pleasant. But instead of changing his actions, he insisted I stop praying for him.

That didn't happen. I prayed harder in hopes he'd realize living for Jesus was far more gratifying than dodging the police.

When he came of age, he moved out and increased his rebellious habits. I still prayed for him. I wanted my son in His arms, no matter what the cost. Addictions and lawlessness landed him in jail and then prison, and to this day he's constantly in trouble. His lifestyle hurts him and me. Yet I have faith that one day my son will abandon his sinful ways, and I live with that hope.

We all have regrets. Past behaviors needle at our consciences with reminders we are living contrary to what Jesus desires. We're all guilty of hiding or justifying what we say, think, and do, to avoid the pain of confession. Our secrets are never safe, and our sins will one day see the light of day. We may devise ways to avoid detection, but nothing is ever concealed from God. Aren't we glad forgiveness and do-overs are part of the divine plan centered on truth?

—*DiAnn Mills*

"There are no secrets that time does not reveal." —Jean Racine

DEAR JESUS, You know all we do, and You love us despite our faults. Thank You for shedding Your blood on the cross, that we might have forgiveness and one day live with You. Amen.

> Then he said, "I tell you the truth, unless you turn from your sins and become like little children, you will never get into the Kingdom of Heaven."
> —Matthew 18:3 (NLT)

Peeking around the corner, I watched with fascination as my eight-year-old son used an invisible sword and battled the villain. It was a mighty battle, full of sound effects and somersaults. He received a few wounds, but in the end he stood in victory. The crowd cheered, and he bowed.

I stepped out and joined the applause, hoping not to embarrass him but wanting in on the grand festivities. He grinned. "I took down bad guys." I commended him on a job well done, and since then I've been invited to participate in several of his battles. We always win.

Children have vast imaginations. They see things adults don't. While he's fighting on invisible mountains, I'm busy fighting the mountains of bills, grocery lists, and doctor's appointments. But Jesus asked us to see Him with the wonder of a child. When the money doesn't appear to stretch and the doctor's report suggests troubling news, I need to take a play from my son's book. I need to pick up my sword—the Word of God—and fight battles with childlike faith with which my eyes see defeat but my faith sees an adventure with Jesus just around the bend and a testimony on the horizon.

My son never shied away from giants. He forged ahead with confidence. I don't have to shrink away in fear either. Because in Jesus's kingdom, the victory is already won.

—*Jessica R. Patch*

"That's the trouble with the world. Too many people grow up."
—*Walt Disney*

 JESUS, I want to see with childlike faith. Take me places I've never been and fill me with wonder. Amen.

> Therefore everyone who hears these words of mine and puts them into practice is like a wise man who built his house on the rock.
> —Matthew 7:24 (NIV)

When my daughter was just six months old, we moved our little family of three from northern Alabama to the Georgia coast. Our ten years there were full of adventure and fun. The beach was just a fifteen-minute drive away, so availing ourselves of the sand and surf became as common to us as a trip to the park might be to other families. Living so near the ocean wasn't all sandcastles and seashells. This raised-in-the-Midwest girl had lessons to learn about hurricanes.

While we were fortunate never to experience a full evacuation during our years on the coast, we did give careful attention to the preparations necessary just in case. We had a list of items we'd need to pack and knew the best route inland. Though we never had to put our plan in action, we knew it was foolish not to have one.

Jesus guides us with His wisdom, preparing for life's storms by urging us not just to hear His words but also to put them into practice. His half-brother James echoed His words by urging us to be "doers of the Word and not hearers only" (James 1:22).

The parables and the miracles were not simply entertainment. Jesus taught with purpose. His intent was to give us the foundation of faith, the basis of wisdom. Just as it would have been foolish for us to have a list of hurricane preparations and never actually prepare, we must act on what we learn from Scripture.

—Teri Lynne Underwood

"The safe place lies in obedience to God's Word, singleness of heart and holy vigilance."
—*A. B. Simpson*

JESUS, I ask for faith to heed Your words and wisdom. May my foundation be squarely found in You. Amen.

Love Letter from Jesus
LESSONS OF JESUS/ BEATITUDES

My Blessed One,

Do you know where the greatest blessing lies? It is in fulfilling your purpose on this earth, and that purpose is knowing Me and then reflecting Me to others. You are blessed when you are at the end of your own resources, because then you tap into My infinite power. Through you, I bring about My kingdom on the earth.

You are blessed when you mourn, because then I can comfort you, and you learn that I am truly enough to sustain you and give you peace. And you are blessed when you hunger and thirst for all that is right and good, because you will find it in Me. You will become what is right and good in the world when you are filled with Me.

I bless you when you show mercy to others. As I extend it to you and you fully receive it. You are blessed when you are pure in heart, when your desire is for Me and you seek Me with all of your heart. You will find me—you will see Me and experience God.

You are blessed when you make peace—with God, with yourself, and with others. Even when others persecute you My blessing is yours. Because I am your Redeemer, you can embrace every lesson that leads you to your purpose. My kingdom belongs to you because you cling to what is good, and in doing this you reveal God's beauty in the world.

I love you forever.

Let me tell you why you are here. You're here to be salt-seasoning that brings out the God-flavors of this earth. You're here to be light, bringing out the God-colors in the world. —Matthew 5:13-14 (MSG)

> Jesus said to his disciples: "Things that cause people to stumble are bound to come, but woe to anyone through whom they come. It would be better for them to be thrown into the sea with a millstone tied around their neck than to cause one of these little ones to stumble." —Luke 17:1-2 (NIV)

My then-six-year-old son rode with me as I pulled into a long line at our bank's drive-up window one busy Friday afternoon, back in the days before ATM machines. In those good old days of the mid-1980s in our New England town, it was necessary to actually go inside a bank or through the drive-through banking facility just to get cash or deposit a check. I desperately needed cash for the weekend, yet I arrived at the drive-up window just a few moments too late. The teller flipped on the "Closed" sign just as I pulled up to the window.

I honked my horn and hollered at the teller, who was still visible behind the shade. I even got out of the car and banged on the window. (Security concerns were less in those days!) Finally, I drove off, vowing under my breath to never darken the door of that "stupid" bank again. Then, I was cut to the heart by the words of my young son: "Hmm. Some way for a Christian to act!"

I learned a hard lesson that day. I realized children hear our pronouncements about faith and God and the golden rule. But more importantly, they are watching our lives.

—David Downs

"The example of good men is visible philosophy."
—*English proverb*

 JESUS, I want my life and actions to point people to You...never away from You. Please help me. Amen.

> Then he took a cup, and after giving thanks he gave it to them, and all of them drank from it. He said to them, "This is my blood of the covenant, which is poured out for many." —Mark 14:23-24 (NRSV)

When I was in my twenties, I joined a volunteer corps for a year and moved to Alaska. They had the other volunteers and me sign a sort of covenant agreeing to uphold certain values the organization espoused. It was a very difficult year for me—probably the toughest in my life—and what I remember most is the way two of my fellow volunteers stood by me in my darkest hour, and how we all found a deeper connection to Christ and to one another. The covenant was no longer a piece of paper I had signed and taped to my wall. Thanks to my friends, it became a relationship that was internalized and lived.

So it is in today's Scripture passage! Jesus offers us covenant not as law or obligation. He offers it as friendship, as shared experience. He offers it as something that can quench our thirst. I see Jesus pouring Himself into His relationship with God and then letting that passion pour out of Him into the lives of all who love Him intimately. And I am deeply touched by the fact that while His covenant is with "many," He lives out the covenant by sharing a vulnerable, honest, difficult moment with close friends. In this world of social media and YouTube and all the rest of it, we can be lured into believing impact is measured by how many views or hits a message garners. But Jesus shared a cup of wine with His friends. That's all it took to initiate a covenant that still lives and grows today.

—Lizzie Berne DeGear

"How did the rose ever open its heart and give to this world all of its beauty?
It felt the encouragement of light against its being,
otherwise we all remain too frightened." —Hafiz

JESUS, let me face life with the gratitude and acceptance You experienced. Today, let me discover Your covenant in a new way, in some simple moment with those I love. Amen.

> But a Samaritan, as he traveled, came where the man was; and when he saw him, he took pity on him. He went to him and bandaged his wounds, pouring on oil and wine. Then he put the man on his own donkey, brought him to an inn and took care of him. The next day he took out two denarii and gave them to the innkeeper. "Look after him," he said, "and when I return, I will reimburse you for any extra expense you may have." —Luke 10:33–35 (NIV)

The invitation to a friend's fortieth birthday party stated participants should each bring a memory to share. As remembrances were shared, I realized my friend is a true "good Samaritan" who unselfishly gives of herself, her time, and her resources to help anyone in need. Story after story demonstrated her creative and generous nature: drawing cartoons to encourage a smile, visiting a friend at the hospital, taking a meal to the infirmed, babysitting for a harried parent, listening to a hurting heart...and the list continued.

Something interesting happened as different folks spoke. My friend remembered very few of the incidents mentioned. She recalled a few, but most memories were fuzzy for her or completely gone. I found this to be an excellent example of the verse that reads, "When you give to the needy, do not let your left hand know what your right hand is doing" (Matthew 6:3).

I want to emulate my friend and the Samaritan in Jesus's parable, generously helping those along my path. I want to adopt my friend's "just do it" mentality, trusting God to provide what I need to bless others just as Jesus taught us.

—*Nancy Sebastian Kuch*

"The time is always right to do what is right."
—*Martin Luther King Jr.*

JESUS, give me a generous heart. Help me reach out and help those in need along the road I travel today. Give me opportunity and courage to "just do it." Amen.

> Then he said to his disciples, "The harvest is plentiful but the workers are few." —Matthew 9:37 (NIV)

The harvest was plentiful in biblical times, and it is now—maybe more than ever. With so much turmoil and uncertainty in the world these days, people are longing for comfort, peace, and meaning.

Yet the workers remain few.

Every church nursery is short of volunteers, even though children are an easy "crop" for spiritual truth (Matthew 18:3, 19:14). Every school has students who could use a little extra attention. Every community has neighbors needy for love, care, or practical support. Ministries around the world serve worthy causes, meeting what seem like endless needs.

Yet the workers remain few.

Sometimes, I feel overwhelmed by my own needs and those of my family. Having considered myself one of the twenty percent, I jealously guard my time, treasure, and affections because I genuinely fear there isn't enough to go around.

But I now know I can start my day by asking the unlimited Lord of the harvest (Matthew 9:38) to make me attentive and available for the harvest. I can trust He will present opportunities and equip me minute by minute to plants seeds of gospel love—one action or word at a time. It need not be an overwhelming worldwide ministry but the smallest gesture, the simplest words, the tiniest gift.

—*Isabella Yosuico*

"Don't judge each day by the harvest you reap but by the seeds that you plant."
—*Robert Louis Stevenson*

LORD of the harvest, equip me to clearly see the harvest before me, every day. Amen.

> Again, truly I tell you that if two of you on earth agree about anything they ask for, it will be done for them by my Father in heaven.
> —Matthew 18:19 (NIV)

Leaving the coffee shop, I waved to my friend and headed toward my car.

Pray with her. The words came as a gentle nudge to my heart.

Typically, Midwesterners—even those newly transplanted to the South—didn't pray with others, especially in public. Over coffee, Tammy and I had discussed struggles with life. I'd listened, offered advice. That was enough.

Pray with her. The words grew more insistent, thundering in my head like a command and cementing my sandals to the asphalt.

In a parking lot, Lord? You know I'm not comfortable with that. Silence. I groaned and turned. "Tammy! Wait!" Rushing to her, I blurted, "Maybe we should pray together. Would that be okay?"

"Sure." Tammy smiled and held out her palms. I placed my shaky hands in hers and released a heavy breath. Recalling details of our chat, somehow my words rolled out into a prayer to Jesus. Tammy's "Amen" followed mine.

I opened my eyes. Tears filled hers. "I needed that," she said. "Thank you."

The Lord had pushed me to overcome an issue, but more than that, I believe He desired to be invited into our midst.

Praying together in Jesus's name assures a heavenly response.

—*Holly Michael*

"Nothing tends more to cement the hearts of Christians than praying together.
Never do they love one another so well as when they witness
the outpouring of each other's hearts in prayer."
—*Charles Finney*

JESUS LORD, never let our fears or insecurities prevent us from gathering to seek the Father's will and mercy. Amen.

> **When Jesus turned and saw her, he said, "Be encouraged, daughter. Your faith has healed you." And the woman was healed from that time on. —Matthew 9:22** (CEB)

I landed in the hospital with a mysterious lung infection the doctors couldn't name. A machine pummeled me with oxygen, but every breath was a struggle. Even worse was my emotional state. "I'm in despair," I told our minister when she visited me that first day in the ICU. "I need hope." She prayed for me, as did many others.

Funny thing, the next day in the hospital I wasn't feeling much better, but something happened to me internally that didn't show up on any test. I knew I would get better. Somehow I was sure I would get out of that hospital for good. And I did.

I had wonderful medical care from a kind, knowledgable, compassionate staff, but I discovered how healing also comes from within. "Your faith has healed you," Jesus said. My faith? I don't think it was so strong, but all the years of trusting, listening, praying, and drawing on others to pray for me were not lost. If anyone asks about my two weeks in the hospital, I say, "The doctors kept me alive; the prayers healed me."

—*Rick Hamlin*

"We cannot rely on ourselves, for we have learned by bitter experience the folly of self-confidence. We are compelled to look to the Lord alone. Blessed is the wind that drives the ship into harbor. Blessed is the distress that forces us to rest in our God."
—*Charles Spurgeon*

 I AM WEAK, Lord, but You are strong, and when I trust in You, I can do more than I could ever do on my own. Keep Your healing touch on me. Amen.

> For whoever is ashamed of Me and My words in this adulterous and sinful generation, of him the Son of Man also will be ashamed when He comes in the glory of His Father with the holy angels. —Mark 8:38 (NKJV)

I waited in line at the department store for fifteen minutes in a standstill. The clerk did her best to move the line along but took too long to answer a customer's questions. The man in front of me shifted from one leg to the other, sighing with disapproval. He cursed the store clerk, and worst of all, he cursed my Savior. He shouted out Jesus's name one too many times.

When he did that, it hit a nerve. I spoke up.

The man pointed at me and told me to mind my own business, raising his voice in an unsettling way. He finally simmered down after the clerk threatened to call security. I was relieved when he paid for his items, and I left sad at having witnessed such an event. I wondered if that man had any idea how much Jesus loves him.

I came close to staying silent due to the fear of speaking up in public, but I know Jesus spoke up in situations many of us wouldn't have dared. I want to be like Him and for Him to acknowledge me, too, in heaven.

—*Kathleen Ruckman*

"Faith is also the means by which we live in response to the commands of God."
—R. C. Sproul

JESUS, help me to know when to speak up, and guide my words. And help those with troubled hearts know You love them unconditionally. Amen.

> Don't be afraid of those who want to kill your body; they cannot touch your soul. Fear only God, who can destroy both soul and body in hell.
> —Matthew 10:28 (NLT)

Scary movies frighten me. When I hear the creepy music that's often a prelude to something terrible, I whisper to the screen, "Don't open that door," or "Don't look behind you." Fear of a movie scene is temporary, but some fears are recurring.

I fear for my children. What if they get hurt or lost? Sometimes, I feel anxious about illness. When I read about crime or terror attacks, fear grips me so tightly I don't want to let my kids out of my sight, or I become a hermit because the outside world seems too dangerous. Many of my fears are tied to physical harm or danger.

Jesus said we shouldn't be afraid of those who can hurt only our bodies. Instead, he said, we must guard our souls because the soul is more important. George MacDonald said, "You don't have a soul. You are a soul. You have a body." I've been thinking about the differences between body and soul. My body is skin, bones, joints, muscles, and organs. I need nourishment to keep it alive and exercise to keep it toned. I cannot see my soul, but it's what makes me a person. My soul is eternal, and my body is temporary. Fearing God is not just about understanding how powerful He is, but also understanding that He uses His power for our good, not for our destruction. He is the One Who rescues my soul.

—*Karen Porter*

"We fear circumstances so much because we fear God so little."
—*Lecrae*

DEAR JESUS, help me see beyond fear. I choose to trust You, because You alone can save and rescue me. Amen.

Heal the sick, raise the dead, cleanse those who have leprosy, drive out demons. Freely you have received; freely give.
—Matthew 10:8 (NIV)

A couple I know volunteers every week with an inner-city ministry in one of the country's poorest and roughest neighborhoods. They hand out food, pray with neighbors, and build relationships with society's forgotten and misunderstood. When I asked why they would put themselves in such a dangerous place, their words convicted me: "Someone needs to look these people in the eyes, treat them with dignity, meet their needs, and introduce them to Jesus."

My friends are following Jesus's instructions to His disciples when He sent them out to share the good news and show His compassion. In that time, caring for the sick, the lepers, and the demoniacs was a humiliating task. But Jesus wanted His followers to carry on His work to care for the neglected, helpless, and friendless. He wanted to show that God loves them, befriends them, and cares about their physical and spiritual needs. Christ has blessed us so much, and He wants us to reach out to others and do the same.

Compassion is important to Jesus, and if we want to follow Him, out of the overflow of our blessings, we can obediently and freely give to others so they can experience the same compassion we experience.

—*Ginger Kolbaba*

"Too often we underestimate the power of a touch, a smile, a kind word, a listening ear, an honest compliment, or the smallest act of caring, all of which have the potential to turn a life around."
—*Leo Buscaglia*

JESUS, thank You for how You show compassion. Help me care for others who desperately need to experience that goodness. Amen.

"Lord, teach us to pray, just as John taught his disciples." He said to them, "When you pray, say:

'Father,
    hallowed be your name,
    your kingdom come.
Give us each day our daily bread.
Forgive us our sins,
    for we also forgive everyone who sins against us.
And lead us not into temptation.'" —Luke 11:1–4 (NIV)

Some of the happiest times in my childhood were the days my favorite children's magazine arrived in the mail. And among my favorite parts was the "find the hidden pictures" page. I loved the challenge of finding things that weren't apparent at first glance.

I often try to do something similar when reading the Bible. I look for things that aren't apparent at first glance. I sometimes wonder why the biblical writer chose the specific words he did. I often ask myself questions like, *What would I have said or done in that situation?* or, *What would I have expected to be said or done?*

When Jesus's first followers asked, "Lord, teach us to pray," His answer was one I find surprising. He didn't talk about prayer. He didn't give them pointers. And He gave them a prayer so short and simple, it might have shocked them. In fewer than fifty words, He told them to call God "Father," align themselves with the Father's agenda, and ask for God's provision, forgiveness, and deliverance. He gave them a simple, profound, elemental, and effective model that has been foundational and transformational in my prayer life—one we can pray easily and often, every day.

—*Bob Hostetler*

"Do you wish to find out the really sublime? Repeat the Lord's Prayer."
—*Napoleon Bonaparte*

 JESUS, teach me to pray as You taught Your first followers—simply, profoundly, elementally, and effectively. Amen.

> **For them I sanctify myself, that they too may be truly sanctified.**
> **—John 17:19** (NIV)

I remember singing a song in children's church a long time ago called "Kids Under Construction." In addition to its catchy tune, the song had a theme that God is not finished with us yet. Once we grow up and become adults, we sometimes forget we're still works in progress.

I get frustrated when I mess up. Instead of remembering the grace Jesus offers, I aim for the unattainable goal of perfection. The sacrifice Jesus made for us on the cross was perfect. Because of His actions, we are granted the gift of grace. Even though we fall short every single day, we can be sanctified through Jesus, not through any merits of our own.

Jesus sanctified us through His sacrifice, and He is the holy example we should always follow. Jesus spent a lot of time in prayer with the Father and, in fact, taught us how to pray. He knew the Scriptures by memory and quoted them often, especially when being tempted. Jesus never hesitated to do what God required. From Him we can learn about the sanctification process in our own lives.

Our walk with Jesus doesn't end at salvation. We are being sanctified, and we're still under construction. Jesus wants to make us more holy over time, but it's a lifelong process.

—*Allison K. Flexer*

"Kids under construction. Maybe the paint is still wet.
Kids under construction. The Lord may not be finished yet."
—*Bill Gaither and Gary Paxton, songwriters*

 JESUS, thank You for Your grace. You are perfect and holy, but we are not. Sanctify us and grant us grace as we walk closely with You. Amen.

> He also told them a parable: "Can a blind person guide a blind person? Will not both fall into a pit? A disciple is not above the teacher, but everyone who is fully qualified will be like the teacher." —Luke 6:39–40 (NRSV)

When I teach Bible studies, the most important thing I say is, "I don't know." And the most important thing I do is sit in silence. As the teacher, it is tempting to offer insights on demand, even when I don't really have them. It takes a mix of courage and humility to honestly say, "I don't know," to a question or sit in silence after we've read aloud some bit of Scripture. But Jesus reminds me that to cover up my not-knowing would be the blind leading the blind.

What happens in that silence or that not-knowing is amazing. The Spirit moves among us then in a special way. In those moments, organically but also magically, someone else speaks. Someone among us responds to the question or to the silence. She or he speaks from personal experience, from hard-earned wisdom, and we all drink it in. We know the Spirit has landed!

From these precious moments in Bible study, I have learned that "fully qualified" does not have to do with credentials, education, or institutional religious authority. It means being fully in the moment, connected to community and to God, and trusting the Spirit as to when to listen and when to speak.

—*Lizzie Berne DeGear*

"I never teach my pupils, I only attempt to provide the conditions in which they can learn."
—*Albert Einstein*

 OH, JESUS, help me not be blind to my own blindness or the blindness of my chosen leaders! Let me be humble enough to let others share my leadership, and let me be courageous enough to share my perspective with those in authority. Amen.

Let your light shine before men in such a way that they may see your good works, and glorify your Father who is in heaven. —Matthew 5:16 (NASB)

Jesus told his followers to shine in a dark world. The "how" part of that command—doing good works—is easy enough to understand. It's the "why" part—seeing God glorified—that gets tricky.

Years ago, a family in our town lost everything in a fire. I convinced our church youth group to hold a rummage sale to raise funds. It was a giant undertaking, but after several arduous days of collecting, pricing, and selling items, we were able to donate almost seven hundred dollars.

Would you believe the destitute family never said a word—not even a simple thank-you? While no one else seemed fazed by this seeming ingratitude, I felt resentful, even angry.

Very quickly a question bubbled up in my heart: *Why exactly did you spearhead this project, Len?*

It didn't take much soul-searching to realize I had done this good work less to glorify God and more to gain recognition for myself.

According to Jesus, our goal in shining—in serving—must always be to give, not to get. We do good works for the same reason He did: to point others to our heavenly Father.

—*Len Woods*

"We are told to let our light shine, and if it does,
we won't need to tell anybody it does. Lighthouses don't fire
cannons to call attention to their shining—they just shine."
—*D. L. Moody*

JESUS, You always served in order to please and bring honor to the Father. Make me more like that, more like You, I pray. Amen.

BRAVE AND BOLD

> Whoever is ashamed of me and my words, the Son of Man will be ashamed of them when he comes in his glory and in the glory of the Father and of the holy angels. —Luke 9:26 (NIV)

One morning, a panic-stricken neighbor stood on my porch, asking if I had seen her daughter. The school had just called to say she was missing from morning attendance.

When I replied that I hadn't seen her daughter, she turned to leave. Before I could stop myself, I said, "Can I pray for you?"

I wasn't certain what she thought about Jesus, but now wasn't the time to wonder if it was OK to speak His name into this crisis.

I put my hand on her shoulder, and asked Jesus to help find her daughter and to make His presence known. As I said, "Amen," her cell phone rang.

The school had found her daughter. She hung up and exclaimed, "He heard your prayer!"

I learned that morning to not be afraid or ashamed to speak His name into every situation, even if I'm not sure what the other person thinks of Him. I've prayed with friends and neighbors over text messages, at the school bus stop, in a crowd, and even while running.

The more I speak up about Jesus, the less timid I become about sharing His truths. And I'm always comforted in knowing even if He doesn't respond immediately to our requests, He always provides His peace and reminders of His presence.

—*Amelia Rhodes*

"God desires for you to be involved in drawing people to
His Word through a dedicated life to Him and an active witness for Him."
—*Paul Chappell*

JESUS, keep me sensitive to Your Spirit and show me who needs to know Your presence in his or her situation today. Amen.

For they all saw him and were terrified. But immediately he spoke to them and said, "Take heart; it is I. Do not be afraid." —Mark 6:50 (ESV)

On the heels of multiplying the loaves and fish for five thousand mouths, Jesus walks on water toward the apostles in a boat that's "making headway painfully" while crossing the Sea of Galilee. We're told He intended to pass them by, until He saw their terror in thinking He was a ghost. It's interesting to note it was Jesus Who'd "made" them get into the boat in the first place.

God has multiplied loaves and fish for me over and over, performing miracles large and small, often at the last possible minute when all hope was lost and I was hungry. And yet, when He shows up again as I'm making very painful headway, I often fail to see Him. I fail to believe He's really showing up again. He seems like a ghost—faint, elusive, hidden to me somehow.

This verse and story comforts me, especially knowing the context. Over and over in the New Testament, Jesus's disciples are often absurdly dense, frequently afraid, and generally disappointing in their lack of perfection. Elsewhere in Scripture, Paul, Mary Magdalene, and others close to Jesus fail to recognize Him when He shows up.

How gracious of God to let me see that even those closest to Him, those who witnessed His power, didn't recognize Him and caved to fear, faithlessness, and failure. For that I say, "Thank You, Jesus!"

—Isabella Yosuico

"It is a terrible thing to see and have no vision."
—Helen Keller

 DEAR JESUS, please open my eyes to look for You and to see You when You appear just as You promised. Amen.

> Jesus answered, "Are there not twelve hours of daylight? Anyone who walks in the daytime will not stumble, for they see by this world's light."
> —John 11:9 (NIV)

Florida Field (now renamed Ben Hill Griffin Stadium) is one of the noisiest football stadiums in the United States. Built in a natural depression, sound echoes within it like a snarling beast. Young children wear protective earplugs, and talking on a mobile phone is impossible. During one game, the explosion of sound after a game-winning interception was louder than a dozen military jets parked at midfield with engines screaming at full power.

This is the world of football's "twelfth man."

The twelfth man—referring to the crowd as one more "player" in a game with eleven men on each team—creates a huge home-field advantage. Over a roaring crowd, opposing teams can't hear plays called or discuss strategy except by hand signals. Only the most disciplined and confident teams succeed in such a hostile environment. To emerge victorious takes countless hours of preparation and tough mental discipline.

Like the twelfth man at Florida Field, the cacophonous world around us is an ever-present distraction, threatening at any moment to cause us to stumble. But the world has no power over us if we walk boldly and confidently in the light of Jesus.

—*J. Mason Williams*

"I make it my rule, to lay hold of light and embrace it,
wherever I see it, though held forth by a child or an enemy."
—*Jonathan Edwards*

 JESUS, please give me the strength and discipline to walk in Your light with confidence that I will never stumble as long as I keep my eyes on You. Amen.

He replied, "Blessed rather are those who hear the word of God and obey it."
—Luke 11:28 (NIV)

From the window of our one-bedroom apartment, I watch a glorious sunset outline a billboard against the fading blue sky. That view can make our life in the big city feel especially small. It seems like the world around me is quick to dramatically point out all the things I don't have. It can feel like some friends and family are getting a special blessing and God has forgotten my portion of His goodness.

And then I come to Jesus's words. Jesus promises the best and most enduring blessing comes when we hear and obey the Word of God. He has not forgotten me! In fact, He has engraved His love for me on His hands. His blessing is not measured with the standards of this world's balances in our bank accounts.

Jesus spoke with the social outcasts, the government officials, the prostitutes, the mentally ill, the wealthy, the religious leaders, and the poor. He spoke hoping all would hear His message of abundant life.

The most established needed the message just as desperately as the most destitute. Jesus does not hold back, though He would have reason, but instead He lavishes love on His creation, heaping blessing on top of blessing.

Any material possession, status, or achievement might glitter, but the blessing that comes from hearing and obeying the Word of God endures like fine gold.

—*Caroline Kolts*

"All that is gold does not glitter,
Not all those who wander are lost;
The old that is strong does not wither,
Deep roots are not reached by the frost."
—*J. R. R. Tolkien*

JESUS, thank You for remembering me today. Help me to desire Your Word, and to believe that hearing and obeying are the most supreme blessing. Amen.

> **Watch out that no one deceives you.**
> —Mark 13:5 (NIV)

My best friend and I arrived late for the lecture and nabbed two empty seats just as the speaker appeared on stage. Gazing at my friend, a new Christian, I smiled. This talk would transport her to a deeper faith. At least that's what I'd been told.

The well-traveled man began his sermon, his voice filled with confidence. The audience nodded and laughed in response to his message, myself included. As time passed, he quoted Scripture out of context and took liberties with parables.

I shrugged it off.

But when he questioned whether a specific event in Jesus's life had even occurred, or had been embellished by early church leaders, the hair on the back of my neck stood on end. Had this man said what I just heard?

I gazed at my friend, her expression rapt. A new believer, she didn't catch the discreet change in direction the lecture had taken—the white lies woven into the truth, the subtle smudging of Christ's divinity. We exited the auditorium, headed for her home.

Parked on a dark lane, we discussed the prophet's half-truths and prayed for discernment. Trusting Jesus's presence to be as real as our own, we quieted. In the silence, He drew us close and spoke wisdom into our hearts—a grateful audience of two, forever changed.

—*Heidi Gaul*

"The trust of the innocent is the liar's most useful tool."
—*Stephen King*

THANK YOU, Jesus, for keeping me centered on You. Strengthen my discernment as You guide me to Your truths. Amen.

A good person produces good things from the treasury of a good heart, and an evil person produces evil things from the treasury of an evil heart. What you say flows from what is in your heart. —Luke 6:45 (NLT)

"Did you see who's moving in down the street?" my neighbor asked.

I said yes with a cautious tone. I had a bad feeling about where this conversation seemed headed. Our new neighbors were of a different race, and I sensed she didn't like that.

"What do you think about it?"

"It's fine," I told her. "They got a nice house. They'll enjoy our neighborhood—it's safe and friendly."

She harrumphed. Her words spoke volumes about her true feelings.

Jesus understands that our words and actions reveal our underlying beliefs, attitudes, and motivations. And what we hold innermost will eventually come out to show our true selves.

I see this happen on social media. People who seem so kind can spew the most hateful language against those who don't agree with them. I want to believe they don't mean those things. But then I consider Jesus's statement: "What you say flows from what is in your heart." Our words are billboards to the state of our hearts.

How many times have we said or done something that doesn't show off our best selves or represent Jesus in a good light? That's when we need to pray as King David did in Psalm 51:10: "Create in me a pure heart, O God, and renew a steadfast spirit within me."

—*Ginger Kolbaba*

"The heart is as the words are, vain or serious; it therefore concerns us to get our hearts filled, not only with good, but with abundance of it."
—*Matthew Henry*

JESUS, give me a clean heart so that what I say and do reflect You and Your kingdom's desires. Amen.

LOST AND FOUND

From then on Jesus began to preach, "Repent, because the kingdom of heaven has come near!" —Matthew 4:17 (HCSB)

"You've got to be kidding me," I complained, as I drove down the unfamiliar interstate while combing the seat for my lost car charger. I'd noticed my cell phone had only 1 percent of its battery life left. That meant GPS was a no-go, and I became unsettled at the thought that I, like my charger, was completely lost.

As a children's author who visits schools, a working cell phone with apps is a priority. I can't afford to show up late and disappoint kids who are expecting me. Initially, I refused to admit I needed an automated voice telling me when and where to turn. After all, I had an old-fashioned map and could figure it out on my own. But while visiting an unfamiliar area, I quickly discovered that just winging it wasn't a good idea. My stubbornness in refusing to seek directions the easy way led to wrong turns and missed opportunities.

In our Christian walk, we often do the same thing. God's Word provides clear direction on right and wrong, yet we often ignore it and face harsh consequences.

I pulled over to get my bearings, and to my delight, I found my phone charger under a pile of books on the floor of my car. After only a few quick taps on the screen, the app instinctively knew where I was and guided me to the school.

May we all plug our hearts into God's Word and allow Him to find us, guide us, and lead us home to the loving arms of Jesus.

—*Angie Spady*

"Divine Direction begins with unconditional submission."
—*Andy Stanley*

JESUS, thank You for loving me even when I appear to be lost. Please guide me with Your Word so that I know right from wrong and live according to Your will. Amen.

> So Jesus answered them and said, "My teaching is not Mine, but His who sent Me."
> —John 7:16 (NASB)

Have you ever felt unqualified to do something you want to do? When I was young, I was terrible at reading, writing, and math. I simply couldn't put it all together, and I struggled my first years in school because nothing seemed to make sense. I even forged my father's name on a report card I was mortified to show to my parents. I got an F in math that I tried to make into a B (this was back when teachers wrote report cards in pen rather than on a computer). Every step I made to cover my embarrassment made things measurably worse!

I smile as I write this, because later in life I became a national consultant for the Public Education & Business Coalition, and guess what my specialty was: reading and writing comprehension. I also run nonprofit ministries in the United States and Uganda—and I still hate math!

When Jesus told the Pharisees His teaching wasn't His but His Father's, it was because the religious leaders couldn't figure out how He was able to speak and teach so well without first learning from them. The answer is simple: when Jesus asks us to do things, He gives the knowledge we need for the task—and that's enough.

—*Gari Meacham*

"God will never lead us to places he's not already present."
—*Jeremy Foster*

 JESUS, You will always equip me for where You send me. Help me to not feel overwhelmed by my tasks. Amen.

> **Stand firm, and you will win life.**
> —Luke 21:19 (NIV)

The grief and horror I felt over another campus shooting were taken to a new level when I read that the gunman specifically targeted Christians. At the time, I had twin nephews in college, a son in middle school, and a niece in high school. How would they respond if someone were to enter their classroom, ask the Christians to stand, and say, "You will see God in one second"? How would I respond? I thought about persecuted believers around the world. Where did their courage come from? I reread the story of that awful day on the college campus in Oregon and realized the shooter's chilling words revealed the answer: "You will see God." All I could do was pray that if the teenagers and young adults I loved were ever faced with that question, the promise of seeing Jesus would be their source of courage, and that the same would be true for me.

Jesus made it clear that faith in Him would be costly. He also promised it would be worth the temporary pain and fear. "Stand firm, and you will win life." Not all of us will be called to answer the life-or-death "Are you a Christian?" question, but Jesus's words have repeatedly reminded me that, at some point, He asks us all to stand for Him. Instead of predicting our response, we can pray for such closeness with Him that boldness is our only option.

—Jeanette Hanscome

"To endure the cross is not a tragedy; it is the suffering
which is the fruit of an exclusive allegiance to Jesus Christ."
—Dietrich Bonhoeffer

 LORD, help me become so committed to You that I can't imagine not standing strong. Give me courage today. Amen.

Do to others as you would have them do to you.
—Luke 6:31 (NIV)

Why won't anyone let me out? I grumbled as I waited to turn off of my street. Glaring at the car now blocking me, I recognized the driver. *Doesn't she know I'm her neighbor?* Then it occurred to me: if we can't extend basic kindness to those we know, how can we hope to live as Jesus commanded us?

Treating others as we would want to be treated is not always as simple as it sounds. Every day, we are presented with little opportunities to do just that—to open the door for someone, pay for a coffee, visit the lonely—yet we often fail. We can blame it on busyness or the multiple distractions of our electronically connected lives—or we can confess that none of it matters. The problem is not what is happening around us but what is happening inside us. When my spirit is most aligned with Christ, following the Golden Rule comes easily. When I'm tangled in a spiritual knot, I can be as rude or grumpy as the next person. The remedy is to see Jesus in each person we encounter. How would we treat Him? How does He treat us? The answer is this: with love. We can always rely on Christ within to teach us how.

—*Andrea Raynor*

"We have committed the Golden Rule to memory; let us now commit it to life."
—*Edwin Markham*

DEAR JESUS, help me treat others as I would want to be treated, regardless of what is happening around me. In every situation, help me act with love. Amen.

> Are not two sparrows sold for a penny? Yet not one of them will fall to the ground outside your Father's care. —Matthew 10:29 (NIV)

I don't know about you, but my tendency is to think the details of my life are just not interesting to God. I mean, half of the time they aren't even interesting to me! But when I'm tempted to fall into this trap of insecurity, I'm reminded of the timeless words of Jesus and one of my favorite hymns, "His Eye Is on the Sparrow."

Jesus reminds His disciples He is the One with the real power, and thus the One to be feared and respected. God cares even for the sparrow, which, according to Matthew 10:29, is worth only half a penny. This is as much a comfort to me as it was to Civilla Martin, who wrote the lyrics to "His Eye Is on the Sparrow." When visiting some dear friends, both of whom were stricken with debilitating physical challenges, Martin heard one of the most recognized lines in all Christendom and made it the basis for the hymn we know and love.

The lyrics speak directly to the truth of the power and love of Jesus in our lives. No matter how insecure we might feel, we are always under the watchful, loving eye of Jesus. If His eye is on the sparrow, how wonderful to know He is also watching me!

—*Wayne Adams*

*"One day while we were visiting with the Doolittles,
my husband commented on their bright hopefulness
and asked them for the secret of it. Mrs. Doolittle's reply was simple:
'His eye is on the sparrow, and I know He watches me.'"*
—*Civilla Martin*

 DEAR JESUS, thank You for reminding me that You are always watching over the details of my life. Amen.

**Blessed are the poor in spirit, for theirs is the kingdom of heaven.
—Matthew 5:3** (NIV)

I have had the pleasure of meeting the Reverend Billy Graham in person. It was a bit intimidating to stand in line with dozens of people who, like I, wanted to meet this iconic preacher. As I waited, I mentally rehearsed what I would say to Billy when it was my turn. But at the moment I looked into his face, the only words that came out of my mouth were, "Can I have a hug?"

It caught me by surprise to find Billy Graham giving me one of the biggest hugs of my life. My teenage son snapped a photo of us both grinning ear to ear. The photograph shows my obvious pleasure, but it does not show my amazement at realizing the spirit of humility that defines Billy Graham as real.

Imagine it! This evangelist, who has traveled around the world bringing millions of people to faith in Jesus, is a humble and generous man. His humility was so powerful it presented a challenge to my prideful spirit.

Our photo is displayed in my family room, as a continual reminder that we all share a spiritual need for Jesus in our lives. It reminds me not to allow my pride to prevent me from humbling myself before Jesus and simply standing in awe of Him.

—Barb Howe

*"If thou desire the love of God and man, be humble; for the proud heart,
as it loves none but itself, so it is believed of none but by itself;
the voice of humility is God's music, and the silence of humility is God's rhetoric.
Humility enforces where neither virtue nor strength can prevail nor reason."*
—Francis Quarles

DEAR JESUS, I stand in awe of Your holiness. Thank You for gently reminding me how powerfully You work through those who are willing to be poor in spirit. Amen.

> For false messiahs and false prophets will appear and perform great signs and wonders to deceive, if possible, even the elect. See, I have told you ahead of time. —Matthew 24:24–25 (NIV)

"Pay close attention when you get to the construction on the interstate in Memphis. It will be easy to miss your turn."

Scott's words echoed in my head as the GPS said, "Recalculating," over and over again while I tried to figure out where I was, where I was supposed to be, and how I was going to get there.

I'd forgotten his warning, as my daughter and I laughed our way through Memphis. I missed the turn and was lost in all the detours. Even my GPS was confused about where we were.

Jesus also sought to prepare His disciples for the hazards ahead. He knew they could be confused or distracted and even deceived. The warning wasn't meant to demean them; it was intended to ready them for what was coming.

Just as some would seek to deceive the early followers of Christ, we have distractions today. Jesus urged them to remember what He had taught them and to compare it to what others taught. We must heed the same counsel.

I navigated my way back to the correct exit in Memphis. But it would have been far less difficult if I'd listened to Scott's advice from the beginning. That's true as well for the wise counsel of Jesus. As I navigate through life, I hope to follow Jesus's instruction and carefully consider whom and what I allow into my heart and mind.

—*Teri Lynne Underwood*

"Readers are advised to remember that the devil is a liar."
—*C. S. Lewis*

 JESUS, in this world with all its distractions and diversions, help me focus on following You. Amen.

> I am coming to you now, but I say these things while I am still in the world, so that they may have the full measure of my joy within them.
> —John 17:13 (NIV)

If you want to understand joy, turn to a child. I recently brought my four-year-old daughter to a park full of inflatable bounce houses, and she spent the happiest morning of her life, jumping, sliding, falling, and shrieking with laughter. At one point she tried to say something to me, but she was laughing too hard to tell me what was so funny. That, my friends, is what joy looks like.

Joy is not something I think much about in my life. I'm mostly concerned with getting through each day. But perhaps I need to think about it more. Jesus wants us to have joy. In fact He wants us to have the full measure of joy. I picture a measuring cup overflowing with joy and spilling every which way because the cup isn't big enough to contain it.

And while I think He wants us to be happy, it's really spiritual joy—the joy that comes from knowing and loving Him—that fills us up. Jesus wants us to be so full of Him that we can't stop our spirits from smiling. He wants us to jump and fall and shriek in knowing He loves us more than we can ever imagine. I sure wish I felt that kind of deep-seated joy in my life. I can't help imagining what would happen if I were to let myself take some time every morning to celebrate the fact that Jesus died for me and that He wants me to be glad about it.

—*Elizabeth Adams*

*"There is not one blade of grass, there is no color in this world
that is not intended to make us rejoice."*
—*John Calvin*

 JESUS, help me to find the full measure of joy in knowing You. Amen.

Indeed, the very hairs of your head are all numbered. Don't be afraid; you are worth more than many sparrows. —Luke 12:7 (NIV)

An incredible thing happened when I got new glasses: I was able to see clearly the number of hairs I was losing each morning! They were scattered on the sink, running down the shower drain, and falling softly on my sweater.

God only knows how many hairs I've left behind in the course of my life.

In fact, God only knows exactly how many hairs are on my head, when I will get them cut, and what color I will choose to dye them. He knows Whose shoulder I will lean my head on the next time I am tired or sad. He knows the thoughts that fill my head, the words whispered into my ears, and the expression that will come from my mouth. He knows where I will rest my head each night, and He knows when I will lay my head down for the last time on this earth.

Only God knows. And that's enough.

As much time and money as I've spent taming the hairs on my head, I've wasted even more energy trying to control circumstances in my life. I fret and worry; I manipulate and speculate. Jesus's words remind me that when uncertainty swirls, He knows. When anxiety arises, He cares. "Don't be afraid," Jesus says.

Jesus counts all the sparrows in the sky, each hair on your head, and every burden of your heart.

—*Amy Lively*

"The God who created, names and numbers the stars in the heavens also numbers the hairs of my head. He pays attention to very big things and to very small ones. What matters to me matters to Him, and that changes my life."
—*Elisabeth Elliot*

JESUS, thank You for caring about every detail of my life and for finding me worthy of Your attention. Help me to not be afraid as I trust in You. Amen.

> Jesus answered, "How can the guests of the bridegroom fast while he is with them? They cannot, so long as they have him with them. But the time will come when the bridegroom will be taken from them, and on that day they will fast." —Mark 2:19–20 (NIV)

For years I based my status with God on the mentality that if I do this "good" thing, I am a good Christian. Even though I wouldn't admit it, my faith was based more on rules than grace.

This is the attitude Jesus ran into when some people, who like I, thought actions mattered more than relationship. They confronted Him because He and His disciples were not fasting. The Law called for people to fast one day a year, on the Day of Atonement. But by Jesus's time, people were expected to fast two days every week. When Jesus and His disciples didn't follow that rule, the Pharisees felt they weren't being sincere enough in their devotion to God. They believed the act of fasting itself was the point.

Jesus understood true fasting was connected with mourning or as a response to disaster. But with Jesus there, what was there to mourn? He was saying, *Why fast? That's like starving guests at a wedding reception! I'm here, so let's celebrate. When I'm gone, fasting will have its place.*

Jesus isn't more impressed with us when we follow rules. He wants us to spend time willingly and joyfully with Him because we want to, because we have nothing to prove. That's when real sincerity and devotion come.

—*Ginger Kolbaba*

*"Whenever faith seems an entitlement, or a measuring rod,
we cast our lots with the Pharisees and grace softly slips away."*
—*Philip Yancey*

JESUS, when I try to impress You with rituals, remind me that I don't have to prove myself to You. Amen.

**Blessed are those who are persecuted because of righteousness.
—Matthew 5:10 (NIV)**

Jesus's beatitudes from the Sermon on the Mount are so exquisite. *Blessed are the meek, those who mourn, the merciful . . .* I know what it's like to be meek, to mourn. I've shown mercy at times. But when I get to "those who are persecuted because of righteousness," I have to admit I haven't had much experience with that. Maybe none.

Ruby Bridges, though, has had experience with persecution. She was a six-year-old living in New Orleans, where she became the first African-American student to desegregate an all-white elementary school in the South. Accompanied by federal marshals, the little girl was greeted by a crowd of angry protesters. On the steps, Ruby stopped, turned, looked at the crowd, and said something that couldn't be heard.

Decades later, Jonathan Kozol, a famous educator and writer, asked her in an interview what she had said all those years ago as she looked out at that frightening crowd.

"I was praying," she answered.

"Praying that God would keep you safe?" he asked.

"No, I was asking God to forgive them. They didn't know that what they were doing was wrong," she answered.

—*Michelle Rapkin*

"It was a prayer not unlike Jesus who prayed when He was persecuted and crucified: 'Father, forgive them; for they know not what they do.'"
—*Ruby Bridges*

DEAR JESUS: Thank You for Your example. Thank You for assuring us that we are blessed when we are persecuted for the sake of right. Help me to be as brave in adulthood as Ruby was in childhood. Amen.

My Dearest,

Sometimes it gets hard to carry on. To keep the faith in the face of doubts. To keep doing the right thing—or trying to—when it just doesn't seem to pay off. But I am here. I listen even as I already know. I teach because I love you. I want you to die to yourself daily, and pick up your cross and follow Me. And I can show you how.

I understand the struggle. Even though I am your High Priest, I am also your brother and friend, Who relates to you because I, too, struggled. My commitment to God—to doing what was right, to being obedient—meant I had to walk a path that took me to the cross. I had to suffer, bleed, and die.

But the autumn season reminds us that, just like the seed that falls to the ground, after we endure death we get to see the resurrection. The season changes. I endured the cross for the joy set before Me. The harvest is your joy—if you don't give up.

With all of my heart, I implore you not to give up. Press on toward the mark of the high calling of God. You can do all things through My strength. People reap what they sow—that's a promise. So go about sowing seeds of kindness, mercy, grace, and love. Stay faithful. In time, those seeds will grow and those beautiful things will return to you. And by My awesome might, they'll also multiply into a harvest that's bigger than just you, a harvest that feeds and fuels the kingdom of God.

I love you forever.

And let us not grow weary of doing good, for in due season we will reap, if we do not give up. —Galatians 6:9 (ESV)

WINDFALL FROM HEAVEN

> Jesus looked at him and loved him. "One thing you lack," he said. "Go, sell everything you have and give to the poor, and you will have treasure in heaven. Then come, follow me." —Mark 10:21 (NIV)

The clerk at the new neighborhood grocery store seemed quite surprised when I turned down a chance to win a thousand-dollar shopping spree. "I can afford to pay for my groceries, but someone else might really need that prize," I said, fondly imagining a family with school-age kids filling their cart.

Years ago, I won a contest at a local department store. The prize was a five-hundred-dollar shopping spree. Our family budget was pretty tight at that time, so this was a big win! My husband and I decided to use the money to buy a bread machine we wanted but could not afford, perfume for our only living grandma, and a few toys in the catalog our son was eyeing.

When the big day came to shop, it didn't take long before the prize money was spent and the thrill of the win behind us. Our son was especially disappointed that our windfall had quickly turned into a memory. But what remained was far greater than the sum total of the winnings. We had those gifts, but we also possessed something even more precious: a reminder that things of this world will never surpass the gift I have through the sacrifice Jesus made on the cross. Those who accept salvation through Jesus's death and resurrection gain eternal life with Him in heaven. His windfall gift is one I would never turn down.

—*Barb Howe*

"Do all the good you can. By all the means you can.
In all the ways you can. In all the places you can.
At all the times you can. To all the people you can. As long as ever you can."
—*John Wesley*

 LORD, remind me this day to be generous unto others without restraint. Nothing on earth compares to the treasure of eternity in Your holy presence. Amen.

> I know your deeds, your love and faith, your service and perseverance, and that you are now doing more than you did at first.
> —Revelation 2:19 (NIV)

My son has a learning disability that makes reading a challenge for him. His tutor told me the other day that the most important part of her job is to monitor progress and point out to him all the specific ways he improves week to week. Otherwise, she told me, he won't even know his hard work is paying off—he will just be aware of all the ways he's still struggling.

When it comes to faith, it seems all humans share a disability. No matter how much we pledge our faith or seek to place our lives in Christ's care, we catch ourselves doing things that hurt ourselves and others. A friend once asked a monk how his community spends time at the monastery, and he answered, "We fall. We get back up. We fall. We get back up." No matter our pledge or commitment to Christ, living a life of faith does not mean smooth sailing.

In Revelation, the Son of Man acts like the faith tutor we all need! While we are too aware of the ways we have fallen short in our faith, He gently reminds us that we are steadily growing in faith. It might not feel like it, but even as we stumble, we are developing new strengths. Sometimes it feels as if we are going in circles to end up right where we started. But Jesus reminds us that the life of faith is a spiral. While we keep coming back around to where we were, we are moving imperceptibly but steadily upward, growing as we go.

—*Lizzie Berne DeGear*

> *"Optimism is the faith that leads to achievement.*
> *Nothing can be done without hope and confidence."*
> —*Helen Keller*

JESUS, remind me of what You see in me today when You look upon me with love. Amen.

"Do you not believe that I am in the Father, and the Father is in Me? The words that I say to you I do not speak on My own initiative, but the Father abiding in Me does His works." —John 14:10 (NASB)

From a worldly view, my senses of initiative, goal orientation, and self-reliance are good traits and, truthfully, they've seemed to serve me well and produced a lot of fruit. But Jesus offers a humbling perspective: Only closeness to Him produces abundant, lasting, high-quality produce. Without Him, I can do nothing.

The word "abide" is full of revealing meaning. Abide means "to dwell, to accept, to comply." Unlike my hard-driving tendencies, abiding sounds restful, passive, submissive even. While being passive is uncomfortable for me, I do want to produce fruit. So what does abiding look like in daily life? The truth is, I don't know, but I have a growing sense of what it's not.

Stressing, straining, frantically controlling to produce good fruit tells me I'm not abiding in Jesus. Maybe that also means the fruit I'm chasing after so hard is not of His vine. After all, fruit doesn't strain to appear! It grows slowly, ripening to beautiful maturity in season.

When I feel that anxious drive, I can turn my thoughts to Jesus, Who gently reminds me to dwell in Him. When I do that, my faith grows, I feel more peace, and I bear the fruit of His vine. Am I willing to trade my striving for abiding in Christ to produce the fruit of his choice?

—Isabella Yosuico

"Stay. Remain. Abide. Dwell. Fix. Delight. When the object
of these verbs is Jesus, He brings the most beautiful
Biblical promises to pass. Jesus. Only Jesus. Forever Jesus."
—Lysa TerKeurst

DEAR JESUS, please remind me that abiding in You produces good fruit without strenuous effort. Help me dwell in You as You dwell in me. Amen.

But the seed falling on good soil refers to someone who hears the word and understands it. This is the one who produces a crop, yielding a hundred, sixty or thirty times what was sown. —Matthew 13:23 (NIV)

My heart is the soil into which the Word is sown. So I have to keep my heart clear of things that will choke the Word and make it unfruitful, and I have to make sure my belief isn't shallow, so the roots of my faith can extend deep and troubles can't uproot it.

Yet the concept of producing a crop that yields many times what was sown makes me question how deeply Christ's roots have extended into my heart. When I read a great author whose words impact the world, or when I think of all the faithful men and women who have done so much for Christ, or when I meet a missionary or hear a speaker the Lord is using to draw many people to Himself, the yield of my faith seems insufficient.

But in the above verse, Jesus doesn't discriminate between the one who produces a crop of a hundred times what was sown and the one who produces sixty or thirty times what was sown. The extent of the yield doesn't seem to be His point, only that the soil isn't fallow. So why do I focus on a number or compare myself to others? Instead, I must focus on keeping the soil of my heart receptive, clear, and deep, and work alongside Him to scatter seed. He's prepared the hearts of others, and with a right heart I can help Him scatter seed.

—*Michael Berrier*

"We are able to persevere only because God works within us, within our free wills. And because God is at work in us, we are certain to persevere."
—*R. C. Sproul*

LORD JESUS, keep my heart right so I can be faithful to Your calling to work alongside You sowing seed. Amen.

> Therefore Jesus said again, "Very truly I tell you, I am the gate for the sheep. All who have come before me are thieves and robbers, but the sheep have not listened to them." —John 10:7–8 (NIV)

When I was in high school, a friend once took me to a "demon gate." At least, that's what he called it. At a break in a barbed-wire fence, his granddad had attached three horizontal strands of barbed wire to a short vertical pole. The pole was placed tight against a standing pole, its base and top secured with wire loops.

"Open it," my buddy said, grinning.

I positioned the gate pole against my chest, wrapping my arms around the standing pole and pulling hard. When the wire loop at the top didn't budge, I pulled harder, the rough wood scraping my skin. My muscles burned as I closed my eyes and pulled with all my might.

My buddy laughed when I broke away panting in frustration. "That," he said solemnly, "is a demon gate."

It took us both working together to finally open the gate. Closing it after us was just as difficult. "It's set too tight," I groused, rubbing where the pole had bruised my collar bone. "Why doesn't your granddad loosen the wire loops?"

"He doesn't want it to be easy," my friend said. "Otherwise, anyone could open it."

Jesus never said life would be easy. But He did say, "I am the gate for the sheep." Since that time I've always been willing to open the gate and let Jesus in.

—*J. Mason Williams*

"A very little key will open a very heavy door."
—*Charles Dickens*

JESUS, please be with me when life gets tough, and help me to always open the gate that leads to You. Amen.

The seed falling on rocky ground refers to someone who hears the word and at once receives it with joy. But since they have no root, they last only a short time. When trouble or persecution comes because of the word, they quickly fall away. —Matthew 13:20–21 (NIV)

It had been one year since my little sister drowned in the pond on our family farm, and I still couldn't reconcile my teenage heart to Jesus. He'd ignored my prayers when I cried out during a desperate attempt to breathe life back into Amy's limp body.

I remembered how as a young child I trusted the Lord with no reservations. At six, in my yellow dress, I laughed and twirled with the dandelion seeds, praising Him and basking in His immense love.

I missed Amy and my joyful self. In my sorrow, I took the advice of a friend and wrote a letter to Jesus. It began with angry words and ended with, *Never let go of me. Help me find happiness again.*

Looking back, Jesus never did let go, even when tragedy threatened to steal my faith. I'm certain He held me through my worst days. Through the years, even if I wandered, He never abandoned me. When my soul became parched, He'd draw me back. My Savior has always only been a heartfelt prayer away.

Though Jesus never lets go of us, when we turn our hearts from Him, our soul—God's ground—becomes dry. When we reach for His Life Water through prayer, church, and Scripture, His everlasting love always nourishes us.

—*Holly Michael*

"Joy is strength."
—*Mother Teresa*

LORD JESUS, we pray that Your Word takes deep root in our joyful, fertile souls, so that when storms come, we will be safe in Your powerful love. Amen.

> Jesus said to him, "Away from me, Satan! For it is written: 'Worship the Lord your God, and serve him only.'" —Matthew 4:10 (NIV)

What begs for your devotion? A television series? Favorite sports team? Even perhaps exercise? One fall I became devoted to anything pumpkin-flavored. I even did Internet research to find where pumpkin treats were sold. That pursuit might seem harmless, but my daily satisfaction had become dependent upon that specific taste in my mouth.

Jesus teaches us that we have power to overcome temptations that would attempt to draw us in with the promise of power, success, wealth, indulgence, or fame. Satan offered Jesus the world if Jesus would bow to him. With a simple "Away from me!" we, too, can stop the lure of that which might turn us from God.

Jesus also shows us how Bible verses give us strength. They speak truth into our souls when we are tempted. And they refocus our attention on God.

Lastly, Jesus shows us that He alone is worthy of our devotion and service. Our work and daily tasks, in fact, reflect that to which we are devoted. After some friends gave me lists of places nearby that sold pumpkin yogurt or muffins, I realized enough was enough. A seasonal pumpkin addiction could turn to a seasonal peppermint addiction and so on. Momentary satisfaction does not fulfill the deepest longings of our hearts. Nothing in this world can give us contentment the way our devotion to the Lord does.

—Janet Holm McHenry

"It behooves us to be careful what we worship,
for what we are worshipping we are becoming."
—Ralph Waldo Emerson

JESUS, thank You for Your reminder that only God is worthy of our worship and our service. Amen.

> **Look! I'm standing at the door and knocking. If any hear my voice and open the door, I will come in to be with them, and will have dinner with them, and they will have dinner with me. —Revelation 3:20 (CEB)**

A group of us guys were getting the church hall ready for our Saturday-night men's dinner when the doorbell rang. I pushed the door open to see a young couple and their baby in a stroller waiting outside. They could have been the holy family. "Is this where you have the soup kitchen?" the young man asked.

"Yes," I said, hesitating, "but that was this morning. We're cooking dinner now for our men's group."

"Oh." The man looked crushed. "We were hoping to get something to eat."

"Wait here for a moment," I said, inviting them in. I dashed back to the kitchen to see how the cooks were doing. Pot roast, pies, salad, mashed potatoes—it smelled delicious. "Do you think we have enough here to feed a couple of extra guests right now?"

"Absolutely," came the response.

We had a great men's dinner that night, full of good food, faith, and fellowship, as advertised, but it got off to just the right start when some needy guests appeared at our door and allowed us to feed them first.

—*Rick Hamlin*

"The world says you gain your life by getting more
and more and more, but Jesus says, No, that leads to death.
You get it back by giving it away and when you give it away you get it back."
—*Philip Yancey*

 JESUS, let me see You and welcome You in all Your guises, especially when You appear as the poor. Amen.

> He who rejects me and does not receive My sayings, has one who judges him; the word I spoke is what will judge him at the last day. —John 12:48 (NASB)

*H*e's back again? I thought. *When will he ever learn?*

This was the fourth time Daniel had walked back into the drug-and-alcohol rehab where I worked as a counselor. He had a wife, a child, a job, and he was on the verge of losing it all because he couldn't control his drinking. Every time he came back to dry out, he said the same old things: "This is so embarrassing. I feel so guilty. I am so ashamed. This time it's going to be different."

Nobody in the group believed him anymore. He needed someone to shake him up. This time I was that person. As soon as he walked in, I pounced: "You again? The last time, we hugged as you left, and you yelled, 'Today is a new day!' Well it is a new day, but you're in the same old rut. What does your family think? Does your name mean anything to you? Know what? I'm done with you. Don't come knockin' on my door after detox. Find someone else to sponsor you."

When I came home from work, I sought the counsel of Jesus on what had happened during that session. Popping a dinner into the microwave, I played my phone messages, and in a whispering voice I heard, "Hey, I thought about what you said today, and my name does mean a lot to me. It keeps me from throwing stones. Oh, this is Dan by the way. Bye."

I was hit with guilt for lambasting Daniel earlier that day and for not remembering that his name means "God is my judge."

—*Erik Person*

"By judging others, you make yourself easy to judge."
—*Brennan Manning*

 JESUS, in my zeal to live righteously, forgive me for playing the judge, jury, and executioner of others. Only you can do that. Amen.

So Jesus said to them again, "Peace to you! As the Father has sent Me, I also send you." —John 20:21 (NKJV)

I rarely saw my mother sit down. She cooked, baked, ironed, rocked seven babies, and gathered our family for church. Mom loved Jesus, and her acts of kindness behind the scenes made the greatest impact on me.

A memory that touched a special chord took place when I was about ten years old—the day I became the delivery girl. Mom filled a bag of folded, clean clothes to give away along with a full meal to go with it and some extra food, too.

"Kathy, will you take this to the Stantons' home?" she asked. "And here's some pretty ruffled curtains Mrs. Stanton might like for her kitchen window."

Mom had her hands full with my younger siblings, so she sent me down the street to the run-down shack that stood by itself amid rows of nicely kept middle-class homes. The Stanton children eagerly ran to the door, their mother behind them, and they graciously received Mom's gifts of love.

Years later, I talked to my mother about her compassion and devotion to this precious but needy family. I asked her how she did it all with such a large family of her own.

"Sometimes you have to just drop everything to help someone," she said. And to this day, I remember her words when Jesus wants to send me to help others, too.

—*Kathleen Ruckman*

"If not now, when? If not me, who?"
—*Hillel the Elder*

JESUS, whether You send me across the sea or down the street, may I go in Your name and love. Amen.

> And the judgment is based on this fact: God's light came into the world, but people loved the darkness more than the light, for their actions were evil. All who do evil hate the light and refuse to go near it for fear their sins will be exposed. —John 3:19–20 (NLT)

My husband, our dog, Isabelle, and I rode out an EF2 tornado, in the bathtub early one morning. When the storm was over, the quiet was deafening, and the darkness felt as if we could touch it. The storm knocked out all lights in the neighborhood. We couldn't see. My husband turned the switch on a small battery-operated flashlight, and this tiniest of lights gave us perspective and vision in that dark place.

Light removes darkness. Jesus, the Light of the World, absorbed the darkness of our sin. After the storm that morning, the light changed our confusion and fear into thanksgiving—we'd survived, and the small damages to our home could be repaired.

Jesus's words go deeper, as He reminds us that we typically embrace the dark. Just as the darkness hid the damage of the storm that early October morning, so darkness hides our secret sins, failures, mistakes, and blunders. I'll be honest. I'd like to keep mine hidden. Wouldn't you?

God's light exposes the truth about our actions, thoughts, and words. We may fear the light, but we need not be afraid, for His light shines with mercy and grace. So we can trust that all is forgiven.

—*Karen Porter*

"I live and love in God's peculiar light."
—*Michelangelo*

 DEAR JESUS, Your light exposes my hidden sins. Thank You for grace, mercy, and forgiveness. Help me walk in Your light. Amen.

> Even now the one who reaps draws a wage and harvests a crop for eternal life, so that the sower and the reaper may be glad together. Thus the saying "One sows and another reaps" is true. —John 4:36–37 (NIV)

We sat in rapt attention as my husband's grandparents told us the story of how they first came to know Jesus.

Grandpa was thirteen when a conversation with his father prompted him to begin a personal relationship with Jesus. Grandma had grown up in church, but it wasn't until attending a youth meeting with a friend at age twenty that she recognized the need for Jesus in her life.

Over the decades, their faith in Jesus grew and poured into their six children through consistent church attendance, reading of Scripture, and family prayer.

My mother-in-law became a missionary and has shared the news of Jesus with children and families across the United States and Canada. Her faith example took root in my husband, and now we are sowing faith into our children.

As one who married into this family, I have gladly reaped the benefit from generations of faith-building that began with my husband's grandparents.

As we share the truth of Jesus with others, we don't always know how these truths will grow. We might invest in a person and generations into the future see the harvest. No matter. I look forward to what will come.

Imagine the joy we will all share in eternity as we see the full crop harvested for Jesus's name!

—Amelia Rhodes

"With every deed you are sowing a seed, though the harvest you may not see."
—Ella Wheeler Wilcox

JESUS, thank You for those who sowed into me. Please enable me to sow Your truth into others. Amen.

HIS LARGER PICTURE

> As the crowds increased, Jesus said, "This is a wicked generation.
> It asks for a sign, but none will be given it except the sign of Jonah."
> —Luke 11:29 (NIV)

I was stunned when a friend, a fellow Bible-college grad, told me she no longer believed in God. My heart broke as I listened to her angst about God not showing up during a major career transition, a family medical emergency, and the loss of a significant relationship. She ended with, "I didn't see a single sign of God through that horrible season of life."

The people of Jesus's day also wanted a sign from heaven. And there He was! Couldn't they see—in the flesh—the Son of God standing right in front of them? No sign can top that one.

I find it easier to focus on Jesus during periods of blessing and ease, as opposed to times of uncertainty when tunnel vision on problems precludes Jesus. When I ask Him for help and then only look where I want Him to act, I miss other ways He is working in the world around me, and that might not include my immediate sense of need. However, when I sit and journal about the larger picture of God's faithfulness, I find comfort and confidence in Him.

Are today's pain and problems clouding your vision? If so, "turn your eyes upon Jesus, look full in His wonderful face, and the things of earth will grow strangely dim, in the light of His glory and grace" (Helen H. Lemmel).

—*Nancy Sebastian Kuch*

"We want big directional signs from God. God just wants us to pay attention."
—*Lysa TerKeurst*

JESUS, keep my eyes trained on You. Enable me to see You clearly so my heart might be filled with hope and joy amid today's challenges. Amen.

> I am the true vine, and My Father is the vineyard keeper. Every branch in Me that does not produce fruit He removes, and He prunes every branch that produces fruit so that it will produce more fruit. —John 15:1–2 (HCSB)

I'm a lousy gardener. No plant is safe in my care. Even so, I've learned the value of pruning. When we bought our house from an elderly widow, the many ornamental shrubs were overgrown—leggy limbs, sparse foliage, and few blooms. Eager to tidy our new yard, I read up on pruning to learn how, what, and when to cut to produce the best results.

As a novice, I found it hard to prune as mercilessly as instructed. It seemed cruel and risky. Would the plants survive my shearing? For instance, butterfly bushes should be pruned nearly down to the ground at the end of each season. The promise is that the following summer, lush and colorful new growth will attract and feed a wondrous assembly of butterflies, honeybees, and hummingbirds.

I recognize Jesus as the Master Gardener. But I must confess, I don't like "Isabella pruning season." OK, it may be the fact that I'm not blooming fully right now, but I really do need to surrender to the idea that somehow a comforting defect hinders my usefulness.

I have learned through my relationship with Jesus that He is a perfectly loving, attentive, and wise gardener. However uncomfortable for me in the moment, Christ's loving intent in pruning me is to promote healthy growth, vital foliage, and beautiful blooms for His purpose and glory.

—*Isabella Yosuico*

> *"God prunes us when He is about to take us into*
> *a new season of growth and expansion."*
> —*Christine Caine*

LORD, I want to yield to Your pruning and trust Your loving intent to help me bloom more fully for Your kingdom on earth. Amen.

> **The seed that fell among the thorns represents those who hear God's word, but all too quickly the message is crowded out by the worries of this life and the lure of wealth, so no fruit is produced. —Matthew 13:22** (NLT)

How can I be that rare kind of Christian who brings immense blessing and life to those around me?

According to Jesus, it all has to do with how I respond to His truth.

In one of His best-known parables, Jesus compares Himself to a farmer, His word to seed, and our hearts to different types of soil. In short, He says that when we pay attention to His teaching, plant it in the depths of our hearts, and root out opposing ideas, we flourish. When we're resistant to His word, or our hearts are overrun by other things, our spiritual lives end up looking like a barren field or a weed-infested mess.

I'm no farmer. However, I have a generous friend with a veritable Garden of Eden behind his house. Why is he able to reap (and share with others!) a bumper crop of fruits and vegetables each summer? Because of all the tilling, fertilizing, watering, and weeding he does. This is Jesus's point: like a garden, our hearts require rigorous maintenance if we are to be fruitful.

When I let bogus, worldly messages take root in my soul—such as, "You need ___ to be happy" or "Let our financial pros show you the way to a secure future!"—I find God's truth is choked from my life. Such lies kill my joy and my spiritual effectiveness.

—*Len Woods*

> *"Where the plow does not go and the seed is not sown,*
> *the weeds are sure to multiply."*
> —*Charles Spurgeon*

JESUS, grant me insight and strength to pull the "thorns" from my heart that are hindering Your work in and through my life. Amen.

> Jesus answered, "I did tell you, but you do not believe. The works I do in my Father's name testify about me." —John 10:25 (NIV)

My teenage son begged his mother and me for a guitar on his birthday. The problem was, he didn't play guitar.

"But I want to learn," he insisted.

We reminded him that he could play his mother's guitars anytime he wanted.

"I want a guitar of my own," he said.

My wife offered to teach him, and we told him we would consider buying him a guitar only after he could demonstrate his interest by playing a song for us. A week later, he had not only taught himself to play—after my wife showed him a few chords—but he also serenaded us like a pro. We bought the guitar.

Some people's words and actions are inconsistent, even contradictory. Jesus is not that kind of person. When His detractors pressed Him to say He was the Messiah, He refused to play their game, insisting His words—and especially His actions—had clearly and consistently revealed His true identity.

I want to do more than say I am a follower of Jesus. I want also the works I do to testify about Him. I want my life to display my true identity as a child of my Father in heaven.

—*Bob Hostetler*

"Don't say things. What you are stands over you the while,
and thunders so that I cannot hear what you say to the contrary."
—*Ralph Waldo Emerson*

JESUS, please help me to show my true colors at all times, and to be clear and consistent in all I say and do, to the glory of Your Name. Amen.

> Then he said to them, "Watch out! Be on your guard against
> all kinds of greed; life does not consist in an abundance of possessions."
> —Luke 12:15 (NIV)

A friend and her husband had accumulated so much stuff that they moved from a 2,300-square-foot house into a 4,600-square-foot one to accommodate everything. After a while, she expended so much energy just dealing with the excess that she couldn't keep up with it all. So they sold their house and downsized.

"I had five toilets to clean!" she admitted. "Everywhere I looked, things needed my attention—to be cleaned or fixed or moved. I just couldn't do it." She realized all that stuff was keeping her from enjoying the life and purpose God created her for.

Her story convicted me, and I evaluated my own "collecting" habits. I wondered, *Do I purchase things because I believe they will make me happy? What do I give up in exchange for investing in these material items?*

It isn't wrong to need or want nice things. But as my friend discovered, stockpiling those things does not make our lives more joyful or abundant, just as having fewer things does not make our lives less whole. Jesus reminds us that possessions will not make our lives more satisfying. Instead, unhealthy attachments to them will keep us from investing in what is truly life-giving: relationships that last.

When we focus on what lasts—relationships with Jesus and other people—we find true wealth and satisfaction.

—*Ginger Kolbaba*

"When wealth is lost, nothing is lost; when health is lost,
something is lost; when character is lost, all is lost."
—*Billy Graham*

 JESUS, sometimes I forget that things won't bring satisfaction. Remind me of the wealth of investing in things that last. Amen.

> Therefore be on the alert, for you do not know which day your Lord is coming. —Matthew 24:42 (NASB)

My kids tease me about my habit of making beds. Each day I get out of bed and neatly tuck the sheets in at the corners of the mattress. I pull the comforter tight and place the throw pillows at just the right angles. I love a crisply made bed, and often my kids say, "Who cares, Mom? If no one is going to see this room today, what's the point?" I understand their thinking, but I don't want to live in a house that I clean up only when I think someone might stop by.

It's easy to get in the same rut with faith. Prayer can become a triage bandage in times of trouble rather than a daily delight. Bible reading, church attendance, and great talks with people can become winks and nods to a God we're ignoring. Jesus talks a lot about being ready. He lets us know we won't know the time of His return, but we should live as if it were imminent. Imagine the difference in our plans and routines if we were to know this was the day we would meet our Lord. I know one thing: I want my bed to be made and my spiritual life in order.

—*Gari Meacham*

"If you're not ready with your house in order, you might miss the presence of God."
—*Mae McGuire*

 JESUS, today I ask You to help me live as if I were going to see You face to face. Loving You is the true purpose of my life. Amen.

THE ETERNAL SPIRIT

> Very truly I tell you, whoever obeys my word will never see death.
> —John 8:51 (NIV)

One of the most powerful stories I've ever encountered about death comes from *A Window to Heaven: When Children See Life in Death* by Diane Komp, a pediatric oncologist who wrote of her experiences caring for children who were battling cancer.

The story is about a little boy who was desperately ill. He'd been in the hospital for months and often asked when he'd get to go back to school and be with his friends and schoolmates, whom he missed terribly. His condition continued to worsen, and he neared death. One particularly difficult morning, he raised his head from the pillow and asked his mom excitedly, "Does Jesus drive a school bus, Mommy?" His mother said she didn't think so. "Oh, yes, He does, Mom!" he said excitedly. "Here's the bus, Mom. And there's Jesus! I have to go now. I'll see you later, Mom!" he said. With that, he closed his eyes and took his last breath.

I am always reassured when I read today's verse and remember that, while my body will surely experience death one day, Jesus promises my spirit will not see death. I don't know how that will happen in that moment, but I do know Whom I'll meet.

—*Michelle Rapkin*

"You're born. You suffer. You die. Fortunately, there's a loophole."
—*Billy Graham*

 DEAR JESUS, thank You for Your promise that You will never forsake Your children, not even in death. Please help me not to be fearful when I think about death but rather to know that, when the time comes, You'll meet me and I'll smile. Amen.

> He also said, "This is what the kingdom of God is like. A man scatters seed on the ground. Night and day, whether he sleeps or gets up, the seed sprouts and grows, though he does not know how." —Mark 4:26–27 (NIV)

I conducted my first horticultural experiment, in Mrs. Aker's kindergarten class. Under her watchful eye, students planted lima-bean seeds in paper cups. Over the next few days, our excitement grew as our cups yielded first a sprout, then a spindly bean-bearing plant. For all but one of us, that is. One friend's project was not so successful. He had planted and watered, yet his bean sprout didn't grow. And, he was confident nothing was wrong with his seed...because he'd dug it up every day to inspect it.

Jesus taught us that the kingdom of God is like a farmer and his seed. God sets the process of growth and spiritual maturity in motion, and we respond by nurturing that growth through the tools He has given us. We spend time with Him daily. We open our hearts to Him in prayer and confession. We fill our hearts and minds with His Word. We seek fellowship with other believers. However, all of this is based on patience and faith. If we cannot trust that our lives are in His hands, we rush in and seek to control each situation we encounter. In doing so we often miss the lesson. We can easily lose sight of His providence. We sometimes even thwart His will for our lives.

—*David Downs*

"Seeds of faith are always within us; sometimes
it takes a crisis to nourish and encourage their growth."
—*Susan L. Taylor*

DEAR JESUS, please give me wisdom to appropriately act and react to the challenges of this day. Help me be patient and to trust that You are working even when I cannot see Your hand. Amen.

A HAND UP FOR GOLIATH

> I am sending you out like sheep among wolves. Therefore be as shrewd as snakes and as innocent as doves. —Matthew 10:16 (NIV)

Standing at the soup kitchen's bread station, I halved each slice to extend the supply. My teenage daughter walked the room, refilling water glasses. She bent to speak with someone just as another yelled to demand more bread.

I recognized the giant—his sheer size intimidating, his name a perfect fit: Goliath.

Her voice shaky, my child explained there wasn't enough for seconds but that she'd see what she could do. She headed for the kitchen.

An idea popped into my mind. Desserts filled the space to my right. I piled some on a plate, and hurried over and offered it to him. "Sometimes Jesus doesn't give us exactly what we want. But when we trust in Him, He gives us something even better." The insensitivity of my unbidden words stung. I didn't want him to think I was making light of his hunger, rather that Jesus can exceed expectations.

Goliath's expression softened. Grabbing the dish, he seated himself.

I returned to my station and studied the assembly of broken people, who seemed vulnerable and dependent as lambs. Possessing little, they asked for even less. Then, I realized something. I, too, was a lamb, part of a larger flock. I prayed for Goliath and all the others. With Jesus's help, I'd search out a way to provide for those in need. And I trusted my Shepherd would show me how.

—*Heidi Gaul*

"Continue. Be loving and be strong. Be fierce and be kind.
And don't give in and don't give up."
—*Maya Angelou*

LORD JESUS, help us hear Your divine wisdom and then give us the courage to do Your will. Amen.

> Whoever believes in me, as Scripture has said, rivers of living water will flow from within them. —John 7:38 (NIV)

I remember watching a children's choir perform "I've Got a River of Life." Their faces beamed as they made hand-motion waves to illustrate the river flowing from within. Arms flung wide, they opened imaginary doors, setting prisoners free. At the chorus, they leaped, reaching for the sky, singing, "Spring up, oh well, within my soul!" What a joyful picture of the Spirit-filled believer.

Is this a picture of me? Or you? Not always. When we receive Jesus as our Savior, He promises the Holy Spirit's indwelling. Yet how easy it is for life to become barren. Hands with too much busywork and heads too full of information combine to deny the heart what it truly needs: communion with Christ. Unless we are filled with Jesus, no channel of blessing will flow from us.

Seeking the living water, we become revived and comforted. It pardons us and offers grace. Out of this abundance, the river flows from each redeemed heart revealed in our actions toward others. And through us, He brings light and life to a hurting, thirsty world.

—Cathy Elliott

"Christ is not a reservoir but a spring. His life is continual, active and ever passing on with an outflow as necessary as its inflow. If we do not perpetually draw the fresh supply from the living Fountain, we shall either grow stagnant or empty. It is, therefore, not so much a perpetual fullness as a perpetual filling."
—A. B. Simpson

LORD, fill me with Your living water so my heart will overflow with love toward others. Amen.

> You did not choose me, but I chose you and appointed you so that you might go and bear fruit—fruit that will last—and so that whatever you ask in my name the Father will give you. —John 15:16 (NIV)

They said the toddler years would be hard. They were right. The season was captured in one photograph: face red, fists clenched, head thrown back in a howl, our daughter's sweatshirt read, "WARNING: I AM 2." My days were measured by countless "no's!" (from both of us!).

They said the teen years would be hard. They were right again. There were still lots of "no's!" (now mostly from me), but we also said "yes!" to new adventures. Prom pictures graced our refrigerator, and we logged hours chauffeuring, cheering on the sidelines, and maneuvering through delicate relationships.

But no one could have prepared me for the adult years. Driving away from her first college dorm wrung my heart, yet it paled in comparison to closing the door on her first apartment—a one-year lease, with no more summers to be spent walking the dog and making pancakes at home. Now we have video chats about careers, politics, and culture.

On those days when I didn't know what I was doing, Jesus answered every prayer period. The toys are long gone, the prom dresses stashed away, and that upset toddler is now a strong, independent young woman who may someday comfort her own child.

It was easy to lose sight of the eternal truths we were both learning, but Jesus gave me grace for each day and wisdom beyond my own experience.

—*Amy Lively*

"Do not confound work and fruit. There may be a good deal of work for Christ that is not the fruit of the heavenly Vine."
—*Andrew Murray*

JESUS, may my daily tasks bear eternal fruit. You chose me for my responsibilities, so please equip me to accomplish them. Amen.

> But when you give to the needy, do not let your left hand know what your right hand is doing, so that your giving may be in secret. Then your Father, who sees what is done in secret, will reward you. —Matthew 6:3–4 (NIV)

Thirty years ago I met a woman who might as well have been an angel. At the time, I was newly single with four young sons. I desperately needed a job, and the day-care costs soared higher than any paycheck. The problem settled on the empty refrigerator and pantry.

Dear Jesus, how am I going to feed my sons?

I phoned a few people for help but got nowhere. Depression hit hard that one afternoon as I tried to figure out what to do for my family.

A knock at the door captured my attention. I made my way there with a heavy heart. I opened the door to a smiling woman. "Hi. God told me the family here needed groceries."

My stomach flipped, and I didn't know whether to laugh or cry. "Thank you," I said. "Please, come in."

"Oh, I don't need to visit. I just want to deliver what I have for you."

My sons heard the conversation and hurried to help. Every item in the bags came from my grocery list. What an amazing victory! Not a single box, can, or cold item was something my sons didn't enjoy.

The next day I received a job opportunity to direct a day care, where my sons could stay free of charge and be fed breakfast and lunch.

Jesus answers prayers.

—*DiAnn Mills*

"Remember that the happiest people are not those getting more, but those giving more."
—*H. Jackson Brown Jr.*

DEAR JESUS, You meet our needs in ways we never expect. Your love is the greatest gift of all. Amen.

SEEDS OF FAITH

Don't you have a saying, "It's still four months until harvest"? I tell you, open your eyes and look at the fields! They are ripe for harvest.
—John 4:35 (NIV)

A while back, I took a vacation to Arizona with my brother and his family. We rented a suite of rooms with walk-out patios at a Holiday Inn Express. Each day, we explored different tourist destinations and favorite family spots.

One evening, we returned to find a motorcycle gang had moved into the rooms adjacent to ours. Armed bodyguards stood at the entrances to their rooms. I was standing on our patio, talking with one of them, when their leader, Buzzy, joined us. Elaborate tattoos extended from below Buzzy's muscle shirt to his wrists. I felt compelled to initiate a conversation with him.

Buzzy said he was in town to visit his sister, who was hospitalized. I asked if I could pray for them both. Buzzy said, "Yes." But as I began to pray right there, the bodyguard snickered. Buzzy bowed his head, and he thanked me after I finished.

I then shared my testimony of faith in Jesus. Buzzy told me he was surprised I was even talking to him. When I asked why, he told me he knew his tattoos and biker image were intimidating. He also admitted he had done too many bad things to be saved. I assured him Jesus died for all our sins and that all he had to do was believe in Him. The seeds of faith were planted, and I prayed they would grow. Only the Holy Spirit can bring Buzzy to salvation. By faith, I anticipate seeing Buzzy again—one day in heaven.

—*Barb Howe*

"We sinned for no reason but an incomprehensible lack of love,
and He saved us for no reason but an incomprehensible excess of love."
—*Peter Kreeft*

DEAR LORD, by faith alone I believe You will bring the ones You have placed in my path to a saving grace through faith in You. Amen.

A good tree can't produce bad fruit, and a bad tree can't produce good fruit. —Luke 6:43 (NLT)

Growing up, I thought my mom coined the phrase, "You are who you hang around with." I wanted to fit in with the "in" crowd, but Mom wouldn't let me.

I always wondered how she knew they were up to no good. Now I know. Trees are known by their fruit. You can tell what a person is like by his or her deeds or behavior. It's true that you are prone to become like whomever you spend your most intimate time with. A friend of mine once told me if I wanted to grow a particular fruit tree indoors, I'd have to buy two because they needed to cross-pollinate to produce fruit. I had no idea!

I'm certainly not saying to befriend only Christians. Jesus was friends with everyone. Still, even He had an inner circle: Peter. James. John. Over the years, I've learned that, like Jesus, my inner circle needs to be made up of people who love Jesus and want to produce good fruit.

But even more so, I need my best friend to be Jesus Himself. Alone, I can't produce anything good. And I don't want to be known for producing bad fruit or no fruit at all! By drawing closest to Him, I know I'll become more like Him. My actions will prove it.

—*Jessica R. Patch*

"My best friend is the one who brings out the best in me."
—*Henry Ford*

 JESUS, let my actions represent You well, and help me to never forget that You are my best friend. Amen.

> Whoever has my commands and keeps them is the one who loves me. The one who loves me will be loved by my Father, and I too will love them and show myself to them. —John 14:21 (NIV)

My mother was a beautiful, faithful person who knew and loved Jesus. She told me of the time she was deathly ill with scarlet fever. Filled with the illness, she called on her angels and lifted up a prayer. Following that, she had a vision of Jesus with his arms spread at the foot of her bed. She awoke completely healed! Another time, my brother was at death's door with an invasive infection. The doctor said my brother's life was in God's hands. As he returned to my brother's side, my mother prayed. Jesus appeared to her, surrounded by smiling children. At that moment, the doctor rushed out of the room, shouting that my brother was healed. "A miracle," he proclaimed.

The Lord appeared to my mother one final time, when he took her home. She was only forty years old. I was ten and heartbroken by the sudden loss, but I still knew Jesus had taken her home to heal her of the cancer that had so ravaged her earthly body.

That day, I promised to dedicate myself to prayer. I've yet to "see" Him as my mom once did, but praying and walking in His way helps me feel His presence more and more each day.

—Mary E. Williams

*"In those times I can't seem to find God,
I rest in the assurance that He knows how to find me."*
—Neva Coyle

THANK YOU, Jesus, for Your great love, which You share so freely with me. I can't wait to see You face to face. Amen.

Greater love has no one than this: to lay down one's life for one's friends. You are my friends if you do what I command. —John 15:13–14 (NIV)

During his first year of college, my oldest son called home and said, "Now I know why I have diabetes."

Jake had been battling Type 1 diabetes since his diagnosis at age fourteen. Managing dangerous blood-sugar highs and stumbling through the lows, he pushed on toward his dream of playing high-school football and then became a starter for the Wisconsin Badgers.

"I think God has allowed me to have diabetes to help others," he said.

Then Jake shared Joey's story. The ten-year-old, newly diagnosed diabetic, contacted him because his mom wouldn't let him play football.

Jake didn't want kids to struggle like he had.

My son continued helping Type 1 diabetic children and their parents while managing his own diabetes, college, and football. During his NFL career, he volunteered at the Juvenile Diabetes Research Foundation.

Jesus made the ultimate sacrifice by laying down His life for us, His friends. Not everyone is called to pay that price, but our struggles with disease, illness, and other sufferings can be used to edify others.

We truly are His friends if we obey His command to love one another.

—Holly Michael

"For God no cost is too high. Anything can be sacrificed
if only we may please Him. Let us daily learn to be obedient children."
—Watchman Nee

JESUS LORD, may we not complain about our sufferings but rather ask that they be used for the greater good. Amen.

When Jesus saw this, he was indignant. He said to them, "Let the little children come to me, and do not hinder them, for the kingdom of God belongs to such as these. Truly I tell you, anyone who will not receive the kingdom of God like a little child will never enter it." —Mark 10:14–15 (NIV)

Teaching children is one of the greatest blessings we can have—and a tremendous responsibility. When I was teaching Sunday school, one little girl was too shy to join in with the rest of the class, and this got my attention. When I helped her tie her shoes, she looked at me with so much gratitude it melted my heart. After class was over, when parents arrived to pick up their children, her mother arrived alone. Later, another teacher mentioned that the girl had no father. I don't remember whether she'd lost him to death or abandonment. I never got the chance to find out the girl's story because she never returned to class, but I remember her well.

We are all like that little girl, needing love even though we might not know how to ask for it. And our perception of love might be warped by the imperfect love we've experienced from others through separation or even abuse. But the pureness in love we receive from Jesus beckons us like children. By rising from the dead, He proved His everlasting and redeeming love, care, and concern for us. I must acknowledge my need for Him, open myself up to His help, and be as grateful as that fatherless little girl.

—*Michael Berrier*

"If childlike dependence on God is the mark of a great soul,
then there are great souls hidden in all sorts of places
where the world sees only disability, decay, and despair."
—*Colleen Carroll Campbell*

LORD JESUS, help me to be childlike in my faith in You and filled with wonder at the miracle of Your love for me. Amen.

On that day you will realize that I am in my Father, and you are in me, and I am in you. —John 14:20 (NIV)

I am an artist. I have been for as long as I can remember. Much more than a hobby or pastime, making art is a way of life for me. Much of the way I see the world around me is shaped by my understanding of art, examples of how artists have responded to their lives and times, and the community of artists I have known in my life. For me, making art is a way of processing and understanding my life.

One photo series, which I began in 2007, is called "Jesus Portraits." I have all types of people pose for my camera while wearing a "biblical" wig and beard I purchased at a local costume shop around Halloween time. It's often a very awkward, and usually pretty funny, experience.

At first, this seems ridiculous, and I must admit it really is rather goofy. On another level, this photo series helps me and, I hope, anyone who sees it to recognize Jesus in other people. When Jesus talks about being "in the Father" and "you in me" and "I in you," this can be rather challenging for me to comprehend. Through these campy pictures of women, men, and children, I find it easier to look at everyone around me and see the Savior.

—*Wayne Adams*

"I see Jesus in every human being."
—*Mother Teresa*

 DEAR JESUS, please help me to see Your face in the people around me and love them with Your love. Amen.

> He told them: "The harvest is abundant, but the workers are few. Therefore, pray to the Lord of the harvest to send out workers into His harvest." —Luke 10:2 (HCSB)

"If everyone could remember to bring extra coloring books and crayons next Sunday, I'd greatly appreciate it." I can't count the number of times I watched Carolyn, my best friend and mentor, make that announcement at church, always smiling from ear to ear. However, it was a phrase that always left me with mixed emotions: happiness, amazement . . . and grief.

Carolyn was a high-school art teacher in a courageous battle with ovarian cancer. She always made it a point to take art supplies to the pediatric cancer ward before going to her chemotherapy appointment. I was always amazed that she had the emotional energy to visit with children and parents while also facing her own fight of her life. But Carolyn used her illness as a means to reach out to others and tell them about Jesus. She considered it a true blessing to work in His harvest.

I can't help but believe that when this command was given, God knew those who were going out into the fields would reap just as many blessings as the very ones they were witnessing to. Carolyn once said cancer was the greatest thing to happen to her. I believe that's when she was transformed into a courageous servant.

Carolyn went to be with the Lord recently. She was given a grim prognosis, but lived another ten years joyfully reaching others for Christ. She left me with a righteous lesson: make every second count. The result is a heaven filled with colorful joy.

—Angie Spady

"Christian courage is the willingness to say and do the right thing regardless of the earthly cost, because God promises to help you and save you on account of Christ."
—John Piper

 JESUS, I praise Your name. Thank You for loving me. Please give me the strength and courage to reach out and tell others about Your wonderful saving love. Amen.

My Cherished One,

Because of Who I am, you truly can give thanks in everything. I hold you in My everlasting arms. Nothing comes into your life without going through Me first. What that means is this—regardless of how things might seem, I am in control. I am working all things together for your good. So you can be thankful in all things, letting your heart rest securely in My love.

Let not your heart be troubled nor afraid. Instead be thankful. God's will for you as a believer in Me is that you trust Him in all things and choose thankfulness over fear. Because I broke My body for you, you can be thankful for salvation. Because I conquered death, you can be thankful for eternal life. Because I forgive your sins, you can be thankful for restoration. Because I never leave you, you can be thankful for My presence. Because My strength is perfect, you can be thankful for your weakness. Because I am the Way, you can be thankful for each step along your journey. Because I am the Truth, you can be thankful you are set free. Because I call you, you can be thankful for your purpose. Because I give you My Spirit, you can be thankful for His comfort. Because I calm the storm, you can be thankful for peace. Because I live in you, you can be thankful for the power to live a godly life. Because I make no mistakes, you can be thankful even for hardships. And because My kingdom never ends, you can be thankful for the future.

I love you forever.

Give thanks in everything, for this is God's will for you in Christ Jesus.
—1 Thessalonians 5:18 (HCSB)

> He said to them, "You are the ones who justify yourselves in the eyes of others, but God knows your hearts. What people value highly is detestable in God's sight." —Luke 16:15 (NIV)

While I had fixed Craig's dinner favorites—steak, fried potatoes, and salad with homemade Thousand Island dressing—I was once again cleaning up the dishes with nary a "thank you."

I shut the dishwasher door with a little more emphasis than usual.

Craig, startled, said from the end of the kitchen counter, "Is something wrong?"

I swiped the dishcloth over the brown granite, then paused, hands on hips. "Well, I just fixed you a great meal, but I didn't get any kind of thank-you."

"I'm sorry," he said. "It was a great meal. Thank you." He started up the nearby stairway. "But—"

"What?" I interrupted. "But what?"

He looked me straight in the eyes. "But you know, I just changed the oil in your car, and you didn't thank me either." Then he headed upstairs.

Ouch. He was right. Not only had I not thanked him, but I also wasn't very nice about it when I asked him to check the oil in the first place.

A relationship with Jesus requires more than lip service. God doesn't appreciate it when we serve or give only when we know others will applaud us. Quietly offering our gifts and little acts of service to God develops Christ-like humility that ultimately favors us in others' eyes.

—Janet Holm McHenry

"Morals and ethics are best learned…in relationship with one who is an impeccable model of morals and ethics. We suggest Jesus Christ."
—Michael Horner

 JESUS, help me live a life of integrity so my actions match up to a life worthy of Your calling. Amen.

> If you abide in me, and my words abide in you, ask for whatever you wish, and it will be done for you. My Father is glorified by this, that you bear much fruit and become my disciples. —John 15:7–8 (NRSV)

"Ask whatever you wish, and it will be done for you." Doesn't this sound almost too good to be true? As if we were children and Jesus were a wish-granting fairy! Well, this is the same Jesus Who suggests we be like children if we wish to enter the kingdom of God. So maybe there's something to it.

I remember when I was first going through my religious conversion in my late twenties. In many ways I did feel like a child, and every day seemed like Christmas morning. I felt Jesus's joyful presence standing over me and eagerly anticipating my opening the next gift—as if He couldn't wait to see my delight at what the day had in store.

What does it mean to abide in Jesus and for His words to abide in us? It is such an intimate, mystical notion, isn't it? And here it also points to the creative nature of our connection with Jesus. Somehow, when we live our relationship with Christ, our creative actions in the world become God's glory! Somehow, when we release ourselves into an intimate, committed relationship with Jesus, our desires become the gravity that pulls us toward the kingdom of God. Not only do our personal wishes come true through this creative connection, but also the world moves closer to fulfillment as we dwell in Christ and Christ's word within us.

—*Lizzie Berne DeGear*

"In our joy, we think we hear a whisper. At first it is too soft. Then only half heard. We listen carefully as it gathers strength. We hear a sweetness. The word is Peace. It is loud now. It is louder. Louder than the explosion of bombs."
—*Maya Angelou*

JESUS, the world pulls me in and fills me up with so much distraction and confusion. Today, help me abide in You. Today, may each breath leave more room for Your words to abide in me. Amen.

**God is spirit, and his worshipers must worship in the Spirit and in truth.
—John 4:24 (NIV)**

The other day I saw a friend from a church I used to attend. As we spotted each other, I felt my heart rate quicken, my tummy flutter, and a burst of joy. I thought of Mary going to Elizabeth's house when she was pregnant with Jesus. Luke 1:41 reads, "When Elizabeth heard Mary's greeting, the baby leaped in her womb." There was no baby in either my womb or my friend's, but we are both believers with the Spirit of God living inside us (Romans 8:9).

Knowing the Spirit of God in us is alive, powerful, and active is cause for rejoicing. We recognize Him, and rejoice and worship Him—and worship with Him. What does worship look like when we consider that the Spirit of God worships with us? Amazing!

Sometimes singing or praying feels boring, lifeless, and unexciting. In reality, our God is anything but boring! Jesus encourages us to worship with His Spirit. When I read a Psalm or sing a praise song, I remind myself that God is worshipping right along with me. My heart rate quickens, my tummy flutters, and I feel a burst of joy. How great is our God!

—*Nancy Sebastian Kuch*

*"And wonder, in turn, is intended to lead us to the
ultimate human expression and privilege: worship."*
—*Steve DeWitt*

 JESUS, You are truly worthy of all praise! Help me remember to employ the greatness and glory of Your Spirit to worship You today. Amen.

> **Jesus answered, "It is written: 'Man shall not live on bread alone.'"**
> **—Luke 4:4 (NIV)**

I focus too much on my own needs and hungers. My prayers too often revolve around what I want. I go through my day, working, spending time with my family, exercising, considering what my next meal will be, or calculating how my pay might not be adequate for my bills. My needs are always at the forefront of my thoughts.

Nothing is wrong with bringing my needs to God. He wants me to. And it is good to be productive at work, be dedicated to my family, and exercise so I can be at my best for Jesus. But I can't live for earthly desires.

Jesus promises to supply my needs. He always has. He always will. And He has given me even more: He has given me His Word, recorded from His very mouth, that He will train me spiritually, intellectually, emotionally, and physically. The same enemy Jesus responded to in the desert sends temptations my way, but temptations are only distractions from the promises of Jesus, which are far more fulfilling. Instead of letting my thoughts focus on my physical hungers, I must hunger for Jesus and only what He has for me.

—Michael Berrier

"The strongest, most mature Christians I have ever met are the hungriest for God. It might seem that those who eat most would be least hungry. But that's not the way it works with an inexhaustible fountain, and an infinite feast, and a glorious Lord."
—John Piper

LORD JESUS, when I'm tempted today, remind me that You'll meet all my needs and that You will sustain me. Amen.

> **Jesus answered, "Whoever loves me will keep my word. My Father will love them, and we will come to them and make our home with them."**
> **—John 14:23** (CEB)

One Sunday morning our church choir felt especially prepared to sing. We'd rehearsed all the music and had gone through all the hymns. Soon the service would begin. But one of the sopranos, thumbing through her bulletin, pointed out to our music director, "The wrong communion hymn is listed here. It should be 'What Wondrous Love Is This.'" The rest of us looked at our bulletins. "I've got it right," someone said. "My bulletin is correct," said another.

The soprano turned a page in her bulletin and noticed a few other errors, lots of them, including the date. She burst out laughing. "It's wrong because I'm looking at last week's bulletin."

I can't remember what the sermon was that morning, but this pre-sermon offered me a pretty good lesson. How many times do things seem wrong simply because I'm looking at the wrong program? Jesus asks me to love, and I decide I'm supposed to judge. Jesus wants to make His home in me, and instead I accommodate Him by being an occasional visitor. I get focused on rules when Jesus says there is another way to keep His word.

—*Rick Hamlin*

"The Christian faith is meant to be lived moment by moment.
It isn't some broad, general outline—it's a long walk with a real Person.
Details count: passing thoughts, small sacrifices, a few encouraging words,
little acts of kindness, brief victories over nagging sins."
—*Joni Eareckson Tada*

 JESUS LORD, let me follow You by simply loving You and loving the Father as You make Your home in me. Amen.

Very truly I tell you, whoever accepts anyone I send accepts me; and whoever accepts me accepts the one who sent me. —John 13:20 (NIV)

"How do you get to heaven, Mom?"

My four-year-old had overheard my phone conversation. I'd spoken earlier with a friend about an elderly Jewish neighbor who passed away. Occasionally I talked to my neighbor, Bess, about Jesus, but she never accepted Christ, so I wondered about her salvation.

How do you get to heaven? While I was contemplating a proper answer for a preschooler, Nick said, "Never mind, Mom. I know."

"You do?" I knelt beside him.

"Yes, Jesus comes and takes your hand." Nick ran off to play. Had God sent him to tell me something?

Bess believed in the God of Abraham. God sent many prophets and priests and then He sent Jesus. The Lord calls us to preach the gospel to all. Had Bess rejected my words and missed Him? I wondered if, in Bess's last moments, Jesus held out His hand, like Nick said. Would she recognize her Savior? I can't know for sure, but I think she would've placed her hand in His.

Jesus's message of salvation is for all. We can lovingly share it and only pray our words take root in the hearts of nonbelievers. Perhaps, when Jesus comes to take their hands, they'll recognize the One we love—the One God sent.

—Holly Michael

"O that our hearts were enlarged in love to God, that we might turn inward, to the blessed comforter, that the blessed Jesus said the Father would send."
—Elias Hicks

JESUS, You are the Way, the Truth, and the Life. No one comes to the Father except through You. Reveal yourself to those who don't know You and lead them to heaven. Amen.

> Looking at his disciples, he said: "Blessed are you who are poor, for yours is the kingdom of God. Blessed are you who hunger now, for you will be satisfied. Blessed are you who weep now, for you will laugh." —Luke 6:20–21 (NIV)

The best meal I ever had was a tray of overcooked hospital food. I'd just given birth to my first daughter, and during the twenty-four hours of labor I hadn't been allowed to eat or drink. By the end of it, I was so hungry—and, OK, so hopped up on hormones—that the soggy spaghetti I shoveled into my mouth felt like the best thing I'd ever eaten. I was hungry, and after two huge helpings, I was finally satisfied.

I know how silly this sounds. Going twenty-four hours without food in an expensive hospital suite is nothing compared to the kind of hunger people face every day around the world. I know how blessed I am. But I also know what it's like to despair and lose all hope. I understand what it's like to mourn, and to long for comfort. To desire, and to have those desires go unmet.

That's why I find Jesus's words in Luke 6 so comforting. Jesus reminds us that what we go through now is not the end. The troubles we face today will be but faint memories tomorrow, because He is with us and comforts us. Because we know what it's like to weep, we find even more pleasure in laughter. Like the relief you feel when you wake up from a nightmare, Jesus promises better things are in store. That's a promise I can cling to.

—Elizabeth Adams

"We were promised sufferings. They were part of the program.
We were even told, 'Blessed are they that mourn,' and I accept it.
I've got nothing that I hadn't bargained for."
—C. S. Lewis

 LORD, help me to remember that I am blessed not in the midst of suffering but because I suffer. Thank You that You are near. Amen.

> Therefore, go and make disciples of all the nations, baptizing them in the name of the Father and the Son and the Holy Spirit. Teach these new disciples to obey all the commands I have given you. And be sure of this: I am with you always, even to the end of the age. —Matthew 28:19-20 (NLT)

A friend was determined to read the Bible from beginning to end, and because my husband and I are Bible teachers, he came to our house each week to ask various questions about what he had read. We didn't always have profound answers, but we pointed him to Jesus.

Another friend resides in a suburb where many immigrants live, so his neighbors come from many religious backgrounds. He lives an upright, joy-filled life, and when people ask him why he is so happy, he tells them about Jesus. Another friend serves sandwiches in the poorest part of a major city, and when people ask her why, she tells them about Jesus. Sometimes Christians preach on street corners. Other times, the best way to share is by living like Christ and waiting for an opportunity before speaking.

Jim Elliot died trying to share the gospel with the Auca Indians of Ecuador. Before his death, he said, "He is no fool who gives what he cannot keep to gain what he cannot lose." Jim Elliot understood that bringing another person to Jesus is the greatest work in the world.

I tell others about Jesus because of what He did—and does—for me. He rescued me from following the wrong path. His love assures and comforts me. I want to tell others about Him.

—*Karen Porter*

"God's command 'Go ye, and preach the gospel to every creature' was the categorical imperative. The question of personal safety was wholly irrelevant."
—*Elisabeth Elliot*

DEAR JESUS, reveal to me a creative way to tell the world about Your powerful and life-changing message. Amen.

> What good will it be for someone to gain the whole world, yet forfeit their soul? Or what can anyone give in exchange for their soul?
> —Matthew 16:26 (NIV)

A mbition is a good thing, right?

Fifteen years ago, I would have said, "Absolutely." But I had a change of heart one afternoon at a writer's conference. I attended a workshop being taught by an editor from National Geographic Kids, a company I wanted to write for. A stack of submission guidelines and sample magazines was making its way to me row by row, the supply was dwindling fast. At that time, such resources weren't yet available online.

As the woman in the row in front of me passed the short stack to the writer beside her, I reached around her shoulder and peeled a packet from the meager remains. If looks could annihilate, I would've been a goner. "Really?" she groaned. "That was so rude!"

Surprised at and shamed by my self-serving action, I agreed with her. In that moment, I learned feral ambition can be just as insidious and corrupting as greed. I had to admit that my heart was susceptible to the pull to pursue gain and chase after favor regardless of the cost.

I asked the two women in front of me to forgive me, then I asked Jesus to forgive my transgression. I sought His perspective on my role in satisfying the passion He's placed in my heart.

—*Mona Hodgson*

"The desire to reach for the stars is ambitious. The desire to reach hearts is wise."
—*Maya Angelou*

 LORD JESUS, help me keep my eyes fixed on You and my heart set on Your ways, not on the ways of the world. Amen.

> Meanwhile, when a crowd of many thousands had gathered, so that they were trampling on one another, Jesus began to speak first to his disciples, saying: "Be on your guard against the yeast of the Pharisees, which is hypocrisy." —Luke 12:1 (NIV)

Sauerkraut is a dish that's a favorite part of my Eastern European heritage. I tried making it recently and found the process to be quite simple: Finely shred a head of cabbage, mix with sea salt until the cabbage begins to give off its juices, and pack it tightly in a glass jar. Carefully place a plate and a weight on top of the mixture, ensuring all cabbage is submerged below the salt brine. Then cover the container with a clean towel, and let it ferment.

In about two weeks, my fresh cabbage was transformed into a culinary delight. I had successfully followed directions and created an environment free from harmful bacteria. I tried it again. But my second attempt was less successful.

Maybe I was careless about following instructions. A bit of mold formed on the top of the brine and infiltrated the cabbage. The entire batch was ruined by a tiny bit of bad bacteria. What made the difference? It was the discipline to carefully follow instructions the first time, and failure to follow them as closely the second time. I'd learned my lesson.

Jesus encourages me to read His Word and follow the instructions. When I don't do that carefully, I become vulnerable to an environment in which human deception can lead me to sin.

—*Barb Howe*

"Most of us are aware of and pretend to detest the barefaced instances of that hypocrisy by which men deceive others, but few of us are upon our guard or see that more fatal hypocrisy by which we deceive and overreach our own hearts."
—*Laurence Sterne*

GUARD my heart and motives, dear Jesus. Help me to remain alert to Your simple truths so I do not become infected by thoughts that lead me to sin. Amen.

> **Watch out for false prophets. They come to you in sheep's clothing, but inwardly they are ferocious wolves. By their fruit you will recognize them. Do people pick grapes from thornbushes, or figs from thistles? —Matthew 7:15–16** (NIV)

It was an election year. I'd studied the candidates, weighing their focus against issues I considered important.

I remembered attending a church meeting centered on answering questions of prospective members. One man kept interrupting the pastor, comparing his previous denomination to this one and pointing out things he didn't like about the way we worshipped, baptized, and took communion. The division he sparked echoed the tension already present due to the upcoming general election.

With great patience, the pastor explained the difference between things that matter and those that don't. If we keep our eyes on the Lord, we won't be distracted or misled by the details mankind has added. Do the words or church practices point to Jesus and His sacrifice? Do they bring glory to the One Who died for all my "stuff"? Are they found in the Bible?

My thoughts zeroed in. My barometer for truth—Christ—is clear about the issues. He knows what I need, and how and where to guide me. He can be trusted with my faith, my family, and my life here on earth and in my eternal home. He is the King of Kings and will reign forever. His wisdom, power, and grace don't require my support—I require His.

—*Heidi Gaul*

"It is the nature of all hypocrites and false prophets to create a conscience where there is none, and to cause conscience to disappear where it does exist."
—*Martin Luther*

THANK YOU, Jesus, for guiding me through tough choices. Strengthen my discernment, and keep me centered on You. Amen.

Jesus answered, "It is written: 'Man shall not live on bread alone, but on every word that comes from the mouth of God.'" —Matthew 4:4 (NIV)

Dad usually carried a limited amount of cash in his pocket, not because he was afraid of losing it but rather because he had a habit of giving it away. Our family lived modestly, and bills were often hard to pay, but that never stopped Dad from seeing Jesus in those in need.

One day, when stopping for gas at a station connected to a small diner, he went inside to pick up lunch for himself and my mom. Upon returning to his car, Dad noticed a man at the next pump was counting his change before quietly saying to a child, "Sorry, son. We only have enough for gas today." Without hesitating, Dad peeked around the pump. "Excuse me," he said. "I just realized I have a couple of extra burgers. Guess my eyes were bigger than my belly. I'd hate for them to go to waste." The boy's eyes widened, darting between his father's face and this stranger's. The man paused and then swallowed hard. "I think we might be able to find a home for those burgers. Thanks, friend."

When Dad came home with nothing but a sheepish smile, Mom just laughed. "I'm guessing you didn't forget to buy lunch." "No," answered Dad, "I remembered. But I traded it for living bread."

—*Andrea Raynor*

"Be faithful in small things because it is in them that your strength lies."
—Mother Teresa

DEAR JESUS, open my eyes and my heart so I can see You in others. Help me feast on Your word and on the promise of Your care. Amen.

CITIZEN OF HEAVEN

> Jesus said, "My kingdom is not of this world. If it were, my servants would fight to prevent my arrest by the Jewish leaders. But now my kingdom is from another place." —John 18:36 (NIV)

I have voted in every election since I was a college freshman in the early '70s. These days, we are bombarded by political ads and media campaigns, pundits and columnists, who remind us we are making the most important decision of our lifetimes.

Yet Jesus did not seem overly concerned about politics. His years on earth were framed by Roman occupation along with all of its bias and brutality, including common crucifixion. Though His followers hoped and expected that as Messiah He would bring political upheaval and government overthrow, He reminded them that He was not impressed by local politics or even geopolitics. In fact, when His life was on the line, He said to Pilate, the Roman governor in Jerusalem, "My kingdom is not of this world."

My pastor recently made an interesting statement regarding his growing disenchantment with the political process. "Remember," he said, "as Christians our affiliation is not with a donkey or elephant. Rather, we are people of the Lamb." The apostle Paul puts it this way in Philippians 3:20: "Our citizenship is in heaven."

—*David Downs*

"Let us not seek the Republican answer or
the Democratic answer, but the right answer."
—*John F. Kennedy*

 JESUS, I pray today for the politicians and judges who have been given authority over us. May their service be marked by Your wisdom, justice, and mercy. Amen.

You have heard that it was said, "You shall love your neighbor and hate your enemy." But I say to you, love your enemies, bless those who curse you, do good to those who hate you, and pray for those who spitefully use you and persecute you. —Matthew 5:43–44 (NKJV)

"Monkey Face!" Mary Ann, an older girl, taunted me again. Every day when I got on the school bus, the fifth-grader targeted me, a first-grader. Sometimes I hid behind my big sister's skirt, as the ridicule went beyond the bus, into the halls of the school or outside on the playground.

Painfully shy, I endured the abuse for weeks, until I finally told my mom and dad. Not long after, my father went to the school and talked to the principal.

The principal called Mary Ann and me into the hall, where my father stood waiting. "Apologize to Kathy," the principal told Mary Ann. "Promise you won't bully her." Papa nodded, satisfied as she obliged, his face filled with love for me.

I went back to the classroom, put my head on my desk, and sobbed. I sensed Jesus was with me as the teacher walked me to the nurse's station because I couldn't stop crying. I realize now, Jesus, my best friend, helped me love and forgive Mary Ann, and He healed my wounded heart.

Decades later, I still think of Mary Ann. Just the other day, I asked Jesus to bless her if she's still on this earth—and if she doesn't know Him as her Savior, that Jesus would draw her to His heart.

—Kathleen Ruckman

"Forgiveness doesn't make the other person right, but it sets you free."
—*Unknown*

JESUS, when others are unkind, help me to love them, pray for them, and forgive them as You would. Amen.

> "Consider carefully what you hear," he continued. "With the measure you use, it will be measured to you—and even more. Whoever has will be given more; whoever does not have, even what they have will be taken from them."
> —Mark 4:24-25 (NIV)

Years ago, I broke my ankle after a church service. I'd like to say I rushed across the wet lawns to heroically rescue a child from the jaws of a pit bull. However, that isn't true. I wanted to catch my friend and compliment her on a new haircut before she left the parking lot. In my haste, I slipped and broke my ankle. The episode resulted in major surgery, fixing me up with a metal rod in my leg and various screws across my ankle. On crutches for a month, I wore a cast for a full six weeks.

When the happy day came to retire the cast, I was appalled to see my leg atrophied from lack of use. No muscle at all, it was the consequence of the natural law: "use it or lose it."

Jesus told His disciples to heed spiritual truth with the greatest care—embrace it in their minds and hearts so they could be effective teachers of the gospel. Based on their efforts, they would reap greater wisdom, truth, and grace to apply for the kingdom.

Jesus builds up my spiritual muscle as I listen to, obey, and embed into my heart His word. Then, should difficulties come, I have only to lean into His truth and draw from a history of His kind provision.

—*Cathy Elliott*

"If we are faithful to God in little things, we shall gain experience
and strength that will be helpful to us in the more serious trials of life."
—*James Hudson Taylor*

LORD, thank You for giving us Your Word. Teach me so I, too, may reflect the Light of Jesus. Amen.

When he had received the drink, Jesus said, "It is finished." With that, he bowed his head and gave up his spirit. —John 19:30 (NIV)

My dear friend, Elia, stopped by today, looking for guidance on how to mark her election ballot. On a small pad she had written, "Tell me how to vote." You see, my friend is ninety-four and suffers from aphasia, a communication disorder that often results from a stroke. She had partially filled in some of the bubbles on her ballot and was determined to finish it on time.

Despite her age, Elia is not finished. She had driven herself to my house and ambled up my seven front steps—without the aid of a handrail, walker, or cane. Earlier that week she also attended my retirement dinner, a Rotary meeting, and my school's scholarship banquet. She went to the banquet because she had written a letter recommending the scholarships to one of her many other service organizations and wanted to see the awards in person.

Jesus finished His earthly tasks in just over three decades of life. He fulfilled His Father's calling—living a perfect life, teaching about His Father, doing His work, and making the final sacrifice for us.

After our short visit, I helped Elia back down my front steps and into her car. Then I wondered, *Am I still about my Father's business?*, even though I know I am not finished until Jesus beckons me to my eternal home. So I will do His business until He says, "It is finished."

—*Janet Holm McHenry*

> *"The death of Jesus Christ is the fulfillment in history*
> *of the very mind and intent of God."*
> —*Oswald Chambers*

 THANK YOU, Jesus, that You finished Your call to bring salvation to all men. Guide me in Your call on my life. Amen.

> Then, turning to His disciples, Jesus said, "That is why I tell you not to worry about everyday life—whether you have enough food to eat or enough clothes to wear. For life is more than food, and your body more than clothing." —Luke 12:22-23 (NLT)

I stood inside an orphanage in Chiang Rai, Thailand, fascinated by the children eating their dinner, which consisted of watery rice and scrambled eggs. They relished each bite.

Laughter and joy filled that rickety table until the children jumped up in mismatched, worn shorts and shirts to hurry after their bath towels. Their giggles left an echo in the room. And conviction in my heart.

My life is not always steak and baked potatoes or expensive clothes. Sometimes it's ramen and Goodwill. And occasionally, I've been ungrateful. But Jesus didn't say He'd clothe me in high-end jeans and feed me the finest cuts of meat. He simply said He'd meet my daily needs and not to worry about the rest. That night, those toddlers and preschool children recited from memory several Psalms. They had a better grasp on the above verse than I. It didn't matter what they wore or what filled their bellies. What mattered was Who filled their spirits.

Jesus doesn't always provide how I think He should. But He never lets me go hungry physically or spiritually. I only need to open my mouth and my heart.

—Jessica R. Patch

"Though troubles assail, and dangers affright, though friends should all fail, and foes all unite; yet one thing secures us, whatever betide, the Scripture assures us, the Lord will provide."
—John Newton

 JESUS, humble my heart. Fill me with joy. Help me to always be grateful for Your provisions. Amen.

For the bread of God is the bread that comes down from heaven and gives life to the world. —John 6:33 (NIV)

When I was a little girl, I was obsessed with my Uncle Bud's amazing magic tricks. Whenever I saw him, I begged him to perform each one over and over. Quite frankly, I wasn't particularly interested in anything about my uncle besides his ability to pull rabbits out of hats or long scarves out of his ears.

In John 6, Jesus feeds thousands with just a few loaves of bread. For the masses, the miraculous feeding was what interested them. Crowds were following Him, but He knew that was because He had just performed a miracle. He may have sighed with frustration at the crowd or scolded His followers for wanting to send the masses away. Instead, He told them He could do so much more for them than just magically produce bread to feed them. He was there to provide sustenance that would last eternally.

Years after my Uncle Bud died, I learned he had led a very exciting life. He'd been a diplomat who traveled the world over and spent time with famous people from all walks of life. I'm sure he'd have been thrilled to tell me stories of the exotic places, fascinating people, and valuable lessons he encountered. He must have been disappointed that I only cared about his magic tricks when he could have shared so much with me that would have had lasting value. I imagine Jesus felt that way.

—*Michelle Rapkin*

"Give us this day our daily bread."
—*Jesus, in the Lord's Prayer*

THANK YOU for being the bread of eternal life. Thank You for Your patience—and please forgive me when I ask You for magic tricks. Amen.

> He replied, "My mother and brothers are those who hear God's word and put it into practice." —Luke 8:21 (NIV)

The tears came quickly, and they would not stop.

I was visiting a new church in our new town. A cross-country move and a new calling meant we left our parents, lifelong friends, and sweet neighbors. We had also left a ministry and memories.

We were called to move away from the church we helped plant, the one where I had been on staff for several years. Each Sunday I had the privilege of welcoming the congregation, looking into the smiling faces of my dear friends and many family members.

So on that first Sunday morning in our new church, I felt understandably alone.

But strangely, I also felt very much at home. The pastor preached from familiar Scripture. We sang songs my grandmother had taught me. The traditions of communion and baptism were shared and celebrated by generations of believers. And the same Spirit comforted me.

The worship team finished, and a singer who had noticed my tears came over and hugged me. "I don't know you, but God bless you," she said.

Oh, He has blessed me indeed. This special place has become my home away from home. New relationships developed gradually over lunch and Bible studies and serving in our community. I'm still awkwardly moved to tears when we worship, but now they are tears of joy and thankfulness for my new family.

—*Amy Lively*

"Church attendance is as vital to a disciple as a transfusion of rich, healthy blood to a sick man." —Dwight L. Moody

JESUS, thank You for giving us the legacy of Your church. I embrace my new family of people who love and serve You. Amen.

All those the Father gives me will come to me, and whoever comes to me I will never drive away. —John 6:37 (NIV)

When I was a young teen, I experienced trauma. One day, I looked down at the ground where my feet stood and wondered, *Why am I taking up this square foot of earth—except to be abused or ignored?* I penned poetry about taking my life. Desperate, I shared my words with anyone who would read them.

But few took me seriously. I felt desperately lonely, longing for a group of fun friends but so absorbed in my pain that I never quite fit in. Then someone invited me to youth group. We popped balloons, ran crazy relays, sang songs, and sprayed copious amounts of shaving cream all over one another! The last minutes of the meeting, though, someone talked about Jesus.

Hearing about Jesus nearly stopped my heart. I had no idea He was God's Son, Whose mission it was to die on the cross for us. So when the leader shared how Jesus loved the abused and folks who felt ignored, I took notice. Could this be true? Was there really a reason for me to live? Was I loved? Wanted?

I committed myself to learning more about Jesus. A year later, I gave my life to Him. I finally understood why I was born—to be loved by Him. And I am forever grateful that I have life. I also know one thing for sure now: He gave me this life and values it more than I ever thought possible.

—*Mary DeMuth*

"I have one desire now - to live a life of reckless abandon for the Lord, putting all my energy and strength into it."
—*Elisabeth Elliot*

JESUS, help me to remember how beautifully You rescued me. I'm grateful You pursued and wooed me. Amen.

> In the same way, I tell you, there is rejoicing in the presence of the angels of God over one sinner who repents. —Luke 15:10 (NIV)

I have to confess that I'm a fan of country music. For most of my youth, however, I wouldn't have been caught dead listening to it. The slow, smooth sounds of a steel slide guitar or a singer's deep country twang didn't appeal to me. As an adult, though, I found myself appreciating classic country artists like Hank Williams and Johnny Cash and, more recently, Dolly Parton, and Merle Haggard.

Country music isn't generally known for its positive and uplifting messages. The old joke goes, "What do you get when you play country music backward? You get your wife back, your dog back, your truck back…" If I'm honest, the hardscrabble tales of woe and misfortune are probably what appeal to me. Something just resonates with me when it comes to people's confessions of hardship and bad choices.

This is why I was surprised to find spiritual exhortation from the same man who wrote hard-knocks country songs like "Mama Tried," "The Bottle Let Me Down," and "Misery and Gin." The late Merle Haggard also covered the Woody Guthrie classic "Jesus Christ," that talks about the people who crucified Jesus: "If Jesus was to preach like He preached in Galilee, they would lay Jesus Christ in His grave." I don't know where Mr. Haggard found himself at the end of his life regarding religion, but if this song is any indication, he certainly knew enough about the life of Jesus Christ to now sing a happier tune in the afterlife.

—*Wayne Adams*

"Faith is the only way we're going to make it.
None of us are smart enough to do it on our own."
—Merle Haggard

DEAR JESUS, please help us to remember that true life comes from You. May we join with heaven in rejoicing over our salvation, and with those who repent and trust in You. Amen.

Give us today our daily bread.
—Matthew 6:11 (HCSB)

I detest dieting. I mean, does anyone enjoy carrot sticks? I much prefer carrot cake.

It's never more than a few days into a diet when my body screams, "I want food! Real food!" But I and countless others who fall off the dieting bandwagon never seem to understand why we fail miserably: we've trained our bodies to yearn for the wrong things.

Our spirits are the same way. Just as the Israelites in the Bible, we often yearn for possessions or experiences that aren't in our best interests. Just a month or so into their grand exit from Egypt, they felt the rumbling in their stomachs. Rather than trust in God to sustain them with manna, they grew angry and accused Moses of trying to kill them. Being filled with greed is never a good thing.

If the Israelites had been thankful and trusted God to sustain them, their days of wandering in the desert would have been shorter.

Just as we make the decision to eat a healthful salad for improved nutritional value, we should also commit to feasting upon God's Word as spiritual nourishment. This type of daily bread not only reminds us of God's abundant provisions but also results in a healthy and thankful spirit.

—Angie Spady

"'Bread' represents four things in the Bible: the basic necessities of life, God's word, the family of God, and salvation. Whatever your need is—physical, emotional, relational, or spiritual—God will take care of it if you will depend on him."
—Rick Warren

JESUS, help me to be content and only yearn for those things that are healthy for my mind, body, and soul. Thank You for daily bread and for the ultimate provision of dying on the cross so that I may live. Amen.

> Then He took the five loaves and the two fish, and He looked up to heaven [and gave thanks] and blessed them. —Luke 9:16 (AMP)

Thanksgiving is often the epicenter of family reunions. Parents typically anchor this annual tradition in the family home. It is where brothers, sisters, and extended family reconvene, sometimes in the very place in which they were raised.

Our family was a little different. As Italian immigrants and naturalized US citizens, my parents tried to embrace the traditional American celebration of Thanksgiving but with a twist—lasagna or some other festive Italian food in lieu of turkey. They sustained the tradition as long as they could, until their struggles overshadowed any semblance of household normalcy.

Soon, loving surrogates filled that void. Family, friends, and neighbors shared their loaves with my brother and me as part of their Thanksgivings. This simple act of neighborly love had a profound and lasting impact on us, and even now inspires the way we relate to the lost and marginalized. Both celebrations helped shape the way I honor Thanksgiving.

It truly is a time to give thanks. What better way to express our gratitude than to extend the love we ourselves received by including someone with no place else to go?

—*Isabella Yosuico*

"Thanksgiving Day is a good day to recommit
our energies to giving thanks and just giving."
—*Amy Grant*

DEAR JESUS, this Thanksgiving, let me give thanks by giving love to someone who needs it this day. Amen.

But the Advocate, the Holy Spirit, whom the Father will send in my name, will teach you all things and will remind you of everything I have said to you. —John 14:26 (NIV)

It had been years since I'd been back to Perry, Florida, to visit my eleventh-grade English teacher. She still looked the same. She had the same twinkle in her eye, the same no-nonsense demeanor, and the same enthusiasm for shaping and molding young teenagers into responsible adults.

"You were my favorite teacher," I said earnestly. "Thank you for inspiring me. I love to write because of you."

"Thank you," she said, smiling. "I loved encouraging you to write. You were always one of my favorite students."

I chuckled at that. I knew she meant it, but I also knew she must have had innumerable favorite students over the years. In fact, most of her students were probably her favorites. She was like that. It was the secret to her success. She loved to encourage us to do our best. She truly cared for every student she ever taught. I know she cared for me.

Her name was Gwen Faulkner. And she was diagnosed with cancer not long after I spoke to her. She died at the age of fifty-one.

I thank God every time I pray. I thank Him for life, for love, and for always being there when I need Him. I thank Him for encouraging me every day of my life.

And today, I thank Him for Gwen Faulkner.

—*J. Mason Williams*

"Promise me you'll always remember: You're braver than you believe, and stronger than you seem, and smarter than you think."
—*Christopher Robin to Pooh, in the words of A. A. Milne*

JESUS, thank You for teaching me all things and for filling me with Your Holy Spirit. And thank You for placing teachers in my life, who have inspired me. Amen.

> Then he said to Thomas, "Put your finger here, and look at my hands. Put your hand into the wound in my side. Don't be faithless any longer. Believe!" —John 20:27 (NLT)

On occasion, I've had a hard time mustering faith to believe, especially when it comes to believing Jesus desires to give me wonderful gifts and longs for me to accept them.

I know my shortcomings better than anyone. I know how often I fail and how utterly undeserving I am. So it's a combat at times for me to let go and trust that Jesus delights in giving me incredible gifts. Promises. Dreams. Blessings. It seems too good to be true.

I wonder if Thomas stood there, staring and thinking the risen Christ was just too good to be true. All of God's promises fulfilled in Jesus were standing right before Thomas! He was a witness. He should have believed. Instead, he doubted.

What ultimately speaks to me in John 20:27 is that Jesus didn't shake His head or leave Thomas. Instead, He asked him to come closer, to touch His hands, His side. I am thankful Jesus is just as patient and kind with me. Always drawing me near through His Word, He leads me to passages of love that prove over and again how much I mean to Him, that every good and perfect gift comes straight from heaven. I can't physically touch Him or see Him, but I feel Him in my heart, and that humbles and awes me. And it recharges my faith with a resounding "I believe!"

—*Jessica R. Patch*

"God doesn't owe us anything—yet in His grace, He still gives us good things."
—Billy Graham

JESUS, Thank You for Your gracious gifts and unending love. Help me receive and use them for Your glory. Amen.

> He replied, "You give them something to eat."
> They answered, "We have only five loaves of bread and two fish—
> unless we go and buy food for all this crowd." —Luke 9:13 (NIV)

Our town has an influx of homeless people in the fall and winter. So our community provides potluck suppers one Sunday a month at a beachside park for these needy friends. We never know how many people we are going to feed, but the Lord does! It always amazes me how many people come. What amazes me even more is that there is always plenty of food. We've learned to trust Him to provide.

The Lord was ever present in my childhood home. Love was abundant, but extras like vacations or a second pair of shoes weren't. So I would sneak snacks such as cereal or cheese. I even ate dog biscuits under the kitchen table with my dog! One time, I devoured a whole bottle of medicine, thinking it was a cherry-flavored liquid snack. After having my stomach pumped in the hospital and enduring a lecture from my parents, I finally came to realize I must trust them to provide for me.

Jesus wants us to trust Him to provide for us. And He will, if we put our trust totally in Him.

—*Mary E. Williams*

"Faith don't come in a bushel basket, Missy. It come one step at a time.
Decide to trust Him for one little thing today, and before you know it,
you find out He's so trustworthy you be putting your whole life in His hands."
—*Lynn Austin*

JESUS, thank You for all that You provide. Please help me to trust You more. Amen.

> **The one who sent me is with me; he has not left me alone, for I always do what pleases him. —John 8:29** (NIV)

Out of the mouth of any other person in history, these words would make me roll my eyes: "I always do what pleases him."

I try to please God every day, but I still fail miserably by getting impatient and angry and acting like I'm more important than others. I want to do what's right, but I so often fail. How can anyone possibly always do what pleases God?

But then, we're talking about Jesus here. He was perfect, after all.

Then again, maybe God doesn't expect the same level of perfection from us as He does from Jesus. I don't expect my two-year-old to sit still throughout the whole church service; she's not capable of it. I hope God doesn't expect me to always speak kindly, put others first, and live every moment to proclaim His truth. I want to do those things, and He wants me to as well. But sometimes I fail, and I believe God realizes we aren't capable of always pleasing Him.

Thankfully, what is true of Jesus in this verse is also true for us: God has not left us alone. Jesus, Who understands our struggles, is with us. We might not always do things that please Him, but He is with us anyway. He loves us in spite of our failures. I find great comfort in that. I might not be perfect, but thank God Jesus was—and is!

—*Elizabeth Adams*

"God's will may not be the perfection of the true
believer's life, but it is the direction of it."
—*John MacArthur*

LORD, thank You for Your direction. Help me to please You in what I do and say. Even when I fail, help me to continue trying to do what's right. Amen.

> Before long, the world will not see me anymore, but you will see me. Because I live, you also will live. —John 14:19 (NIV)

I still treasure the last hug from my friend, Ethel, before leaving a writers' conference. She was wearing the scarf I'd crocheted for her.

"I love you," I said.

She squeezed me tighter. "I love you, too, my dear."

We kept hugging, as if we both knew this might be the last time we saw each other. And it was. Ethel passed away from cancer a few months later. She was one of my dearest friends, writing mentors, and prayer warriors. The next year's conference had a sad hole in it. When my new book came out, I longed to tell Ethel. Instead I thanked God for the part she'd played in my writing and faith journeys, and pictured her being the first friend to greet me in heaven.

Jesus was more than a mentor, teacher, and friend to His followers—He was their source of eternal life. When I remember moments like my last hug from Ethel, I wonder what it must have been like for Jesus to count down the days until He left His friends. He knew the end of the story, but they didn't, so He did His best to remind them. How many times after He left this earth did His disciples say, "I wish Jesus were here"? Like we do, they had to trust His promise that they would see Him again. It is a gift Jesus gave by leaving them—and us—with hope. It's a gift for which I am truly thankful!

—Jeanette Hanscome

"With Christ as your friend and heaven as your home,
the day of death becomes sweeter than the day of birth."
—Max Lucado

THANK YOU, Lord, for the promise that I will see You someday and for the life I have through You. Amen.

Do not judge, and you will not be judged. Do not condemn, and you will not be condemned. Forgive, and you will be forgiven. —Luke 6:37 (NIV)

*H*onk! *Honk!* "That turkey just cut me off," I said out loud. From his backseat child carrier, my seventeen-month-old grandson laughed as he said, "Turkey." I had forgotten how much children learn from the things we do and say. His little voice reminded me how quickly I can be offended, especially compared to significant injustices others suffer.

Louis Zamperini went from juvenile delinquent to Olympic athlete in 1936, before his life detoured during World War II. On a routine US Air Force mission, his plane crashed in the Pacific, and Louis survived forty-seven days adrift only to be captured by the Japanese and tortured in a POW camp. Louis was eventually liberated into a nightmarish existence of anger, alcoholism, and night terrors.

On the brink of divorce, Louis's wife convinced him to attend a Billy Graham crusade. Louis came to faith in Christ and went on to establish numerous ministries centered on forgiveness and healing. In 1998, Louis returned to Japan during the Olympics. And he personally forgave the very guards who had tortured him as a POW.

I felt a sense of shame, considering the injustices Louis had forgiven in contrast to my highway mishap. Then I laughed and repeated the word "turkey." Silently I thanked God for using a baby's voice to remind me to forgive as Jesus has forgiven me.

—*Barb Howe*

"I think the hardest thing in life is to forgive. Hate is self-destructive.
If you hate somebody, you're not hurting the person you hate, you're hurting
yourself. It's a healing, actually, it's a real healing…forgiveness."
—*Louis Zamperini*

JESUS, help me to remember that You were nailed to a cross for my sins. Teach me to forgive others with the same loving spirit You show. Amen.

> Many will say to me on that day, "Lord, Lord, did we not prophesy in your name and in your name drive out demons and in your name perform many miracles?" Then I will tell them plainly, "I never knew you. Away from me, you evildoers!" —Matthew 7:22–23 (NIV)

"I don't understand why Jesus died for my sins," the Christian leader said. She smiled as she said it, while we ate our lunch.

"I don't either," I said. "It's just so amazing."

"No, you don't understand. I understand why He died for that guy over there." She pointed to a man drinking coffee a few tables away from us. She looked at me. "And I know why He died for you. But I don't sin, so why would He have to die for me?"

I am sure I must've looked shocked as I stumbled over my response. I couldn't believe she couldn't acknowledge her own sin. But as I unpeeled the layers of someone I thought knew Jesus, I grew sad. On the outside, she looked like a Christian. She said Christian words. She raised her children to go to church. She prayed to Jesus in public. But her heart seemed far from Him.

Her relationship with Him seemed more ritual than real. My heart told me to pray for her. Jesus wants a relationship with us all, but we have to acknowledge that His purpose in our lives is to wipe away our sins.

It's a gift I am thankful for and one I hope to teach others to cherish.

—*Mary DeMuth*

"A Pharisee is hard on others, and easy on himself,
but a spiritual man is easy on others and hard on himself."
—*A. W. Tozer*

JESUS, I want to know You and be known by You. Thank You for dying on the cross for me. Amen.

My Beloved,

I came into the world for one reason: because God loves you. And My sole purpose then and now and forever is love. I know what it feels like to be happy, to have fun, to be bored, to suffer loss, and to be betrayed. I know how it feels to fear. I know how hard it is sometimes to do what's right, to stand up for what you believe, to keep silent in the face of insults, to trust, to have self-control, and even to make peace. I know what it means to be lonely. Applauded. Welcomed. Rejected. Loved. Hated. Ignored. I know all the contradictions of the human experience, all the challenges of the world. I know.

But in all of this, I am more than a conqueror, and so are you through Me. Just as I understand you, I want you to breathe in My spirit and understand what you have when you have Me. Because in Me you're given everything you need for this life. When you feel weak, remember My power is made perfect in weakness. When you feel alone, remember I am with you always. When you feel sad, I weep with you. And when you celebrate, I'm cheering you on. You are precious and honored in My sight, and I love you. I redeem you. Defend you. Help you. Stay with you. And love you no matter what. Remember that. There's a banner over you called Love. You are Mine.

I love you forever.

For God so loved the world, that he gave his only begotten Son,
that whosoever believeth in him should not perish, but have everlasting life.
—John 3:16 (KJV)

"I am the Alpha and the Omega," says the Lord God, "who is, and who was, and who is to come, the Almighty." —Revelation 1:8 (NIV)

I love to travel. I enjoy planning a trip to a place such as the Black Hills, San Francisco, Jerusalem, or Machu Picchu. I enjoy the anticipation of an upcoming trip—though not always the process of getting there. I revel in experiencing the unique and often enchanting characteristics of a location. And, of course, I treasure the memories of such an excursion long after it has ended.

Each part of a journey has its own charm. The beginning is different from the end, but there is not only variety but also beauty in the difference. I think a person's life is similar.

Jewish rabbis often used the first and last letters of the Hebrew alphabet to express wholeness or completeness. For instance, "Adam transgressed the whole law, from Aleph (א) to Taw (ת)." Alpha and omega, the first and last letters of the Greek alphabet, similarly convey the completeness of Jesus's beauty, character, holiness, and power. But often, when I think of the Lord referring to Himself as Alpha and Omega, I think also of my past, present, and future. Jesus was there, even when I was in the womb (Psalm 139:13). He is with me every moment (Matthew 18:20), and I often sense His presence when I am driving or watching a grandchild play. He will be there, too, when I draw my last breath (John 14:3).

—*Bob Hostetler*

"God be at mine end, and at my departing."
—*Sarum Primer*

 JESUS, thank You for Your constant and continuing presence with me. Keep me as the apple of Your eye and hide me under the shadow of Your wing, all the way to my last moments on earth. Amen.

> But he said to me, "My grace is sufficient for you, for my power is made perfect in weakness." Therefore I will boast all the more gladly about my weaknesses, so that Christ's power may rest on me. —2 Corinthians 12:9 (NIV)

I don't like to boast about my weaknesses. Honestly, I try to hide them. I want others to perceive me as smart, professional, and capable, and so I'm less inclined to admit my flaws. But at times I've had to pretend to have it all together.

As I've gotten older, I realize something important: I can be myself. Flaws are part of my character, and they make it easy for people to relate to and connect with me. If we show vulnerability, we allow others to see we're real and flawed, just like them.

We can be real with Jesus, too. During His time on earth, Jesus surrounded Himself with imperfect people. Thomas doubted. Martha was too busy to sit at His feet. Many of the disciples struggled with their faith, even with daily access to Him. Some even fell asleep after Jesus asked them to keep watch and pray.

Our weaknesses become the tools that allow the power of Jesus to shine through. Instead of trying to accomplish everything on our own, we can lean on Jesus. It's not all about us. The gospel is all about Jesus and His grace. It covers us and allows us to be a light for Him.

When we become less, Jesus has room to become more in our lives. He can use our weaknesses, if we don't keep them hidden.

—Allison K. Flexer

"Peter stuck his foot in his mouth. Joseph was imprisoned in Egypt. The Samaritan woman had been married five times. Jesus was dead in the grave. Nevertheless, Peter preached, Joseph ruled, the woman shared, Jesus rose—and you?"
—*Max Lucado*

LORD JESUS, let Your power shine through my weaknesses. Pour Your light in a dark world today. Amen.

> Then he said to them, "The Sabbath was made for man, not man for the Sabbath. So the Son of Man is Lord even of the Sabbath."
> —Mark 2:27–28 (NIV)

Birthdays are a big deal at my house. Celebrations typically cover all the bases: decorations, cake, candles, singing, and gifts. After years of practice, I now understand the value of the celebration.

For my birthdays, I enjoy relaxing with loved ones, reflecting on all that has happened during the past year, and anticipating what lies ahead. Doing so gives me time to reflect so my spirit can be rejuvenated. I noted a similarity between the way I celebrate "my day" and the way I observe the Sabbath.

Each week, I join fellow worshippers in singing hymns and songs. When my thoughts are quieted, I am open to hearing Jesus speak to me through a sermon. As I allow the ordinary stuff of life to fade away, I am more able to listen intentionally and to rejuvenate my spirit in His presence.

Jesus was present when the first Sabbath was introduced after the work of creating the world was finished. Jesus later observed the Sabbath, as the Son of Man, giving Him a unique understanding of our human need to rest. No wonder He spoke with such authority about "His day"!

In the same way I enjoy spending my birthdays with my family, Jesus enjoys spending every day with me.

—*Barb Howe*

"Sabbath observance invites us to stop. It invites us to rest. It asks us to notice that while we rest, the world continues without our help. It invites us to delight in the world's beauty and abundance." —Wendell Berry

LORD, You have given the Sabbath as a day set apart to remember that I was created to experience a personal relationship with Jesus. I welcome Your presence. Amen.

> Look, I am coming soon! My reward is with me, and I will give to each person according to what they have done. —Revelation 22:12 (NIV)

The elderly woman tugged her threadbare coat tight, stepped off the senior-transit bus, and then shuffled over an icy patch near the church's ramp. My husband and I, in the midst of a tsunami-relief fund-raising effort, rushed to assist her.

"I'm a widow and don't have much." She opened her purse and handed over a generous amount of cash. "But here's what I've saved from my Social Security. I'm sure there's a widow in India who needs this more than me."

A week later, in Nagapattinam—the worst-hit area along the coast of southern India—a wide-eyed little girl in braided pigtails stood in our host's doorway.

Mr. Rethinam turned to us. "Her father died, and according to the local Hindu custom, her mother must shave her head and remain in mourning for one year sequestered outside of the community as a bad omen."

My jaw dropped. "How will she survive?"

"From the generosity of others," Mr. Rethinam said.

Thoughts of the transit-bus widow returned to me. After a quick word with my husband, we offered the child what the widow had given us. It would bless the mother and child for many months. Jesus would surely reward the giver's generous sacrifice.

While on earth, Jesus said to feed the hungry, give drink to the thirsty, care for strangers and the sick, clothe the naked, and visit the lonely and those in prison. Upon His return, the Lord will reward our acts of love.

—*Holly Michael*

"For it is in giving that we receive."
—*Francis of Assisi*

 JESUS, instill in our hearts a willingness to support Your kingdom so true religion may be revealed. Amen.

You are the light of the world. A town built on a hill cannot be hidden. Neither do people light a lamp and put it under a bowl. Instead they put it on its stand, and it gives light to everyone in the house. —Matthew 5:14-15 (NIV)

I love living in New York City. I love its excitement and opportunities. But for all its glamour, it is not always a place where it's easy to be a Christian. My faith is often seen as quaint, weird, or, in some cases, threatening. My admission that I write Christian books is often met by an awkward silence or a polite, "Oh, that's nice." Typically, I can see that the person is already looking for an escape route. I've been asked, "So are you one of them?" Once, a girl I was talking to about my faith turned on her heel and walked away without a word.

I know I am not the only one who has been judged. I think it's something every believer has faced. But I also know God places us where we are for a reason.

And so I must believe we are the light of the world. Jesus says Christians are the light of the world. I am called to bring light into dark spaces. I am supposed to let the light of Jesus shine through me. Even when my instinct is to shrink back, to gloss over what I do for a living so conversations at parties don't get awkward, I need to remember that Jesus has placed me where I am so I can bring His Light to those who need it. Sometimes it's challenging, but in the words of that song I learned in Sunday school, "This little light of mine, I'm gonna let it shine."

—*Elizabeth Adams*

"Darkness cannot drive out darkness: only light can do that.
Hate cannot drive out hate: only love can do that."
—*Martin Luther King Jr.*

LORD, please help me be a light for You. May I be a blessing to those around me. Amen.

> Therefore consider carefully how you listen. Whoever has will be given more; whoever does not have, even what they think they have will be taken from them. —Luke 8:18 (NIV)

In our multitasking age, I sometimes catch myself trying to engage a lunch companion in conversation while I carry on a text exchange or unobtrusively check my email or glance at Facebook, Instagram, or Twitter or even slyly track several games on the restaurant's big-screen TVs! The irony is that in trying to pay attention to all those people and things at once, I'm incapable of listening— really listening—to any of them!

It's not just me. Listening is an endangered life skill for this entire generation.

Jesus mentioned a similar tendency in the spiritual realm. He warned that it's possible for us to hear His words without taking them to heart. I do this. Sometimes I catch myself mindlessly reading Scripture. Though I'm staring at eternal truth, my mind is absorbed with trivial matters. The result of such distraction and indifference is that unless I catch and correct myself, over time I begin to lose the ability to appreciate His teaching at all.

On the other hand, when I perk up and welcome Jesus's words, they liberate me and impart life. When I ponder and practice them, my spiritual fervor increases. My insight grows. With such gifts, I'm able to serve others and be effective in the process.

—*Len Woods*

"We need to listen to God because it's not what we say,
but what He says to us and through us that matters."
—*Mother Teresa*

JESUS, give me grace to listen. Then reveal even more truth so I can give freely to those around me. Amen.

Most assuredly, I say to you, he who believes in Me, the works that I do he will do also; and greater works than these he will do, because I go to My Father. —John 14:12 (NKJV)

I love to read about the miracles Jesus performed. Blind eyes could see, the lame walked, and He raised Lazarus from the dead. Bread and fish multiplied when Jesus prayed, and He commanded the tempest to be calm. Yet Jesus told us we will do greater things.

When my two baby grandsons visit, I become young at heart. I dance and sing to them. My children are amused to see their mother waltz cheek to cheek with the boys and twirl them around.

"Can't Help Falling in Love," by Elvis Presley, is a favorite. When I sing and dance, and dedicate the words to each little fellow, I sense he knows he is loved.

I sing "Jesus Loves Me" when the boys are cradled in my arms. They can't talk yet, but their smiles let me know they recognize the song. When I sing, "The B-I-B-L-E—yes, that's the book for me," I believe it's being recorded in their hearts.

Every time I share the gospel with or sing about Jesus to my grandsons, I know this is the greater work Jesus talked about, because its message is eternal—and it is the work Jesus commissioned us to do. When I pray my little ones will know the Savior, I can trust Jesus hears me, because prayer is the greater work, too.

—*Kathleen Ruckman*

"I am unworthy of You, Jesus, but I can become a miracle of Your grace."
—*François Fenelon*

JESUS, may I be a vessel to share the gospel of salvation—the greatest miracle of all! Amen.

> He replied, "You must love the Lord your God with all your heart, with all your being, and with all your mind. This is the first and greatest commandment. And the second is like it: You must love your neighbor as you love yourself. All the Law and the Prophets depend on these two commands."
> —Matthew 22:37–40 (CEB)

John used to sit on the standpipe outside the cafeteria near the corner of Thirty-Fourth Street and Park Avenue on Friday afternoons, waiting for the free food offered at the end of the week. For a while he'd been homeless, but at the time he had a room in Harlem for which he was tremendously grateful.

He often wore a coat and tie, and usually had a Bible with him. I'd chat with him before heading back to the office from lunch. We talked about the weather, some sports team, his grandkids, or Scripture. He could quote a verse or two without even having to look it up.

"I wish I could memorize Bible verses like you," I once said.

"You have the Bible right where it belongs," he said. Then he gestured toward my heart.

It was one of the loveliest things anyone has ever said to me. I walked back to the office, his words ringing in my ears. Yes, it's important to know Scripture by heart. But isn't it better to have it in your heart?

—*Rick Hamlin*

"If you wish to befriend someone, look for a person who loves first God then themselves. If they love God, they will be able to love their neighbor, too."
—*Peter Deunov*

 JESUS, may I live in such a way that it is apparent to all my neighbors that I have You in my heart. Amen.

I will not judge those who hear me but don't obey me, for I have come to save the world and not to judge it. —John 12:47 (NLT)

When I was learning to drive, my daddy allowed me to borrow his new car. I drove carefully, trying not to scratch the shiny, blue Ford. I stopped at a red light and felt the jolt as a truck crashed into Dad's car from behind. When I saw the huge dent in the trunk, panic filled me. *What will Daddy say?*

Daddy was a powerful, formidable man who loudly expressed his opinions. He saw the world as black and white, right and wrong, and he didn't like excuses. I wasn't afraid of him, because I knew he loved me, but I never wanted to displease him. As I walked in the door that night, tears filled my eyes. I told him about the car, anticipating his judgment. Instead, he folded me into his mighty arms and asked if I had been hurt. When I told him I was OK, he said, "Cars can be fixed, but daughters are more important."

It seems easy for us to think Jesus came into the world to condemn and judge us for sin. He came because of our sin, but He does not condemn; He rescues. He does not judge; He offers pardon. He is the Savior, not an executioner. From the beginning, His plan was to save and rescue, not convict and sentence.

—*Karen Porter*

"God proved His love on the Cross. When Christ hung,
and bled, and died, it was God saying to the world, 'I love you.'"
—*Billy Graham*

DEAR JESUS, Your forgiveness and kindness are priceless. Thank You for salvation, for rescuing me, and for loving me instead of judging me accordingly. Amen.

> **Believe me when I say that I am in the Father and the Father is in me; or at least believe on the evidence of the works themselves.**
> **—John 14:11** (NIV)

Two of my grandchildren were born with the genetic condition known as cystic fibrosis. Among the measures that keep them healthy are twice-daily treatments for which they wear vests connected to hoses that are in turn connected to machines each the size of a small carry-on suitcase. Those vest treatments clear their lungs and breathing passages of mucus to prevent infection and aid their breathing. Like everyone else, they wake, sleep, eat, and live in an oxygen-rich environment. They are in oxygen. But their health is contingent upon the oxygen also getting in them—into their lungs, bloodstream, and organs.

I think of that reality when I read Jesus's words to His first followers: "I am in the Father and the Father is in me." Though the words probably mystified Jesus's disciples, they depict a mystical reality I want my life to reflect—one mentioned often in the New Testament—that I may be "in Christ" (2 Corinthians 5:17), even as Christ is in me (Colossians 1:27). I am simultaneously surrounded by and enveloped in Jesus and His creative, protective presence, even as I need His power in me to spread through every impulse of my mind and every beat of my heart.

—*Bob Hostetler*

"I must first have the sense of God's possession of me before
I can have the sense of His presence with me."
—*Watchman Nee*

JESUS, thank You that I am in You and You are in me. Fill my life with Your presence as fully and constantly as my lungs fill with oxygen. Amen.

> It will be good for that servant whom the master finds doing so when he returns. Truly I tell you, he will put him in charge of all his possessions. —Luke 12:43–44 (NIV)

I'd never been close with the single man living down the street. But last year I discovered he was diagnosed with a malignant brain tumor, and that changed everything. Having dealt with a serious illness myself, I remembered the fatigue and nameless terrors that plagued me. I knew how reassuring it felt to have someone take care of things. Postsurgical mega doses of my friends' love sped my recovery and strengthened my faith.

Now it was my turn to serve. I delivered hot meals. My husband did the man's yard work. And I prayed for our neighbor, for his healing and his salvation.

One day I offered him a special item: a Christian book I hoped would help him find his way to Jesus, since he didn't like "talking religion." I hesitated as I handed it to him, but he accepted the gift.

A few days later, as I answered the door, my jaw dropped. There stood our neighbor. He'd walked over to show his gratefulness for all we'd done—and also for the book. And to tell us he'd begun to pray.

Nothing can replace the satisfaction I experienced looking into his eyes and seeing the Lord's peace reflected in them. I can only imagine the Giver's joy when He looks into our hearts and sees His love reflecting back.

—*Heidi Gaul*

> *"To love someone is to show to them their beauty,*
> *their worth and their importance."*
> —*Jean Vanier*

JESUS, help me find ways to share Your love through service to others, especially those in need. Amen.

> What do you think? If a man has 100 sheep, and one of them goes astray, won't he leave the 99 on the hillside and go and search for the stray? And if he finds it, I assure you: He rejoices over that sheep more than over the 99 that did not go astray. In the same way, it is not the will of your Father in heaven that one of these little ones perish. —Matthew 18:12–14 (HCSB)

I was never good at math. Permit me to rephrase: I was never good at geometry. It didn't help that I was surrounded by classmates who seemed to easily understand it and aced every test. I'd resigned myself to accept that I'd most likely fail the class and be grounded at home for all eternity. But my teacher refused to give up on me.

Mr. Slone was one of the most patient teachers I'd even known. He spent countless hours tutoring me after school. Not only did he make sure I finally understood those confusing slope equations, but he also ended every tutoring session with, "I'm not giving up on you. I'm always here to help."

In the parable of the lost sheep, Jesus emphasizes the importance of each and every one of us in the eyes of God. He explains that even when one sheep goes astray, the Shepherd is persistent in finding and protecting it. In fact, He is overjoyed to lovingly place the lost one back into the fold.

I've still haven't practically applied the Pythagorean theorem, but I did pass geometry. More importantly, I learned that regardless of whether I felt like a failure, I was cared for despite any weakness. In this same way, allow Jesus to search you out wherever you are right now. Rest in knowing He's completely overjoyed to have you in His fold and will never leave you behind.

—*Angie Spady*

"The wolves come to scatter the sheep…but Jesus comes
against anything that comes against His sheep!"
—*T. D. Jakes*

JESUS, thank You for Your relentless search for my heart. I praise You as my Shepherd and for Your unconditional love for me. Amen.

He sighed deeply when he heard this and he said, "Certainly not. How many more miracles do you people need?" —Mark 8:12 (TLB)

Several years ago, I was speaking at an event that ended with time for attendees to come forward for prayer. As I hugged and prayed for countless women, I was struck by the body language of one particular woman, who hung back until most of the crowd had filtered out. She strutted up to me, full of assurance, and said rather loudly, "I liked what you had to say tonight about Jesus, but I need more proof that He is real. I need to see something more substantial if I'm going to believe in Him."

I asked what she'd consider substantial. She said she needed to see a miracle or some kind of sign from heaven. I explained to her that miracles look like all kinds of things: restored relationships, forgiveness that heals, freedom from bondage, breakthroughs in faith, and breakouts of joy! She wasn't buying it. She wanted a flamboyant miracle or nothing at all. The woman walked out of that place, unchanged. I would imagine she'd rather spend her life asking God to prove Himself.

Jesus faced people who asked for signs and wonders yet had no intention of believing or changing. Some hearts seem to become so hard that no amount of wonder can unthaw them. When I encounter those people, I know it's time to simply step aside and let Him have His say.

—*Gari Meacham*

"Be careful when you look for big miracles—you may miss the miracle right under your nose."
—*Brooke Masotti*

JESUS, help us to never get so caught up in spiritual drama that we forget You are the real story. Amen.

> But you will receive power when the Holy Spirit comes upon you. And you will be my witnesses, telling people about me everywhere—in Jerusalem, throughout Judea, in Samaria, and to the ends of the earth. —Acts 1:8 (NLT)

I've never met Mulu, and I probably never will. She was born within a week of our daughter, but their lives could not be more different. According to the organization that transforms our monthly gift into food, education, and medical care for Mulu, she spends her days hauling water, tending to the family's goat, and walking to school in their Ethiopian village—tasks that are not on our first-world agenda.

We exchange letters and get a new picture of Mulu for our refrigerator every year. Her caregivers share the gospel with her as they meet her basic needs.

Inspired by the people who care for Mulu, I realized I needed to move out of the comfort of my home into the lives of my neighbors. But this was scary!

My neighbors sometimes have an agenda that is foreign to me. They dress in different styles and talk differently than I do. They vote for different candidates and play different music. They have different worldviews and ways of life.

Thankfully, this nudge came with a boost of supernatural power that could have been only from the Holy Spirit. He helped me overcome my fears and gave me compassion for the people I see every day.

My family will care for Mulu until she's grown, and then we'll find another child to support. In the meantime, we love our neighbors around the world and right next door.

—*Amy Lively*

"His voice leads us not into timid discipleship but into bold witness."
—*Charles Stanley*

 JESUS, I want to tell people about You…but I need Your help. Please send Your Spirit to give me power and opportunity in my corner of the world. Amen.

When Jesus spoke again to the people, he said, "I am the light of the world. Whoever follows me will never walk in darkness, but will have the light of life." —John 8:12 (NIV)

Living at five thousand feet in the Sierra Nevada mountains can be challenging, especially when snowstorms knock out the electricity. While other families have woodstoves, we do not, so when the power goes out, we typically hunker down in bed with a host of candles carefully placed in the corners of our bedroom.

One winter, the younger two of our four kids crawled into bed with my husband and me, while our two oldest decided to play hide-and-seek in the dark downstairs.

When I asked Bethany, then three years old, why she didn't want to play with her older siblings, she said, "I think Jesus will take care of me better up here."

When she said that, I felt His gentle nudge. Jesus guides us when we pursue His Light, because He is the Light of life. But we cannot benefit from Jesus's Light unless we actually follow Him. Light guides us. Scientifically, life on earth could not be sustained if not for light. Additionally, light gives clarity to our surroundings—we see the truth more clearly. And the light of Jesus attracts others to us. However, we can slip back into darkness and its confusion if we do not pursue Jesus and His life of holiness. Just knowing about Him, or even just knowing Him, is not enough—we need to try every day to be more like Him.

—*Janet Holm McHenry*

"Jesus is the light of the world because he comes from the Father and speaks for the Father and is going to the Father and is one with the Father."
—John Piper

JESUS, I want to stay in the light that You offer me. Keep my eyes focused on You alone. Amen.

FAITHFUL MANAGERS

> **The Lord answered, "Who then is the faithful and wise manager, whom the master puts in charge of his servants to give them their food allowance at the proper time?" —Luke 12:42 (NIV)**

Every month I arrange the medical charts for the patients who will visit La Clinica Cristiana, a free medical clinic for those without health insurance in our community. I pray over each name as I place those files in order. Each patient is an opportunity for our staff of volunteer physicians, nurses, pharmacists, and translators to use their training to build the kingdom.

A few months ago, the pharmacist noticed that one of our regular patients, an elderly Hispanic man, was not his normal, smiling self. We got him in to see the doctor quickly, concerned about his symptoms. The physician sent our friend to the emergency room, believing he'd had a stroke.

Just as the medical staff was quick to recognize and respond to the situation in front of them, Jesus encourages us all to be willing to use our abilities and resources to notice others' needs and take action to help. He invites us to engage with those around us by using what we have and know to benefit others.

Last month, as I added the hospital records to that patient's chart, I whispered thanks to Jesus for giving us the opportunity to help others. When our elderly friend hugged the doctor and pharmacist, I was reminded what a gift it is to serve others with the abilities Jesus gives us.

—*Teri Lynne Underwood*

"Faithful servants never retire. You can retire from your career, but you will never retire from serving God."
—*Rick Warren*

 JESUS, may I be a good manager of the abilities You have given me, always using them to build Your Kingdom. Amen.

Are not five sparrows sold for two pennies? Yet not one of them is forgotten by God. —Luke 12:6 (NIV)

With modern telescopes, we can see into distances so vast that they're impossible to comprehend. I'm amazed by the scale of the universe, the abundance of galaxies, and gravity so powerful that it bends time and light.

The Bible says it is Jesus Who created all this, and yet for all the vastness and incredible variety and distant grandeur of the universe, He is capable of remembering the smallest bird fluttering through the sky on this little, blue planet. And not only does He remember each one, but He also cares for them. His love seems boundless, especially once you consider the care and concern He's extended to us all.

He came as a human being, emptying Himself of the glory of heaven, to become the sacrifice for me. Because of this, I can live in His superabundant, overflowing, and infinitely creative love, knowing Him and being known by Him. When I see pictures of faraway galaxies and stars being formed, of towering nebulae too huge to fathom and at distances beyond what I can imagine, I'm reminded that although He is inconceivably powerful, awesome, loving, and imaginative, He is so great and His mind so infinite that nothing can escape His care, even me.

—*Michael Berrier*

"Worry does not empty tomorrow of its sorrow, it empties today of its strength."
—*Corrie ten Boom*

LORD JESUS, I have no reason to worry when I am in the hands of one so imaginative and powerful. Thank You for caring for me! Amen.

> They were casting a net into the lake, for they were fishermen.
> "Come, follow me," Jesus said, "and I will send you out to fish for people."
> —Matthew 4:18–19 (NIV)

Living in New York City, I am surrounded by fame and significance. My friends are designers, performers, and artists who have excelled in their crafts and are known by many. Sometimes, I feel especially "regular." I get caught up in the drudgery of household chores, daily routines, and unrealized dreams.

Reading Matthew 4, I am glad the fishermen probably had calloused hands and sunbaked skin. I am glad Jesus decided to step into dull routines to remind us that living with significance is about being our regular selves.

What a relief! Regular household chores are not wasted on Jesus. He delights to find me—in the middle of whatever I am doing—and extends an invitation to follow Him. He delights to step right into my most mundane days so I can become part of His significant story.

Follow Me as I walk toward the broken. Follow Me as I bring peace. Follow Me as I invite outcasts to dinner. Follow Me as I speak truth in love. Follow Me as I offer the hope of eternal life. You are qualified for this work.

No work is more significant than that of sharing the good news of Jesus, and no joy is greater than that of knowing I am qualified to do that work.

—*Caroline Kolts*

"[Jesus] matters because of what he brought and what he still brings to ordinary human beings, living their ordinary lives and coping daily with their surroundings. He promises wholeness for their lives."
—*Dallas Willard*

 JESUS, thank you for inviting regular people like me to follow You. Give me courage to respond in faith so that You can use my gifts for the kingdom. Amen.

> But Jesus said to him, "Follow Me, and let the dead bury their own dead."
> —Matthew 8:22 (NKJV)

When Mom died at sixty-five, I found it hard to let her go, but the promise of heaven gave me comfort. But when Dad died at ninety, it was just as difficult, and in many ways harder because now I felt orphaned.

I flew to Pennsylvania to care for my father for five weeks. After he died, I reminisced about his yearly visits to Oregon. I wished I had one more day with Papa.

As I focused on how much I missed my parents and other loved ones who had died, I realized that while I was focusing on the dead, I was wasting the time I've been given to do good on this earth. I must bury the dead and look forward to seeing my loved ones in heaven. Jesus's words to look forward and follow Him returned me to proper thinking.

Recently I pictured Mom, her tender love for all, and Dad, witty with a sparkle for life, and his words echoed in my mind, "Don't worry; be happy." His little quote is a reminder that dwelling even on cherished memories can turn into unhealthy mourning if I keep looking back.

I will follow what Jesus has for me to do with a willing spirit, and in due time, I'll see my loved ones again.

—*Kathleen Ruckman*

"With Jesus, even in our darkest moments,
the best remains and the very best is yet to be."
—*Corrie ten Boom*

JESUS, be my vision each new morning. Let me be enriched by my past but gazing upward as I follow You. Amen.

> **The Spirit alone gives eternal life. Human effort accomplishes nothing. And the very words I have spoken to you are spirit and life.**
> **—John 6:63** (NLT)

All you need is mind over matter, I've been told. "Stick with the weight loss plan. Exercise. You got this."

Time and again, I've failed. I didn't have what it took. Whether it was working to lose that extra weight, a great idea for women's ministry or writing my first novel (which will never see the light of day), I've discovered the truth of Jesus's words: Human effort accomplishes nothing. If I try to do anything in my own power, it'll tank. I'll give up. I'll go right back to old patterns and habits. I can't uphold the goal.

Many times we jump in with the right heart to do something for God but forget it's not about us or our ideas. It's about Him and what He wills. Daily, I begin with prayer and ask this of the Lord: *What do You want to do through me?* Because if it's from Him, His power through the Holy Spirit enables me to accomplish each and every task He assigns and provides me with everything I need to succeed for His glory. That's why it's critical to be in the Word daily, to receive life—real life—so I can be sustained in order to do the things that last eternally.

—*Jessica R. Patch*

"God's work done in God's way will never lack God's supplies."
—*James Hudson Taylor*

JESUS, fill me with Your Spirit so I can accomplish what You ask—in Your strength and not my own. Amen.

However, do not rejoice that the spirits submit to you, but rejoice that your names are written in heaven. —Luke 10:20 (NIV)

When our youngest daughter was in second grade, she had a hard time adjusting to our new life in France. She kicked her brother and sister, and often was belligerent toward her father and me, not characteristic of her affable personality. We figured she was battling culture shock, so we prayed for her and helped her process our move to the unfamiliar.

Eventually she confided in us through tears that nightmares had woken her at night and that angry voices were telling her to do mean things to us.

So we prayed. And we prayed some more. But she continued to struggle.

During this time, my husband and I attended a leadership retreat in another European country, so we shared her struggles with our friends.

My daughter shared with one of our friends that she wanted to be free of the nightmares. They told her about Jesus and how to meet Him. With their kindhearted guidance, she prayed to invite Jesus into her life.

The change in her was immediate—no more nightmares, unkind words, or lashing out. She interacted well with her siblings, and the happy-go-lucky girl we knew returned. Later, her father baptized her in the Mediterranean Sea.

While we were grateful Jesus had triumphed over Satan's schemes, we rejoiced more so that now she was forever secure in Jesus's love forever.

—*Mary DeMuth*

"The one concern of the devil is to keep Christians from praying.
He fears nothing from prayerless studies, prayerless work, and prayerless religion.
He laughs at our toil, mocks at our wisdom, but trembles when we pray."
—*Samuel Chadwick*

JESUS, I'm grateful You're bigger than the enemy. But I'm even more grateful that You saved me. Amen.

> **If you, then, though you are evil, know how to give good gifts to your children, how much more will your Father in heaven give good gifts to those who ask him! —Matthew 7:11 (NIV)**

I will never forget the year I spent planning a large conference for women. At the time, I was homeschooling my eighth-grade daughter, and one beautiful spring morning, the two of us went for a prayer walk around the neighborhood. The stress of anticipating the upcoming event weighed on me, and I lamented to Jesus about its huge financial challenges. I asked Him for peace and assurance that God would provide.

Just before my daughter and I reached home, I happened to glance down through a sewer grate and spotted some money. I stopped to really look. A hundred-dollar bill? My daughter and I ran home for a stick and some gum (yes, it really works!), and then retrieved an actual one-hundred-dollar bill.

"Can't you see, Mom? It's a sign from Jesus saying He's got that money thing covered." My daughter made the connection first. Jesus gifted us both that day.

A prayer walk and pouring your heart out to Jesus are excellent activities for a worried soul. The key, however, is looking for how and where He uniquely provides for your need. God's gifts are good and perfect for each situation.

—*Nancy Sebastian Kuch*

"Looking at a deficit fuels our fear and drains our hope…
Looking at a surplus, on the other hand, fuels our courage and fills us
with hope…if you're a Christian, you no longer have any deficits. None."
—*Jon Bloom*

JESUS, thank You for good gifts. Thank You for surprising me, encouraging me, and providing for my needs. Help me not to overlook the gifts You have for me today. Amen.

> "Believe in the light while you have the light, so that you may become children of light." When he had finished speaking, Jesus left and hid himself from them. —John 12:36 (NIV)

One of my favorite worship experiences every year is the Christmas Eve service. As we enter the church, ushers hand out the familiar stubby candles.

We sing old carols and listen to the nativity story we all know by heart. The lights dim, and the pastor gently tips his own stubby candle toward a larger one already lit on stage. As the flame flickers from one candle to the other, he reminds us that Jesus, the baby in a manger, called himself "the Light of the World." The pastor turns to light the candles of others, recalling the command of Christ to us that we also are the light of the world.

Slowly, the flame moves from one candle to the next, down rows, across aisles. Just as the Holy Spirit's flame spread among the disciples on Pentecost, the flickers of light brighten the room, displacing the darkness.

Every year my eyes fill with tears as I consider the call to be light, to shine brightly against the backdrop of heartache and sin around me. Jesus knew the cost, the price we'd pay for our flickering faith. And yet He called us to this noble task.

We shine not our own lights but His. We lean into His bold flame and feel the spark as He empowers us to stand against the darkness as children of light.

—*Teri Lynne Underwood*

"Dare to reach out your hand into the darkness, to pull another hand into the light."
—*Norman B. Rice*

 JESUS, may I be faithful to shine Your light into the darkness around me, living as a child of light. Amen.

> **Be dressed ready for service and keep your lamps burning, like servants waiting for their master to return from a wedding banquet, so that when he comes and knocks they can immediately open the door for him. —Luke 12:35–36 (NIV)**

A frowning young man came into church on Christmas Eve. He pulled at his collar, obviously uncomfortable, as he sat next to a silver-haired woman. Behind him, a scowling man settled into a seat by his wife, crossing his arms like a shield. Next came a trio of girls, one festooned with tattoos, her brow pinched in a frown.

Why are they here? I thought.

Maybe the young man was there to please his grandmother. The other man was easy—his wife had made him come. Maybe the girl had come just to be with her friends.

But then it struck me. They were seekers. They might have thought otherwise, but they came to this warm, loving place on Christmas Eve, seeking answers to questions they could barely voice. They were drawn by a grandmother's love, a wife's hope, and a friend's invitation. They all had said yes, opening the door to possibilities they had yet to imagine. In all the world, they had consented to come to this church, on this holiest of nights. And Jesus was there, waiting for them to ask Him into their lives.

I shivered, suddenly realizing I, too, had been waiting for them. This was the reason I was in church on Christmas Eve.

I stood and went to greet them, hoping I could open the door.

—*J. Mason Williams*

"Opportunity doesn't make appointments, you have to be ready when it arrives."
—*Tim Fargo*

 JESUS, please help me to be ever watchful for those moments when You are near and to seek Your will in all things. Amen.

> **The Son of Man did not come to be served, but to serve, and to give His life as a ransom for many. —Matthew 20:28** (AMP)

It's a truism often repeated at Christmastime: we need to keep Christ in Christmas. "Jesus is the reason for the season," people say, implying that Jesus often gets left out. OK, I understand it. We probably see more images of Santa Claus, sleighs, and Christmas trees in December than of the baby in the manger. But isn't it possible Jesus makes some seasonal appearances anonymously?

Like when you go to the mall, wracking your brain to find just the right present for someone, and the sound of a carol in the loudspeaker and the kindness of the overworked cashier make you feel glad. Or when you reach in your pocket for a buck to put in the Salvation Army kettle, and you drop in a ten instead...because it's Christmas. Or a long-lost relative you haven't spoken to in years calls just to say hi. Or something you hear, on the car radio brings tears to your eyes and because of it, you don't yell at the driver who cuts you off on the highway.

"Emmanuel," we sing. "God is with us." He feels awfully close just now.

—*Rick Hamlin*

"Want to keep Christ in Christmas? Feed the hungry, clothe the naked,
forgive the guilty, welcome the unwanted, care for the ill, love your enemies,
and do unto others as you would have done unto you."
—*Steve Maraboli*

JESUS, You came to serve, and in everything I do, may I be Your servant and the servant of peace. Amen.

The greatest among you will be your servant.
—Matthew 23:11 (NIV)

I moved to New York City after finishing graduate school, where I studied art. I was young and determined to make it in the art world. At first, my goals were simple: I wanted to always be able to make art, and deep down, I also wanted to achieve greatness. I think most people want some level of success. But I had my sights set pretty high. I wanted to be like the iconic painters I had studied in class—Van Gogh, Cézanne, Picasso, Warhol. Historians have named them the greats, and society values their artwork at millions of dollars.

More than twenty years later, I'm still in New York and still making art, but my perspective on greatness has shifted dramatically. I am now influenced more by the words of Jesus and a quote by William Shakespeare than my youthful aspirations. Shakespeare reminds us that greatness is as much a product of one's circumstances as of one's hard work. Better still, Jesus tells us the greatest among us will be servants. What a difference from the naive ideal of my youth!

Our culture and media tell us greatness means winning, achieving, and being wealthy, while Jesus tells us the opposite. No matter what our circumstances, we can strive for and achieve the true greatness to which Jesus calls us. Now that's really great!

—*Wayne Adams*

"Some are born great, some achieve greatness,
and some have greatness thrust upon them."
—William Shakespeare

 DEAR JESUS, please help me to see greatness through Your eyes and to become a servant of others. Amen.

He said to them, "Make room, because the girl isn't dead, but sleeping."
—Matthew 9:24 (WEB)

A wise man once told me, "The only difference between an old coal and a hot coal is the heat." It's impossible to tell the difference sometimes between a cold, charred coal and one that merely looks cold and black, only to find it glowing red underneath. This is why it is important to stir an outgoing campfire with a stick, so as to reveal the "live" coals from the "dead" ones. Jesus has a knack for knowing what is actually dead and what is merely dormant.

That pretty much summarized my career.

I interviewed at twelve places and got no callbacks. Resume was pristine. Recommendations were glowing. Experience was extensive. Why hadn't I landed a job in the profession? My dream was dead. Dejected, I stopped looking for openings. I felt I'd become a cold, black, charred, leftover coal from a fire that blew out long ago.

But Jesus is the Lord of the ashes.

A year went by, and after dutifully making ends meet through multiple unrelated jobs, a little heat stirred in my heart after a former colleague invited me to apply for a position I believed I was born to have. The heat increased, flaking off the rough exterior cinders. The glow turned into an ember, and as the heat rose into a small flame, I got the callback, a second interview, and the position, ushering in a sense of appreciation for Jesus, the Lord of the ashes.

—*Erik Person*

"So if I stand let me stand on the promise that you will pull me through;
and if I can't let me fall on the grace that first brought me to you."
—*Rich Mullins*

 LORD JESUS, help me remember that You are able when I am willing. Thank You for loving me so much that no amount of soot can stain me in Your eyes and only You can extinguish a flame. Amen.

> In everything do to others as you would have them do to you; for this is the
> law and the prophets. —Matthew 7:12 (NRSV)

The Golden Rule! Jesus offers it right when He's teaching us to trust God with our deepest desires and basic needs.

I'm thinking of the man I met in a train station one cold December day when I was collecting coats for the homeless. This man had lost his job and his apartment. He was desperate to get down to Florida, where his sister lived, as he was in search of a new start. This man needed God's help in the worst way...and this was his prayer: He took off his leather jacket and handed it to me. He said, "I know how the man upstairs works. Someone out there needs this coat more than I do. I trust that God will get me to Florida. This is my act of faith."

I was stunned. In this man's hour of need, he was praying by taking care of someone else. He was offering exactly what some stranger needed—someone willing to sacrifice for another's well-being. As he walked away, he seemed confident, but I worried about his being homeless—and now coatless—on a cold December day.

Sometime later he came back, almost jumping with excitement. His sister had accepted his collect call. She would pay for his train ticket and welcome him into her home. "I knew it!" he said. "God is good."

—*Lizzie Berne DeGear*

"If we don't manage to implement the Golden Rule globally,
so that we treat all peoples, wherever and whoever they may be,
as though they were as important as ourselves, I doubt that
we'll have a viable world to hand on to the next generation."
—*Karen Armstrong*

JESUS, what is Your deepest desire for me? Today, please give me the opportunity to respond to that same desire in someone else. Amen.

But Jesus overheard them and said to Jairus, "Don't be afraid. Just have faith." —Mark 5:36 (NLT)

As I flip through the pages of my life, I find that uncertainty has been the greatest roadblock to the divine plans prepared for me. Every time God is about to do something new, my heart's default seems set to fear.

I was terrified to lead a women's ministry. Terrified to write my first novel. I almost backed out of going to my first writers' conference because I'm afraid to fly alone. I'm the person who reads the online menu before I ever set foot in a restaurant. I want to know what I'm getting into before I ever get there. But that's not faith.

As I've matured in Christ, knowing Him more intimately, I've learned to trust Him, to believe, and to be obedient to walk with Him wherever He leads, even to places where I see no hope or positive result on the horizon. If Jairus hadn't trusted Jesus's words—"Don't be afraid. Just have faith."—he wouldn't have experienced the miracle of seeing Jesus raise his daughter back to life. I wouldn't have witnessed the joys of ministry, the blessings of peace, or the resurrection of lifeless circumstances. Oh yes, Jesus still brings dead things back to life. But to see it unfold, we have to be willing to replace fear with faith and go with Him into the unknown places.

—Jessica R. Patch

"Never be afraid to trust an unknown future on a known God."
—Corrie ten Boom

 JESUS, remove my fear. Fill me with faith to go with You to unknown places and to trust You with uncertain circumstances. Amen.

> When anyone hears the message about the kingdom and does not understand it, the evil one comes and snatches away what was sown in their heart. This is the seed sown along the path. —Matthew 13:19 (NIV)

Two years ago, I had the pleasure of listening to a female speaker who'd worked in Africa and the United States to show other women how to discover the Jesus Who loves them. She'd spent hours learning their cultures. Her goal was to help women experience a relationship with Jesus Christ. But her transparency allowed us to understand all we needed was a willing heart to follow God's lead. We could minister to others and not be afraid of making mistakes. We laughed and cried with her, cheering on her triumphs and committing to pray for her family and ministry.

By exploring the worlds of those we're seeking to reach with the love of Jesus, we cultivate new and lasting friendships. We show our genuine desire for each of them to have a personal relationship with Him. The task is laborious, and we can't be sure those who need Jesus will surrender their lives to Him. But our mandate is to share His love.

Many of us pray for family members and friends who have no desire to walk with Jesus. But as long as we have breath, we'll continue communicating to these people through our words and actions. Oh, the joys of being a Jesus follower and experiencing His amazing blessings.

—DiAnn Mills

"Radical obedience to Christ is not easy… It's not comfort, not health, not wealth, and not prosperity in this world. Radical obedience to Christ risks losing all these things. But in the end, such risk finds its reward in Christ. And he is more than enough for us."
—David Platt

DEAR JESUS, we are honored to tell others about You. Give us strength when we tire and wisdom to know we are but a vessel for You to use for Your kingdom's glory. Amen.

> But Jesus said to him, "No one who puts his hand to the plow and looks back is fit for the kingdom of God." —Luke 9:62 (HCSB)

Who can follow Jesus? You can. I can. Any and all are welcome.

What's the catch? There's no catch... just one requirement: absolute surrender to His will.

Without hesitating, stammering, blinking, or apologizing, Jesus spelled out the high costs of discipleship to three potential followers in Luke 9. To paraphrase, He told the first, "Following me will not be easy or comfortable. Can you handle a whole life of 'unpredictable'?" To another guy who was wrestling with the inconvenient timing of Jesus's call, the message was essentially, "Sorry, but the time is now!" To a man who first wanted to tie up some loose domestic ends, Jesus basically said, "Quit looking over your shoulder, and focus on your future with Me!"

Reflecting on these blunt words of Christ always makes me gulp. I know all too well the strong pull of family. And nightly I face the choice: I could kick back and watch my favorite TV show, or I could serve someone else—my wife, my neighbor, a friend. How powerful the impulse to rationalize Jesus's authoritative call. And how dangerous!

Jesus is Lord! He does not exist to further our worldly interests; we exist for His eternal purposes.

—*Len Woods*

"[Beware of] the supreme tragedy of following a Christ
who is merely a Christ of convenience and not the true Lord of glory."
—*A. W. Tozer*

JESUS, forgive me for treating Your words like advice I can take or leave. Rule in my life right now. Make me fit for Your kingdom. Amen.

CONTRIBUTORS

ELIZABETH ADAMS lives in Brooklyn, New York, with her husband, Wayne, and two young daughters. When she's not writing, she spends her time cleaning up after two devious cats and trying to find time to read. She graduated from Princeton University and has a master's degree in English from New York University. Elizabeth is the author or co-author of more than twenty-five novels under various pen names, which she will reveal for the right price. She has written for Guideposts' fiction series including *Sugarcreek Amish Mysteries, Tearoom Mysteries,* and the *Mysteries of Martha's Vineyard* series.

WAYNE ADAMS is a Brooklyn-based painter and photographer whose Christian-based exhibits have been seen throughout the Midwest and New York, and even in Vienna, Austria. Shows include "Wayne Adams is Speaking in Tongues: A show of objects and images organized by the unrelenting voice of interpretation" at the Barrington Center for the Arts, Wenham, MA (2014). He received his bachelor's in fine arts from Calvin College and master's in fine arts from Washington University in St. Louis. In addition to sharing his faith through art, he also writes hoping to inspire with his stories of his own walk of faith.

As a chaplain **DR. ELIZABETH BERNE DeGEAR** offers pastoral care to individuals and groups in church and hospital settings, and does memorial services for people who have experienced homelessness. Lizzie is also a Bible scholar and has been teaching Bible study at her local church for many years, and is the author of *For She Has Heard,* which explores the role of the standing stone in the book of Joshua. She has lived in Rhode Island, New Mexico, Alaska, and France, and now makes her home in New York City with her husband and two children.

MICHAEL BERRIER became aware of his need for Jesus Christ as a twenty-four-year-old man. In the decades since then his need for Jesus has only deepened. Michael is now a financial executive who also writes about his relationship with Jesus. His daily journal entries are influenced by Scripture, and he writes devotionals inspired by the Bible as well. Michael is a lifelong California resident, and the author of six novels for adults. Under the pen name, Curtis Walker, he is also the author of a series of novels entitled *Book and Key*, for young people. Visit Michael at www.michaelberrier.com.

MARY DeMUTH has written thirty-five books translated into five languages over her career as a writer, including: *The Wall Around Your Heart: How Jesus Heals You When Others Hurt You* and *Worthy Living: How God's Wild Love for You Makes You Worthy*. She's also an international speaker and podcaster who loves to help people re-story their lives. Mary has been writing for twenty-five years and has mentored many writers though the Rockwall Christian Writers Group. She lives in Texas with her husband of twenty-five years and is the mom to three adult children. Find out more at marydemuth.com.

DR. DAVID DOWNS is a district superintendent for the Church of the Nazarene. He lives in Fort Worth, Texas, where he has served the West Texas District since 2011. Before being elected to that assignment, David served as superintendent for the East Ohio District for ten years. He previously pastored Dallas First Church of the Nazarene before moving to Ohio to serve as senior pastor of Canton First Church of the Nazarene. David's path in ministry has also taken him abroad. Prior to serving in Dallas, he and his wife, Susan, were missionaries in Seoul, South Korea, where he was a professor at Korean Nazarene Theological College.

CATHY ELLIOTT, retired from her day job as a Library Information Technician, became a speaker and full-time writer. Now she spends much of her time creating cozy mysteries including her latest novel *A Stitch in Crime,* which was released in tandem with the companion book, *A Vase of Mistaken Identity.* Her gorgeous daughter, Heidi, and handsome son-in-law, Eric, have blessed the family with two, treasured grandgems: Sidney Anne and Nicholas Scott. Cathy is a member of Mystery Writers of America,

Sisters In Crime, American Christian Fiction Writers, the Oregon Christian Writers, and Writers' Forum. She calls northern California home.

GWEN FORD FAULKENBERRY has a sincere passion for Jesus and the devoted family He has given her. She enjoys traveling the world with sixteen-year-old Grace, riding the range with fourteen-year-old Harper, baking with nine-year-old Adelaide, and discovering wondrous books with four-year-old Stella. She is also an author of five novels and four devotional books and loves to connect with her readers. Gwen holds a master's degree in liberal arts, and enjoys teaching literature, writing, and playing the piano at her church. She lives and writes in the mountains of Ozark, Arkansas. Check out her personal blog at gwenfordfaulkenberry.com.

ALLISON K. FLEXER is passionate about communicating the love of God to others. She is the author of *Truth, Lies, and the Single Woman*, a groundbreaking book designed to combat the lies that destroy the joy and confidence of single women. Until age thirty-eight, Allison was single and fought her share of challenges, but through seeking God's grace she learned to replace them with His truth. Allison also served as contributing writer for *Fulfilled: The NIV Devotional Bible for the Single Woman* and *Devotional Ventures*. You can learn more about Allison at www.allisonflexer.com.

HEIDI GAUL lives in Oregon's Willamette Valley with her husband and the furry members of her family. Winner of the 2015 Cascade Award for devotionals, she's written several devotions for *The Upper Room* and is a contributor for Guideposts devotionals, including *Mornings with Jesus 2019*. Her stories are included in ten *Chicken Soup for the Soul* anthologies, and she's a staff writer for The Great Commission Project. Her current project is a devotional/craft book titled *Redeemed and Restored*. A self-confessed foodie, she also loves to travel, both around the block and throughout the world.

RICK HAMLIN is the executive editor of Guideposts magazine, where he has worked for over thirty years. He's published three novels, most recently *Reading Between the Lines*. Rick is also the author of two books on prayer, *Ten Prayers You Can't Live Without*, which was published by Guideposts in the spring of 2013, and *Pray for Me,* which came out in September 2017. Rick has also been a contributor to *Daily Guideposts* since 1985 and blogs about prayer at Guideposts.org. He and his wife, Carol, live in New York City and sing in their church choir. They are the parents of two grown boys.

JEANETTE HANSCOME has written five books, including *Suddenly Single Mom: 52 Messages of Hope, Grace, and Promise.* Most of her writing comes from her experiences as a single mom who has lived with visual impairment since birth. Jeanette also writes about how God reveals His love for us through everyday experiences. She pours her leftover creative energy into singing, knitting, crocheting, and anything that allows her to use her calligraphy and lettering pens. Jeanette and her younger son enjoy living in the same East Bay Area city where she grew up. You can read her weekly blog at jeanettehanscome.com.

MONA HODGSON has written forty-two books during her career, including historical novels and novellas for adults and children's books for infants and kids up to twelve years old. Her writing credits also include several hundred articles, poems, and short stories, which have appeared in fifty different publications. Mona speaks for churches, schools, and conferences, including: YWAM, Mount Hermon Christian Camps and Conference Center, and MOPS groups. Mona currently lives in Arizona with her husband, Bob. And with each passing day, Mona's appreciation for taking time to play, belly laughs, and burbling brooks grows deeper roots.

Pastor **BOB HOSTETLER** has been in the Christian publishing industry for thirty years. He's an award-winning writer and author, executive editor for the new Christian Writers Institute, and recently became an agent with the Steve Laube Agency. His fifty books, which include *Don't Check Your Brains at the Door* (one among a dozen he has co-authored with Josh McDowell) and *The Bard and the Bible: A Shakespeare Devotional,* have sold millions of copies. Bob and his wife, Robin, have two adult children and five grandchildren. They live in Hamilton, Ohio. Visit Bob at www.bobhostetler.com.

When **BARBARA (BARB) HOWE** isn't occupied writing blog posts or weaving story ideas into novels, she keeps herself busy preparing gourmet meals, leading Bible Study discussion groups, or participating in her grandson's school. Barb also pursues a pretty active leisure schedule. Her favorite shared pursuits with author husband, Dave Howe, include attending operas, bicycling, and exploring new destinations. Barb's dual passions are encouraging others to share their faith legacies with grandchildren, and writing adventure stories for children. Barb's website www.SpiritualLegacyMemoir.com offers faith lessons for grandparents to help those embracing that phase of life identify the spiritual gifts that come with their new title.

GINGER KOLBABA is an award-winning author and speaker. She has written or contributed to more than thirty books, including *The Old Fashioned Way* and *The Impossible*, and more than four-hundred articles. She has spoken at national and international conferences, guest lectured at universities, and has appeared on national media outlets such as CNN Headline News, Moody Midday Connection, and Family Life radio. She's also been in national news outlets, such as Newsweek and Chicago Sun-Times. A "humorous contemplative," Ginger loves seeing the joy of God in all situations and desires to share His gift with others. You can visit her at www.gingerkolbaba.com.

CAROLINE KOLTS wasn't always focused on writing. After graduating from Hope College in Michigan with degrees in Communications and Psychology, she worked as a service coordinator in Texas and then a guidance counselor at a bilingual school in Tegucigalpa, Honduras. She briefly worked in farming, youth ministry, and foster care counseling, and then found her way to Atlanta, Georgia, where she spends time writing. Caroline is currently working on several creative collaborations with her husband, a freelance photographer. On a sunny day, you can find her in the park chasing her precocious two-year-old with a newborn strapped to her chest.

NANCY SEBASTIAN KUCH (pronounced "cook") passionately speaks and writes about real life, real people, and making real connections and how to embrace real hope in Him. As a speaker, coach, educator and author for over twenty years, Nancy tackles many topics including marriage and divorce. Nancy uses God's word in all aspects of her career to offer hope and help for all people who may feel they are "stuck" in their lives. She describes her personality as "playful" and loves to infuse wit and wisdom in her writing as well. She lives with her husband in Pennsylvania.

AMY LIVELY is the author of *How to Love Your Neighbor without Being Weird* and the creator of The Neighborhood Café, an international ministry helping people open their hearts and homes to their neighbors. She blogs about her mission and shares tips and tools with others about how to carry out Christ's command to love our neighbor. Amy lives on a dude ranch in the High Rockies of Colorado with her husband, a holy dog, and an unsaintly cat. She also has a daughter who is in college. Learn more about Amy at www.howtoloveyourneighbor.com.

JANET HOLM McHENRY is a speaker and author of twenty-three books, including the best-selling *PrayerWalk: Becoming a Woman of Prayer, Strength and Discipline* and *The Complete Guide to the Prayers of Jesus: What Jesus Prayed and How It Can Change Your Life Today*. She and her husband, Craig, enjoy spending time with their four children and ten grandchildren in the Sierra Valley of northern California, where Craig is a rancher. Janet enjoys reading through the Bible and creatively journals in the margins of a new Bible, which she offers as a birthday gift to her grandchildren. She enjoys hearing from readers through her website, www.janetmchenry.com.

GARI MEACHAM, a popular speaker and writer, travels the globe speaking at conferences, retreats, and events for women. Her highly acclaimed books, workbook, and DVD series, *Spirit Hunger*, *Watershed Moments*, and *Truly Fed* are used in book groups and churches across the country. Gari is President and Founder of The Vine, a ministry to orphans and widows in Uganda, and SHINE, a trendy YouTube show she hosts with her daughter, Ally. She is married to former New York Yankee Bobby Meacham, and together they have three children. Bobby and Gari have been in professional baseball for over thirty years and call Houston their home.

HOLLY MICHAEL has enjoyed a writing career as a journalist, features writer, and a regular ghostwriter for Guideposts magazine. She's the author of the novel, *Crooked Lines,* and non-fiction books, including *First and Goal,* a devotional she wrote with her on, former NFL player, Jake Byrne. Holly is married to Anglican Bishop Leo Michael and together they have three grown children, Jake, Betsy, and Nick. She lives in the Kansas City area, where she writes and works as a realtor. You can learn more about her writing on her website at www.HollyMichael.com.

Author **DiANN MILLS** believes her readers should expect an adventure when they pick up one of her books. She creates action-packed, suspense-filled novels to thrill and delight. Her titles have appeared on the CBA and ECPA bestseller lists, won two Christy Awards, and have been finalists for the RITA, Daphne Du Maurier, Inspirational Readers' Choice, and Carol Award contests. Library Journal presented her with a Best Books 2014: Genre Fiction award in the Christian Fiction category for *Firewall*. DiAnn is a founding board member of the American Christian Fiction writers and a member of Advanced Writers and Speakers Association. Connect with DiAnn at www.diannmills.com.

JESSICA R. PATCH writes to bring the hope of Jesus Christ to readers through her non-fiction and fiction books. She's the author of the *Seasons of Hope* series and several *Love Inspired* suspense novels, including *Fatal Reunion, Concealed Identity*, and *Deep Waters*. When she's not watching too much Netflix, you'll find her on Pinterest collecting recipes for dishes she'll probably never cook. Jessica is married to her college sweetheart, and is the mom of a college-bound daughter and a son in middle school. You're welcome to visit her blog at www.jessicarpatch.com for Forward Friday Devotions.

A life-long New Englander, **ERIK PERSON** lives in rural Connecticut, and has an affinity for the Boston Red Sox. Having sampled a variety of career pursuits, from sports outreach, working for FedEx shipping company, coaching, and counseling services, he's settled on high school teaching. He has been married to his wife, Danelle, for twenty years and together they have four children. In his off time you'll likely find Erik buried in a *9 Marks* book. Erik earned his doctorate in 2015 and whimsically walks around his house calling himself the professor.

KAREN PORTER enjoys being an international speaker, a successful businesswoman, and the author of seven books, including *Speak Like Jesus* and *I'll Bring the Chocolate*.

She is president of Advanced Writers and Speakers Association as well as the First Place 4 Health boards, and serves on several other national boards. Karen coaches aspiring writers and speakers. She and her husband, George, own Bold Vision Books, a Christian publishing company. Among her greatest achievements, Karen says, is her marriage. In her spare time, she follows her lifelong quest to find the perfect purse. Connect with Karen at www.karenporter.com.

MICHELLE RAPKIN is a freelance editor and writer who has worked at Bantam Books, Macmillan, Doubleday, Guideposts, and Hachette Book Group in a variety of editorial roles during her career of more than thirty years. She was also Editorial Director and founding editor of Crossings Book Club for a decade. A cancer survivor, Michelle is the author of *Any Day with Hair is a Good Hair Day*, a companion guide written to inspire those going through cancer treatment. She lives in Ocean Grove, New Jersey, with her adorable dog, Maxie.

ANDREA RAYNOR, a graduate of Harvard Divinity School, is a United Methodist minister, hospice chaplain, and author. In the aftermath of September 11th, she served as a chaplain to the morgue at Ground Zero, offering blessings over the remains and support to the workers there. Her books include *The Voice That Calls You Home*, *Incognito: Lost and Found at Harvard Divinity School*, *A Light on the Corner: Discovering the Sacred in the Everyday*, and *The Alphabet of Grief: Words to Help in Times of Sorrow*. She lives in Rye, New York, where she also serves as the Chaplain to the Fire Department.

AMELIA RHODES is the author of *Pray A to Z: A Practical Guide to Pray for Your Community* and *Isn't It Time for a Coffee Break: Doing Life Together in an All-About-Me Kind of World*. She loves to write and speak on topics of spiritual growth, friendship, and community, offering practical tools for living our faith in the everyday. Amelia lives the small town life in Michigan with her husband, two tween children, and two wild puppies. You can often find her hanging out with friends at the local coffee shop. Connect with her online at www.ameliarhodes.com.

KATHLEEN RUCKMAN is a published author of inspirational articles, short stories, poetry, and five children's picture books. She and her husband, Tom, make their home in the beautiful Willamette Valley of western Oregon. Kathleen is the mother of four adult children and grandmother to five little ones, her greatest joy. Some of her favorite things to do are taking country drives to explore small towns, visit museums, and go on nature walks with Tom to see the beauty of God's creation. Kathleen teaches women's Bible studies and reminds women that the Bible is "God's Love Letter" to them. Visit her at kathleenruckman.com.

ANGIE SPADY is an award-winning Christian children's author of *The Channing O'Banning Series* and *The Desperate Diva Diaries*, an active blogger, and a jewelry artist. Drawing on her experience of deep grief from the passing of a loved one and healing after a car accident, Angie writes a blog and articles regarded by critics as "raw, truthful, and real for today's women." She and her husband, Steve, are co-founders of Give Back to Humanity, a non-profit organization dedicated to serving children in India and Africa. As a mom of two adult daughters, Angie has learned to live life fully and focus on deepening her relationship with Jesus.

TERI LYNNE UNDERWOOD is a wife and mother who wears many other hats. Idea slinger. Word lover. Lopsided living encourager. Grace dweller. In 2015, Teri founded Prayer for Girls, an incredible community of moms built around praying Scripture every day for their daughters. This led to her book, *Praying for Girls: Asking God for the Things They Need Most*. Teri is also the author of the book, *Prayers from the Pews: The Power of Praying for Your Church*, where she explores the connection between embracing Scripture, evaluating personal experience, and experiencing the power in praying for your church. Visit Teri at www.terilynneunderwood.com.

J. MASON WILLIAMS is a lawyer, musician, and writer living in sunny Cocoa Beach, Florida. He's been married to his beautiful wife, Mary, for thirty-six years and they have two adventurous and fun-loving sons. He is considered a Florida Super Lawyer and was honored as a Best Lawyer in America in 2018. He has fueled his passion for music as soloist, choir director, praise team leader, and bass guitarist at various churches in East Central Florida. He is the author of a well-received novel, *And Angels Hovered*, and is hard at work on a sequel.

The consummate entertainer, **MARY WILLIAMS** has for decades performed the Merry Puppeteer, Dot the Clown, and the Merry Magician, and served as children's ministry director. Mary has been married to her loving husband, Mason, for thirty-six years, has two wonderful sons, and celebrates a sweet daughter in heaven. She loves gardening at her family farm in Georgia, walking and talking with God along Florida's beautiful Cocoa Beach, and volunteering with children. Mary is very excited about her most recent project, writing and illustrating a series of children's books.

Louisiana native **LEN WOODS** is married with two grown sons. He holds two degrees, a bachelor's from LSU and a master's in theology from Dallas Theological Seminary. A former writer/editor at Walk Thru the Bible Ministries, Len served for more than twenty-five years in pastoral ministry. In 2014, he left vocational "church world" to write full-time. The author, co-author, or ghostwriter of more than twenty books, Len has contributed to numerous other books and resources for spiritual growth. When not at his keyboard, he enjoys coffee with friends, a well-told story, any sort of road trip, and daydreaming about Colorado waterfalls.

ISABELLA YOSUICO is a longtime health, wellness, and inspirational writer, who most recently contributed to *Guideposts Mornings with Jesus 2018* and *2019*. Her *Embracing Life: Letting God Determine Your Destiny* workbook helps people navigate major life challenges with renewed hope, purpose and faith. With an M.S. in PR management, Isabella is also founding president of MightyTykes, a special needs product company inspired by her youngest son. Her heartfelt belief is that we are all different by design, and God does work all things for the good. Isabella and her family live on Florida's beautiful Suncoast. Connect with Isabella at isabellayosuico.com, mightytykes.com or on Facebook.

SCRIPTURE REFERENCE INDEX

TOPICAL INDEX

death, 54, 86, 126, 205, 289, 302, 321, 343

deception, 183, 242, 271

dedication, 243

    to faith, 89, 199, 243, 248

    to friends/friendship, 101

demon gate, 288

dependence, 121

Deunov, Peter, 354

devotion, 156, 377

DeWitt, Steve, 318

diabetes, 311

Dickens, Charles, 216, 288

Dickinson, Emily, 109

dieting, 337

disabilities, 285

disappointments, 110, 145, 244

discipline, 16

discomfort, 44

dishonesty, 326

Disney, Walt, 250

distractions, 209, 275, 278, 300, 319, 352

dogs, 41, 178

Dostoyevsky, Fyodor, 201

doubt, 26, 84, 201, 235, 238, 270, 283, 297, 340, 359

Dukes Lee, Jennifer, 26

E

Eareckson Tada, Joni, 212, 221, 320

eating habits, 90

Edwards, Jonathan, 81, 268

Einstein, Albert, 264

elections, 326, 328

Eliot, George, 165

Elliot, Elisabeth, 78, 217, 224, 231, 280, 323, 335

Elliot, Jim, 323

Emerson, Ralph Waldo, 36, 155, 239, 290, 299

encouragement, 153, 285, 339

English proverb, 253

Epictetus, 174

eternal life, 31, 284, 333

eternal spirit, 302

eternal treasure, 223

evangelism, 112

exclusion, 180

F

failures, 102, 366

faith

    acceptance and, 10

    belief and, 5, 58, 67, 124, 168, 196, 239, 340

    childlike, 250, 312

    children and, 144, 146, 148, 152, 245

    clarity through, 11, 24, 145, 298

    dedication to, 89, 199, 243, 248

    distractions from, 209, 319

    doubt and, 201, 235, 270, 283

    fear and, 134, 233, 267

    finding, 9, 23, 39, 91, 93, 116, 232, 295, 335

    friends/friendship and, 170

    lost, 296

wisdom, 251, 270

Wolterstorff, Nicholas, 64

Wonder, Stevie, 158

Word of God (see God's Word/Word of
    God)

work
    of God, 244, 342, 366, 376
    of Jesus, 84, 108, 135, 136, 163, 167, 261,
        304, 314, 327, 331, 357, 370, 372
    looking for, 373
    missionary, 84, 112
    place issues, 13, 76, 219
    in progress, 263

World War II, 162

worry/worrying, 18, 25, 83, 141, 208, 210,
    246

worship
    expressions of, 44, 195

joy and, 316

making time for, 150

power of, 369

quality of, 8, 24, 107, 120, 281

ways too, 63, 305

writers/writing, 153 (see also journal
    writing)

Wurmbrand, Richard, 131

Y

Yancey, Philip, 110, 123, 219, 281, 291

Young, Sarah, 10

Young, William Paul, 185

Z

Zamperini, Louis, 344

Zola, Emile, 119

Zwingli, Ulrich, 193

A Note from the Editors

We hope you enjoyed *Every Day with Jesus* published by the Books and Inspirational Media Division of Guideposts, a nonprofit organization that touches millions of lives every day through products and services that inspire, encourage, help you grow in your faith, and celebrate God's love.

Thank you for making a difference with your purchase of this book, which helps fund our many outreach programs to military personnel, prisons, hospitals, nursing homes, and educational institutions.

We also create many useful and uplifting online resources. Visit Guideposts.org to read true stories of hope and inspiration, sign up for free newsletters, download free e-books, join our Facebook community, and follow our stimulating blogs. We also encourage you to become a prayer partner by visiting us at Ourprayer.org or on the OurPrayer Facebook page.

To learn about other Guideposts publications, including the best-selling devotional *Daily Guideposts*, go to Guideposts.org/Shop, call (800) 932-2145, or write to Guideposts, PO Box 5815, Harlan, Iowa 51593.